Hearts
of
Darkness

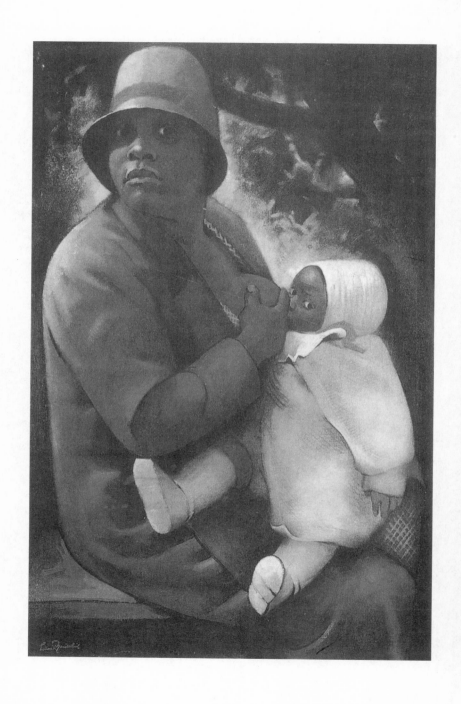

Hearts of Darkness

White Women Write Race

Jane Marcus

RUTGERS UNIVERSITY PRESS

NEW BRUNSWICK, NEW JERSEY, AND LONDON

Cover and frontispiece: *Negro Mother* (1931), by Ernst Neuschul. New Walk Museum (*Courtesy of Leicestershire Museums,* UK) and the Bridgeman Art Library.

Library of Congress Cataloging-in-Publication Data

Marcus, Jane.
  Hearts of darkness : white women write race / Jane Marcus.
    p. cm.
Includes bibliographical references and index.
  ISBN 0-8135-2962-X (alk. paper) — ISBN 0-8135-2963-8 (pbk. : alk. paper)
1. English fiction—20th century—History and criticism.   2. Race in literature.   3. American fiction—Women authors—History and criticism.   4. English fiction—Women authors—History and criticism.   5. Cunard, Nancy, 1896–1965—Views on race.   6. Woolf, Virginia, 1882–1941. Waves.   7. Postcolonialism in literature.   8. Barnes, Djuna. Nightwood.   9. White women—Attitudes.   10. Sociology in literature.   I. Title.
  PR888.R34M37   2003
  823'.91209355—dc21   2002068044

British Cataloging-in-Publication information is available from the British Library.

The publication program of Rutgers University Press is supported by the Board of Governors of Rutgers, The State University of New Jersey.

Designed by Karolina Harris

for Lillian Robinson,
whose *Race, Class and Culture* showed the way

Contents

Acknowledgments

First, my thanks to the editors who first published some of these essays or parts of them: Margaret Higonnet and Joan Templeton, Karen Lawrence, Mary Lynn Broe, Florence Howe, and Mae Henderson and the Harvard English Institute. Second, thanks to the many audiences in the United States and abroad who responded to these ideas when they were presented in lecture form. Thanks as well to the University of Texas, and the City College of New York, which generously supported this work with University Research Initiative (URI), Professional Staff Congress/City University of New York (PSC/CUNY), and Eisner Scholars grants from the Simon H. Rifkind Center. In addition I want to thank the Guggenheim Foundation, the Camargo Foundation; Clare Hall, Cambridge; Anglia Polytechnic University; and the Harry Ransome Humanities Research Center at the University of Texas (for an Andrew Mellon Foundation Research Fellowship). Thanks to Michael Marcus and his colleagues at the mathematics faculties and institutes at the University of Paris VI, at the University of Strasbourg, where much of this book was drafted and revised, and in Calcutta, India, where the chapter on *The Green Hat* and *Coolie* was written; to the research facilities of the Harry Ransome Humanities Research Center, the truly helpful and devoted staff (Tom Staley, Cathy Henderson, Barbara La Borde, and Ann Paterra), and the trustees for permission to quote from the manuscripts consulted there, also to the curators of the Photography Collections, who went out of their way to be helpful. Thanks are also due to the University of Maryland Library for Djuna Barnes materials; the libraries of Cambridge, Oxford, and Strasbourg Universities; and Anthony A.R.A. Hobson, for the Nancy Cunard Literary Estate, for permission to quote from the manuscripts. I thank my students at the University of Texas, CCNY, and CUNY, and those who argued and asked questions when these ideas were tried out in talks, to the organizers of sessions at MLA and elsewhere, to my colleagues and friends who supported these inquiries in various ways, and especially to my daughter, Lisa Marcus, whose writing about race inspired my own—to Lillian Robinson, Louise De Salvo, Sabine Broeck, Alan Fried-

Hearts of Darkness

1

The Empire Is Written

Like it or not, the fall of empire and the rise of fascism are written into modernism. Treated separately by historians and literary critics, empire and fascism deserve to be looked at not only in terms of each other, as they doubtless were experienced, but also in terms of race and gender. *Hearts of Darkness: White Women Write Race* is a book about race, gender, and reading at a moment in which the end of empire and the rise of fascism coincided in Europe's twenties and thirties—a moment that led to the long "night wood" of Nazism. What Djuna Barnes's novel *Nightwood* (1936) has come to stand for is a proleptic vision of Hitler's concentration camps in a text that is a "waste land" for the thirties. The writing of the racial "weakness" of Felix, the "non-Jewish Jew," and his child with an indifferent Aryan lesbian reads now as a prediction of how, as Hannah Arendt argues in *The Origins of Totalitarianism,* the racial fascism generated by a lost German empire and the rise of the third Reich as an empire turned into mass extermination of the Other.[1]

THE CHARACTER OF ONE'S COOK

In the terms of this book we are going to imagine that, on or about April 1934, to paraphrase Virginia Woolf's remark in "Mr. Bennett and Mrs. Brown" (1924) about the *Post-Impressionist Exhibition* in London in December 1910, "human character changed." I relocate that moment of great upheaval to 1934. It was in that year that Nancy Cunard's monumental Anthology *Negro* was published. It was printed by Wishart, the Left publisher in London, but paid for by damages from racial slurs against the author in the press. (Wishart was also the publisher of Mulk Raj Anand's *Untouchable* after it had been turned down by nineteen other publishers in four years.) *Negro,* as a collective documentary about African cultures on the continent and in the diaspora, was both the agent and evidence of that change. Not only did human character change, as Woolf argued the case for 1910, but, more importantly, the Enlightenment concept of what it was to be human changed utterly—to include people of color. For Woolf the change she observed in 1910, which had begun with Samuel Butler's attack on the English patriarchy in *The Way of All Flesh,* was most evident "in the character of one's cook":

> The Victorian cook lived like a leviathan in the lower depths, formidable, silent, obscure, inscrutable; the Georgian cook is a creature of sunshine and fresh air; in and out of the drawing room, now to borrow the *Daily Herald,* now to ask advice about a hat. Do you ask for more instances of the power of the human race to change? . . . All human relations have shifted— those between masters and servants, husbands and wives, parents and children.
>
> Virginia Woolf, "Mr. Bennett and Mrs. Brown"

What had not yet changed, and showed little chance of changing, was the relations between white people and people of color. Woolf and her cook shared the same nationality, race, and gender. (I do not say they shared religious beliefs, for Woolf was anti-Christian and agnostic.) Woolf was highly conscious of their differences, however, and she worried about the class gap that still divided them. Since they both read the *Daily Herald,* their politics were probably very similar. But the cook was obviously white and working class. For her the word *character* meant something other than its universal application in the quoted passage. A "character" for a servant was a letter or reference from her employer indicating that she was honest and hardworking. She spent most of her time in the kitchen, not the drawing room, had very little privacy, and was paid a miniscule salary. It is not clear that the servant had the same view of an apocalyptic change in her mistress's human character in 1910, although Woolf has shown servants in *The Voyage Out* and *The Years* performing a working-class nostalgia for the old days below stairs.

People of color, on the other hand, still lived like leviathans in the lower depths of European cities. And Woolf's adjectives—"formidable, silent, obscure, inscrutable"—are accurate in describing the European view of people of color. She and her husband, Leonard, lived in a state of alternating denial and fear because of his Jewishness. In *Empire and Commerce in Africa* (1920) and other powerful works condemning imperialism, Leonard Woolf failed to see the problem, which he considered to be entirely economic, in racial terms.

The *Negro* anthology is a major cultural landmark, awkward, imperfect, idealistic, and out-of-date. But it changed the way Europeans and North

Americans were to regard Africa and it introduced people of color and their cultures to Europeans. The things that strike us now as racist and embarrassing in the volume are precisely the points where we may enter the tangled depths of the white heart of darkness in the two decades between the European wars. We may cringe at William Carlos Williams's fond memories of black maids, but we are impressed again each time we see his work included in a black text under the rubric "White Poets." But the *Negro* anthology marks the moment when certain white Western intellectuals met African intellectuals and artists on their own terms, with respect and admiration. Their enthusiasm for the Other and the Other's arts and culture, for his body—and I say *his* advisedly—is indeed marked by a primitivist curiosity that was often erotic and sometimes exploitive. As a collective documentary involving hundreds of authors, black, brown, and white, from many different countries all over the globe, *Negro* is as contradictory and problematic as any other kind of interracial relationship, personal or political. But the impact of the anthology's integrated pages in a segregated world, the cultural gesture made by its multicultural, black-and-white Atlantic mix, is astonishing. Yes, I repeat, on or about February 15, 1934, human character changed. I want to mark the moment with a twist of Virginia Woolf's words, noting for the record that it was still possible for her to mean white Europeans when she said "human character." We must turn to the work of another woman of her generation, Nancy Cunard, who gave her heart to the struggle for racial freedom, as Woolf had given hers to the struggle for women's emancipation, to find a contemporary multiracial meaning of the words "human character" in the collective noncommercial making of *Negro*. The worlds of empire and colonialism on the one hand, and the African struggle for independence and Left antifascism on the other, come together in this volume in 1934. It would be a barefaced lie to argue that this book alone could have dispelled European darkness of spirit about race. What is so surprising is that we have a record of that moment of social hope, and if we revive and circulate that record, we may learn a great deal from studying its sources and its making in 1932–1934.

Woolf wondered what genius might be like when caught and tangled in a woman's heart. It now occurs to us that the heart she sought might have been black, but the woman she was seeking was white. She had no concept of the black woman artist, someone who could be her sister or her friend, someone with whom to share a room or a laboratory. The darkness of Virginia Woolf's otherwise enlightened heart is explored later on in this book in the chapter called "A Very Fine Negress." As we shall see in "Britannia Rules *The Waves*," Woolf, like her husband, Leonard, in *Empire and Commerce*

in Africa (for which she did a great deal of the research), had a powerful political and economic analysis of imperialism and absolutely no understanding of the "human character" of racial subjects—except as the experience
of difference allowed her to construct herself.[2] Otherness was not a lived reality to her, but a metaphor through which she could explore the oppression of women. She failed to feel her cook's class alienation, as she did her
husband's denied racial Jewishness.

It is the project of *Hearts of Darkness* to explore women's writing of the
end of empire and the rise of fascism. I want to relocate the heart of darkness in London and Paris, away from those light-filled lands of Africa and
India where it has lodged in the Western imagination. In *Nightwood's* Paris
pissoirs, churches, and bars, the hearts of Djuna Barnes's characters are black
and blue with desire, envy, and spite. In Michael Arlen's romance novel *The
Green Hat,* white woman's honor is celebrated by an Armenian writer who
is treated as a racial Other by the people he writes for. Things have fallen
apart, and, ominously, things are about to be cleaned up by the military.

Other texts from this period that are not discussed in this book might be
examined in the same way. Jean Rhys is another writer in whose novels we
find the end of empire and the rise of fascism colliding, especially *Good
Morning Midnight.* Phyllis Lassner is studying other contemporary women
writers who explore this historical moment in women's writing, including
Phyllis Bottome in *Under the Skin* and Martha Gellhorn in *Liana.*[3]

In fiction, worlds are created that serve as an alternate, often more reso-
nant history of the times than the facts allow. The characters from *A Passage
to India* and *Kim* have, it seems to me, an aura of historical reality that shapes
our vision of the real events in terms of racial and gendered fantasies some
of us share or come to share with their creators. The current wars in
Afghanistan and Iraq have revived *Kim* once again, as the West plays another
set in the "Great Game." The hero of *Coolie* comes from the same fierce
"warrior races" reinforced by the myth and the fictions. I'd like to see the
mythmaker's response to what imperialism does to him. It should be made
required reading for reporters who recycle the stereotypes. Iraq is the latest
imperial destination for players of the Great Game.

Can Kim be replaced in our imagination by untouchables in the Indo-
Anglian novel? Can Robin Vote and Dr. O'Connor, the perverts from
Nightwood, represent human character? Is it human character in the desperate white poet, Bernard, in *The Waves* that makes him feel he can't go on
producing literature unless we make it clear we are listening to him with all
our hearts? Just as Shakespeare's plays create an alternative history of England and antiquity, and nineteenth-century opera creates yet other worlds

from that source, our heads are full of scenes and characters from the Raj and the bush, from the jungle to the bazaar. The physical reality of that world of empire has been so lovingly created in fiction and memoir that we are all educated in savoring nostalgia for the oppressor and his way of life.

It cannot yet be said that the end of empire has been written into the social imagination with the same kind of authority as its heyday. There is indeed already a canon of great books, and many not-so-great ones, in which one may trace the literary ways in which the empire fought back and wrote back, from C.L.R. James to Bessie Head, Buchi Emecheta to Salman Rushdie. And Zadie Smith's *White Teeth* (2000) and Hari Kuzru's the *Impressionist* (2002) makes clear that there is much still to be said in the new English language that writers are constantly creating in their old countries and new cities. The number of brilliant writers, especially women, from India, Africa, and the Caribbean is astounding. For example, the Feminist Press is about to publish its first volume in the Women Writing Africa series, having already pioneered the publication of women writers from southern Asia. Although the struggle has been recorded (or is often still in the first stages of being recorded), its classic scenes and passionate heroics have yet to be absorbed into cultural memory as part of our collective human past. The whites of Western eyes have been so indelibly imprinted with images of black bodies as sexually charged with primitivist desire that only the West's most concerted effort to see whiteness everywhere seems to endow them with human character.

We know from film and television adaptations of the novels of empire, and their popular fellow travelers—boys' stories and adventure narratives— just how the hero dresses for dinner in the wilderness and how the lazy and incompetent natives cannot right an overturned bullock cart. They (we) need the discipline and order empire imposes. Americans, approaching their own postcolonial period, take vicarious pleasure in nostalgia for the fictional dignity and charm of the (white) people and places of the British Empire. African safaris and trips to the Indian hill stations give the tourist a taste of of what it was like to be white in a world of obedient and dependent dark-skinned people—without guilt for one's possible complicity.

What seems to me most disturbing is that it is not only Kipling and the classics of imperialist writing, the memoirs and biographies of white "explorers," narratives of "discovery," and conquest or Conrad's tales of "horror" on the Congo that invent and sustain the world of empire. Despite my reading of *The Waves* as an anti-imperialist novel, there is no question that it can be—and still is—read as a poetic paean of nostalgia for the Raj. It is that reality that insists we bring Mulk Raj Anand back to Bloomsbury, where he wrote *Coolie* and *Untouchable,* and into the university classroom, reading these novels alongside *A Passage to India* and *Kim.* In the multicultural classroom all students, and students of color in particular, need to see that the empire was writing back before Salman Rushdie. These are the texts in which the writing of empire emerges in response to both the Conrads and Kiplings and Woolfs and Forsters, if one accepts the continued critical endorsement of *A Passage to India* as an anti-imperialist text, something I find increasingly difficult to do. For readers of color there is very little difference in register between sympathetic white writers of empire and diehard imperialists. But the critics do not yet agree with the challenges to a canon of classics. Anand's novels have been categorized for easy dismissal as social realism and have not yet entered the discourse about empire. Both V. S. Naipaul and George Lamming must be introduced into class to break the power of the classic texts, to allow competing registers of colonized voices to be heard—the damaged and the survivors telling their versions of the story. When Anand's novels and early Lamming and C.L.R. James are read with the "classic" colonial texts, English literature is enlarged by the effort. They are often as difficult and slippery as Woolf or E. M. Forster, less uncompromising in writing the empire than the now canonical postcolonial writers. And Gayatri Spivak's work gives us a critical and intellectual model. Mahasweta Devi and Ken Saro-Wiwa are there to show us how the colonized learn counterterror to use against their own tribal peoples.

VIRGINIA WOOLF WEPT

In the popular construction of empire in fiction colonialism is so benevolent that native rebellion can only be construed as either terror or biting the hand that feeds. What seems surprising now is that we can see that the empire was also written by Liberals who opposed it. The racial fantasies, often sexual, that drive Kipling also drive the popular novelist Michael Arlen. The empire lives. And its afterlife is often prolonged by the living fictions of artists who seriously wished for the end of empire as well as by critics who continue to dwell on the same texts. Virginia Woolf wept at a film about the Mutiny.

Virginia Woolf wept. The anti-imperialist who later wrote *Three Guineas* wept despite herself. That should perhaps be the epigraph for *Hearts of Darkness.* While she published with her husband (at the Hogarth Press) Edward Thompson's *The Other Side of the Medal* (1925) a scathing critique of English literary misrepresentations of the Sepoy Mutiny and a warning to British readers of the consequences of not dealing through atonement with the

wounded ghost of past bloodshed and slaughter, she, too, was shaped by
the same propaganda that demanded patriotic pity for raped and murdered
Englishwomen and children. As John MacKenzie points out in *Propaganda
and Empire* (1984), ethnographic and anthropological films, documentaries,
as well as Hollywood fantasies of Imperialist Pastoral, British epics, and
Kipling films all shared nostalgia for the empire, even when made by Left
intellectuals during wartime. Patriotism and censorship controlled visual
propaganda for imperialism in Britain.

STILL UNTOUCHABLE?

The writers under discussion here—the socialist and anti-imperialist Virginia Woolf and Nancy Cunard, left-wing champion of the rights of blacks
and celebrator of the arts and cultures of the African diaspora—have also to
some extent written the empire into our cultural imaginary Some white
writers, like Nancy Cunard, shed their British identity altogether and
openly supported African revolution. But the high price paid for her rejection of her mother country is that she and her major anti-imperialist work,
the *Negro* anthology, are forgotten. She is not yet listed in the *Dictionary of
National Biography*.[4] Cunard's absence as an model of another way to act as
an antiracist public intellectual deprives the generations of political women
who come after her of an example of the committed activist's life in
struggle. It was necessary for her to deny England in order to embrace an
Africa of the future instead of the imperialist past. Her compatriots need to
know the story of her protests.

Cunard's work, like that of her colleague George Padmore, is openly
polemical, and between them (Padmore was instrumental in the making of
the book) and their hundreds of contributors, they create a vast panorama
of different African cultures and struggles in *Negro*. As an activist Nancy Cunard always mistrusted fiction as a vehicle for the story of resistance; she
wrote poetry and journalism. Perhaps she was right. It is clear that the pur-
ported radical critiques of empire by British writers continue to install and
sustain a world view they supposedly despised, although why this should be
so is not clear at all. The total rejection of a national and specifically English
class-based gender identity as a "lady" that Cunard bravely undertook was
not possible for other white liberals and radicals whose books critiqued the
empire but not their lives. Those books often live because they offer the
reader a way of reading other plots than adventure and conquest, plots that
complicate gender and race. But Virginia Woolf's Outsider was white.

For Michael Arlen, an Armenian writing in England, Iris March, the heroine of the "wildely" popular romance *The Green Hat,* acts with the honor of an English gentleman in a society that never really accepted the author as a gentleman at all.[5] Despite her claim to having no country, because she was a woman Virginia Woolf was profoundly English-identified and very conflicted about it. Djuna Barnes's exile in France and her ties to her English family heritage gave her insight into the tremendous shifting of national identities, and made her an American by default. Mahasweta Devi records how disturbed the multi-identified Indian national subject becomes when caste, class, color, and gender certainties are disrupted by the end of empire. For Anand and Cunard, writing in the thirties when communism made such a dream conceivable, an international identity becomes possible in a commitment to social justice that goes beyond nation. Neither figure is fashionable today. Their books are not in print. They sometimes take a harsher tone about imperialism than the writers who wrote for empire while ostensibly writing against it—Forster, Conrad, Leonard Woolf. The rage of Anand and Cunard against injustice is more socialist realist than experimental modernist. Reading them both, even in their most vulgar Marxist moments, makes clear that there is a twentieth-century literature of protest outside the canonical texts, and it works exceptionally well in the classroom. Some of my American black students were traumatized by reading Anand's *Untouchable.*[6] But they found a place for themselves in a larger world culture of pain and struggle than stories of the oppression of their own people had given them. There is no nostalgia to be found in slavery or other denials of humanity. None is there in Anand or Cunard. To them the empire is merely monstrous. Their heroes die or go to jail.

The stories, however, that create and recreate the empire are authored by conservatives and radicals alike. The emphasis may fall on different scenes, and the racial slurs may be fewer, but the plot always allows a certain writer (and reader) to get beyond that troubling figure of the "very fine negress" and on to imagining a white working-class woman as England's future Shakespeare. This is a class narrative that allows Virginia Woolf to imagine the creative writer in her cook, who is home washing the dishes while she is speaking. But what about race? We need to help our students to see that Judith Shakespeare is already here and she is called, for the moment, Jackie Kay or Zadie Smith. Am I saying that the political unconscious of the literature of empire and racial difference in modern Britain is always aready complicit in glossing over the evils done to colonized peoples and places? Yes, with some qualifications.

Otherwise how do we explain the intense power of Anand's *Coolie* or *Untouchable* or the works of Mahasweta Devi, Bessie Head, or Buchi

Emecheta, to move us and to instruct our consciences as well? The empire is not reinforced in their books, willingly or unwillingly. Like their British counterparts, they write of cross-racial sexual fantasies, but the reader is not encouraged to forgive the memsahib who toys with her servant boy and then destroys him.

There is a terrible and disturbing passage in C.L.R. James's early novel, *Minty Alley,* where the hero watches and listens to a child being beaten by its mother and does not interfere to stop it.[7] The beating is vicious and uncalled-for, and it recalls the famous scenes of the beating of innocent animals in classical modern novels from Dostoevsky to Zora Neale Hurston. But the abjection experienced by the reader has a resonance for those raised in the shadow of empire that it does not have for others. Anyone from the islands recognizes that scene, my students say. Brutal and senseless beatings are part of the culture; they explain the heritage of slavery. The subjects of empire were taught to write the empire on each other's bodies. A moral position that condemns the mother and feels that the hero should have interfered is foreign to the people of Minty Alley and their descendants. They understand the reasons for the mother's action as well as the hero's inability to act. This violence marks the people with the evil practices of their former masters. James's fictional mother beating her child both mimics the ways of white folks and hardens the child for facing white abuse. All these troubling issues are found in the outrageous contradictions in the work of Jamaica Kincaid and her complicated angers directed at mother and mother country, her combined angst and arrogance about her brother's AIDS. Above all Kincaid seems to be a modern version of Claude McKay's Bita Plant, in *Banana Bottom,* a returned colonial. In some books Kincaid appears to be working out her bitter rage at the imperialist botanical rape of her homeland and her own colonizing desire to make a tropical garden in stony Vermont and then she reverses direction to gather the forbidden fruit of endangered species and their seeds in China. Kincaid is the black version of Miss Parry in *Mrs. Dalloway.*

Miss Parry's Glass Eye

Toni Morrison, who wrote a thesis on Virginia Woolf, was, perhaps, thinking of Miss Parry, "one of nature's masterpieces," when she wrote *The Bluest Eye.* Helena Parry is to readers today a perfect example of the female imperialist, eco-terrorist or Victorian role model for botanical rape, whom we imagine as the first ravishers of the wilderness. To Peter Walsh and the people gathered at Mrs. Dalloway's party, Miss Parry's imperiousness invokes a statue of Britannia: "She belonged to a different age, but being so entire, so complete, would always stand upon the horizon, stone-white, eminent, like a lighthouse marking some past stage on this adventurous, long, long voyage, this interminable [. . .] life. "Stone-white" plays, of course, on "stone-cold," suggesting a marble memorial, a tomb dedicated to the virginal imperial aunts whose bequests enabled Virginia Woolf's generation of Englishwomen to afford the independence to write. The passage, like its author, is ambivalent about the feminist imperialists, who retain their stature as adventurous women while simultaneously serving as reminders of the horrors of empire and Englishwomen's complicity in it.

Miss Parry stands in for Mrs. Dalloway's mother. It was she who insisted on Clarissa's reproduction of motherhood and conformity to normative heterosexuality. Like Marianne North, the eccentric botanical painter of Kew Gardens, Miss Parry paints the orchids she has violently torn from their native habitats. Septimus imagines orchids as the "Greek" flowers that bloom for the dead Evans. Orchids in the text are the flowers of death and destruction. The gaze of the female artist in this case withers the lives of plants as well as budding homosexuals:

> For at the mention of India, or even Ceylon, her eyes (only one was glass) slowly deepened, became blue, beheld, not human beings—she had no tender memories, no proud illusions about Viceroys, Generals, Mutinies— it was orchids she saw, and mountain passes and herself carried on the backs of coolies in the 'sixties over solitary peaks; or descending to uproot orchids (startling blossoms, never beheld before) which she painted in water-colour.
>
> Woolf, *Mrs. Dalloway*

The uprooter of orchids, the blue-eyed plunderer—is an embodiment of what we may call "white sight." Her glass eye is a good metaphor for the half-blindness necessary for carrying on the mission she and Peter Walsh share, the imperial vision. Now she watches over the home front. No longer a soldier of British biology in Burma, in the Darwinian battle at Kew to control the growing things of the world, she remembers her victories over the jungle as well as over as the unruly desires of young Clarissa, Sally, and Peter, who appear at the party as the products of her pruning and shaping. Like Dr. Bradshaw she is a member of the social police who enforce the rules of empire, state, and family. She is neither a harmless old lady, nor a superfluous spinster. Her work is part of British imperial conquest of the natural world. She is picturesque: (Only one was glass.) It is in a parenthesis like this that Virginia Woolf captures a world. Was Miss Parry wounded on her expeditions to the jungle? Did the artist give her eye for her country? Did native people object to her gaze, her white sight?

At the party, the botanist is guarded by Lady Bruton, a black stone Britannia presiding over "barbarian hordes." Together Miss Parry and Lady Bruton form an ever-vigilant monument to empire in the center of the party where the fate of the Indian Uprising is being decided in the other room. We might see them as the Britannia Sisters, Home and Colonies, white and black, like the figures in Peter Walsh's dream (of un-fair women) guarding the empire. The bullying general's daughter and the blue-eyed botanist are exhibits in Woolf's gallery of characters who "force the soul." Miss Parry may only force the souls of rare oriental plants, but she is as much a part of the social-darwinian plot as Lady Bruton and her Aryan emigration schemes for Canada.

Woolf's critique of women's complicity in empire and war includes the expose of Mrs. Dalloway's appalling ignorance of the plight of Albanian refugees as well as the Holocaust of a million Armenians by the Turks (while her husband Richard signs the treaty betraying the Armenians.) There is, of course, an element of parody in the portrayal of the person without a cause, as it reminds us of those political friends of the Woolfs (and ourselves) who insist on our hearing about their causes. But in the novel, Mrs. Dalloway's lack of interest in the Armenians indicates how unready women of her class are for the citizenship that suffragettes had been fighting for.

Now the West is having to deal with the creation of the state of Iraq at Versailles by diplomats like those gathered at Mrs. Dalloway's, after World War I, as Harold Nicolson and his friends, including Maynard Keynes, spoke behind the scenes at social occasions just like this one. While they discuss responses to the passive resistance movement in India in one room, Lady Bruton, like E. M. Forster's Mrs. Turton, is the voice of articulated racism against the people of India in the novel. No one speaks for the Albanians, the Armenians, or the Kurds at this postwar party, although their fates and their present problems were all determined in just such an atmosphere of ignorance. In a way *Mrs. Dalloway* may be read as a London Home Front fictional version of the Treaty of Versailles, where so many vital decisions for the world were made callously and without knowledge of the history of the peoples and cultures involved. Mrs. Dalloway may not care about the fate of the Armenians, but her ignorance actually causes less damage than the ignorance of Britain's negotiators at the peace conference.

The denial of the political texts of *Mrs. Dalloway*, however complex they are, in the middlebrow insults to Woolf in Michael Cunningham's novel *The Hours* and the film it inspired, is important for the reader to notice. In one sense *The Hours* is as boring as the title Woolf discarded from one of her drafts because it chooses only the personal to leach out of the mother text, as it were. *The Hours* in both forms denies the antiwar and anti-imperialist texts of *Mrs. Dalloway* to emphasize the suicidal inner lives of modern women. The misogyny which represents a powerful, pacifist public intellectual as a weak and crazy woman walking not once but twice into the river is obscene. One is forced to notice that *The Hours* has appeared at a moment when the culture wants to demonize strong women, preferring to see them crazy or dead by their own hands. Even AIDS is presented as a personal problem, whereas Woolf's novel indicts the medical incompetence of the state in dealing with Septimus's shell shock. Cunningham and Meryl Streep give us lesbianism lite (and really she is in love with a gay man) in comparison to the devastating portrait of Miss Kilman in *Mrs. Dalloway,* a German academic whose career is ruined by the war, her dirty mackintosh a reminder to Clarissa of what she might have become if she had followed her desire. But the relentlessly apolitical novel and film derived from such a major anti-war novel reinforce a public conception of Woolf as the madwoman in the attic.

Virginia Woolf, body and mind, has long served as an icon of the latest in medical pathographies of women writers, from childhood sexual abuse to eating disorders. And her image has been used to represent the upper-class Englishness of country houses and their faded floral chintzes as evidence of gentility. But the extraordinarily misinformed designers of the film have deliberately defaced the classic English beauty by disfiguring Nicole Kidman's equally lively face with a prosthetic piece of putty for a nose—as boneless as Virginia Woolf's was finely boned, as someone's idea of "Jewish" as Woolf's was English. The nose was necessary to the film's creation of the madwoman as an ugly misfit and so she is given the signs of her husband's "Jewishness" just as his trembling hands are transformed to an incessant hand-wringing unimaginable in the real Virginia.

But why should the filmmakers want to do this? Leonard is normalized and his wife is pathologized. The outsidership Woolf chose did not have physical manifestations, except insofar as the Bohemianism of their lives would not have allowed for flower-patterned Liberty lawn dresses. (Vanessa looks particularly awkward as a young society matron dressed in white when surely she would have been in a paint-covered smock.) The film revels in the madwomen's problems with food. The fifties housewife throws away a badly made cake and makes another; the Meryl Streep character falls apart in the kitchen, then throws away enough food to feed all the AIDS patients in her neighborhood, and Virginia Woolf is seen sadistically manipulating uniformed maidservants in a bourgeois mansion completely out of character with their austere lives. I suppose she would have hooted with laughter, and remarked that Shakespeare has survived many centuries of such remakes, revisions, and rewrites of his masterpieces.

The Waves does write the empire, despite what I argue in "Britannia Rules *The Waves*." At the same time Virginia Woolf's own racial and sexual fantasies, I now believe, also encourage the apolitical readings the novel has always attracted. The overdetermined radical reading of the chapter that forms the center of this book is derived, I now think, from the cultural need to produce a white English feminist voice of modernism that is not totally racist and makes a certain critique of imperialism. Woolf does indeed do that, and I have been complicit as a critic in producing a radical and sympathetic "Virginia Woolf" for readers who want to hear that voice. Woolf gives us the text for this reading. But that is not all she gives us. She gives us texts for many other readings, including one that mourns the loss of empire. Do we have a right to ask that *The Waves* offer itself to only one reading? Is it Woolf's responsibility to prevent the reader from reading anything else but the anti-imperialist texts of her novels and essays? Is it my responsibility as a critic to insist on Woolf's radical anti-imperialism?

It is not, I think, that Woolf is trying to serve two masters, politically. I believe she was even more of a convinced socialist, pacifist, and feminist at the end than she was at the beginning of her career. But her overwhelming fear of and attraction to a vision of "a very fine negress" fills her texts with the stuff of unacted cross-racial lesbian desire. Her own national identity as English is so strong that she cannot imagine Judith Shakespeare reborn as black. As Robin Hackett argues, racial and sexual fantasies produce an ambivalence that spreads to other parts of the text as well as merging with and displacing one another, so that race can be read as lesbian desire, and that desire can be read as white women's (racialized) desire for autonomy or freedom. Again, it is sometimes constructed as freedom from an Englishness that creates a fantasy of exile—"As a woman I have no country." In *The Waves* the political text is sometimes swamped by this passion, as Rhoda sees Africa when she jumps from a cliff to her death. But nothing weakens the attack on patriarchal culture and its cult of heroes that is blamed for the state of the postcolonial world, the brooding masses and the fear of assegais attacking England's sheep.[8]

To break the grip of nostalgia for the empire on ourselves and our students, we need to take other books than the favorites into the classroom, books like Anand's *Coolie* and *Untouchable,* for example. If they turn out to be the right books to be teaching in Harlem, while *Kim* and *The Heart of Darkness* are not, they will be read just as avidly elsewhere. And we may leave Virginia Woolf in tears.

It's Not About India

Unacted desire and racial and sexual fantasy also fuel Forster's *Passage to India.* As Woolf blames patriarchy, Forster blames feminism for preventing international male bonding. An English mother figure, Mrs. Moore, carries the frightening weight of sex and death for both cultures. And Adela, obviously a spinster suffragette figure, is tortured and mocked in court for having had a sexual fantasy about a man of color.

Let's be serious here. Perhaps George Padmore and Nancy Cunard were right to fear what fiction might do to the story of empire. Deep in E. M. Forster's dark heart, I would argue, lies a fear of the emancipation of white women in his own country. He uses a fiction about empire to prove how uncivilized white women are, compared to native gentlemen. Mrs. Moore takes on the attributes of Hindu women as a kind of Kali figure whose willed death may be seen as a kind of *sati.* The absent Muslim woman—signified by Aziz's fetishized photograph of his dead wife, the mention of a quite unimaginable hunger strike by Muslim women over his imprisonment, and his plan to devote himself to the cause of education of Muslim women—is invoked by the text as a truly heroic figure compared with the problematic Hindu and English women. Nostalgia for empire is amazingly spun out of the refusal to accept the Englishman's historical agency in creating it. The process is the same as the one Edward Thompson described regarding the memory of the Sepoy Mutiny in the Hogarth Press volume, *The Other Side of the Metal,* not in terms of the thousands of Indian dead, but in the few dead white Englishwomen. No tears for the thousands of Indian dead at the hands of the British. Forster is inventing an imperial India in which all the trouble was caused by white women (Adela and Mrs. Moore). In *A Passage to India,* one may argue, he is creating a revised cultural memory of the Amritsar massacre, ignoring British male violence and focusing on white women as so troublesome a presence in India that they well may be cause of violent uprising. Precisely because it denies or writes over the Amritsar massacre, *A Passage to India* retains its hold on the English reader's imagination and that of those critics and readers who have inherited nostalgia for the empire.

But it was women in England just then who were creating a public furor over the struggle for their political rights. Just as film and fiction had created the story of the Mutiny as an attack on white women and children, *A Passage to India* allows the Western reader to forget the Amritsar massacre. White women, whose plight was earlier used to bring tears to the eyes of Virginia Woolf, were now fair game to the British male reader whose cross-race sexual fantasies are addressed by Forster.

Imagine the possiblity in reality of a white woman being humiliated like the fictional Adela Quested in an Indian colonial court. Imagine the supposed rapist Indian man going free. Given the reliance on notions of some unreal fantasy of English "democratic" treatment of women, a certain "respect" that was to be afforded "the sex" when it was embodied by women of certain classes, that underwrote colonization of an India in which *sati* was allowed and women treated "savagely," the novel is also a social fantasy. Aziz could not have been freed in real life. It would have weakened English power in the area. And it would have flown in the face of the philosophy that explained their presence in India in the first place, to control bestial Indian men and save the women. I believe that Adela (surely the contemporary reader knew that the name Adela was both a reference to Virginia Woolf as well as to one of the suffragette daughters of Emmeline Pankhurst—the one, in fact, who won women's suffrage in Australia.) is scapegoated in court to remind readers of the uproar in English courts—not Indian colonial ones—over Englishwomen's struggle for the vote at home in Britain. Forster feared Englishwomen as citizens, and as sexual subjects who might use their newfound freedom to stand between him and an imaginary Indian lover. *A Passage to India* is a romance novel for white men. It demonizes white women by identifying them with death and sexuality in the way that heterosexual fictions of empire usually characterize native women. The novel's popularity with white male readers, I would argue, is due to its successful shaming and blaming of white women for the evils of colonialism. Just as the narrator of *A Room of One's Own* announces that only men are imperialists and that she has no desire to make an English-woman of the negress, E. M. Forster turns the tables and blames racism on some white women and shames others as avatars of sex and death, while acquitting English gentlemen of bad faith or the crimes history tells us they did indeed commit. For the misogynist Forster's English mothers and virgins are like Woolf's mysterious leviathan cook, "formidable, silent, obscure, inscrutable," and responsible for social unrest in the colonies. He does introduce Indian Muslim women into the text in a way that was possible only in fantasy. They go on hunger strike to protest Aziz's imprisonment. The hunger strike was indeed a political tactic developed by Ghandi and his followers, who were not Muslims. But the hunger strike in the headlines at the time was the one of the the Pankhursts and the English suffragettes who were jailed for protesting for the vote and were using Ghandi's tactics in Britain.

The tactics of the hunger strike were part of the politics of the weak. As I have argued elsewhere, Hindu freedom fighters and English suffragettes, and later Irish political prisoners, were dependent on the goodwill of the liberal state to recognize the human character of their actions. Sinkwan Cheng argues that the brief mention of the Mohammedan women hunger strikers in *A Passage to India* indicates a challenge to the liberal law based on property rights, with a demonstration of the law of desire (Lacan) defining their action by lack.[9] If that is true it is also true of the English women hunger strikers. It seems to me to be the utmost historical fantasy on Forster's part to attribute the tactics of the hunger strike in India, where mass starvation was not a notable occurrence, an act which has to be public to have any effect, to veiled Muslim women in purdah who were not allowed to appear in public. Those women who did go on hunger strike were Hindu followers of Ghandi. This is as much a myth as the myth of ferocious Muslim manhood (proud Aziz on his horse in the filmic end of the novel) which is its counterpart. *A Passage to India* in fact reinforces a conception of the Muslim woman as more advanced than the Hindu woman as a way of explaining Aziz's celibacy, his devotion to the photograph of his dead wife, and his future as a Muslim champion of women's education. The emancipated Muslim women and the emancipated Englishwomen are then figured together as the reason the Englishman and the Indian cannot make their lives together.

The accumulated past of historical oppression by generations of Englishmen against generations of Indians is wiped out by Forster's fantasy of love between master and colonial subject. It also allows him an escape from any responsibility as an Englishman for the excesses of empire, because of his own (homosexual) difference. The stubborn reality of class and national identity stood in the way of his own happiness as it stood in the way of his sympathy with the oppression of women.

The white women are blamed for destroying an imaginary vision of goodwill among men, governors and their governed, as are their supposedly comic colonial counterparts, Mrs. Burton and Mrs. Turton, blamed for showing in public the (vulgar) racism that British imperialism demands. It's all the fault of the women. Otherwise the white male racial fantasy of India as a homosocial paradise might prevail. Cross-racial friendship is only possible for upper-class/caste males of both societies. But the interracial rape never happens, and the hero's love affair with Aziz never happens, although the terrifying mother and the bride depart for England leaving the field clear for Fielding. Forster's class identity, fixed in his fellowship at King's College, prevented him from regarding his love for a man of color as more than a holiday diversion. It was a privilege he could not give up.

Nancy Cunard's *Negro* anthology is not fueled by unacted desire, racial, sexual, or political. The author worked with and had sex with black men. Her private fantasies were separate from her daily life and from her work. The primitivism of her project does not derive from unacted desire but from identification with the downtrodden, with romantic excess and passionate communism in sharing a dream of freedom. For her England and its empire are always the enemy. She has no patience for its demand for history's forgiveness. Her works were made to blow up the empire and all it stood for, with no regrets. Fiction might have softened the impact of the bloody historical facts of the histories of slavery, exploitation, murder, and lynching with which the *Negro* anthology is spattered. It is still too real for anything but the banning, censorship, bowdlerizing, mockery, and dismissal that have been the book's career.

Because of its unique place as a biracial text, *Negro's* place as version of partly what Mary Louise Pratt calls a contact zone and partly an "autoethnography," "in which colonized subjects undertake to represent themselves in ways that engage with the colonizer's own terms," is problematic. But even more groups are represented in the making of the anthology and its reception than emerging African intellectuals and European and American anthropologists. Working against simplistic accounts of conquest and domination, Pratt says that a "'contact' perspective emphasizes how subjects are constituted in and by their relations to each other. It treats the relations among colonizers and colonized, or travelers and 'travelees,' not interms of separateness and apartheid, but in terms of co-presence, interaction, interlocking understandings and practices, often within radically asymmetrical relations of power." [10] If we read *Negro* as creating a cross-cultural and cross-racial contact zone that connects Harlem and Paris with Zimbabwe and Haiti, Alabama and Brazil with lynching in America, and the history of African art with hundreds and drawings and photographs—it will perhaps emerge with all its contradictions intact as a way of understanding race relations in Europe and the black Atlantic between the wars.

THE WHITENESS OF *THE WAVES*

My essay "Britannia Rules *The Waves*" first appeared in *Decolonizing Tradition: New Views of 20th Century British Canons*.[11] Karen Lawrence carved it out of my manuscript about printed voice in *The Waves,* and the novelist's contemporary power struggle with the BBC over fiction's cultural authority. It was called "Radio Days," and dealt with Sir James Jeans's broadcasts about relativity theory and their influence on Woolf, a subject since treated brilliantly by Gillian Beer. Jane Goldman's *Critical Guide to Virginia Woolf*[12] contains extracts from "Jane Marcus's ground-breaking essay on *The Waves* as anti-imperialist text," and says it points the way to a new era in studies of the modern novel. Goldman sees the essay as representative of "1990s Post-Colonial Criticism." It was one of the first examples of "whiteness studies" in an engagement with the historical representation of race and identity in the English novel. According to Goldman, "Marcus . . . has confronted us with new ways to read that Ur-modernist text, *The Waves*" (149).

The essay declares, and here I am quoting myself,

> that *The Waves* is a thirties novel that is concerned with race, class, colonialism and the cultural politics of canonicity itself. In *The Waves* Woolf interrogates the color problem, setting a metropolitan 'whiteness' against the colored colonial world as a vast desert against which an intellectual elite like the Bloomsbury Group creates itself as culture. *The Waves* might have been called *Waiting for the Barbarians* because of its emotional evocation of white fear and guilt for colonial and class oppression, the national dream of being assaulted by the assegais of the savage enemy as "white sheep."

The Waves, in my view, insists that the modernist epic-elegy is a melodrama for beset imperialists (*The Waste Land, Ulysses,* etc., might be read in the same way.) It marks the end of empire, but to read it this way, as part of what I call the "postcolonial carnivalesque," one must be willing to read the comic and ironic and perhaps even regard with relief the death of the author which it enacts.

The essay on *The Waves* began to take shape when I was first teaching Virginia Woolf in an M.A. class at the City College of New York, but it could not have been written without stimulating contact with my students and colleagues at the University of Texas, where many of the ideas and readings in this volume originated—in particular the many-years-long struggle to articulate what a white racial subject position, in which class and gender matter, was and is, and the extent to which I cannot escape particpating in race privilege, although I may place myself deliberately in critique of it. I tried to imagine then how people of color could read the novel with pleasure and, in the process, developed for myself a workable postcolonial reading strategy. I was excited to find that this strategy revealed an anti-imperialist text of *The Waves* that had been ignored or obscured by decades of "high cultural" readings, including the feminist.

"Britannia Rules *The Waves*" has then found a certain place in literary history because it argues that *The Waves* is about whiteness. Though it makes no claims to be the only possible reading of the text, the reading has clearly provoked as much hostility as it has praise as a landmark in post-colonial studies. I cannot help but wonder what might have happened if I had instead published "Radio Days."[13] Its reception indicates to me now the way the critical text of empire is written. Whose interest is served by the representation of Virginia Woolf as a radical critic of imperialism? (Am I responsible for the fact that this essay was published in a Norwegian collection of feminist essays that arrived today?)

I am, in a sense, arguing with myself and my work of the past decade here as, earlier, I gained some distance on feminist recuperative work of the seventies and eighties. The problem as I see it is to try to understand the extent to which the circulation of some of these readings served the interests of "Britannia," widely construed as British/American/First World excolonial cultural hegemony. Is the empire written again in this writing? Do I do it too?

The previously unpublished chapters in *Hearts of Darkness* are now placed in an intense dialogue with "Britannia Rules *The Waves*," "Laughing at Leviticus," and "Bonding and Bondage." What is at stake is not only my critical conscience but the passing of the torch of socialist-feminist criticism to another generation of critics, whose new strategies for reading will decide how much of these techniques survives ethically and politically to pass on to their students.

One emphasis in "Britannia Rules *The Waves*" is on the figure of Bernard as part of Woolf's strategy of writing the postcolonial carnivalesque. I can see now that it quite clearly derives from my attempt to extend Bakhtin's insights to texts inscribing the racial Other. Following the scene of the overturned bullock cart in Kipling's *Kim,* Bernard's (now classic) ignominious fall from a donkey in India is also prefigured by the fall from a horse of the narrator's aunt (while taking the night air in Bombay) in *A Room of One's Own*—a death that gives the narrator the money and freedom to write, and forever marks the modernist middle class English woman writer as implicated in colonialism.[14]

The most effective anticolonial texts, like *The Waves,* Nancy Cunard's *Black Man and White Ladyship,* and the studies of oppression and slavery in the *Negro* anthology, examine whiteness as well as blackness.[15] But racial fantasy propels the novel as well as the political pamphlet. *Negro*'s dated rhetorics remind us of what garbled responses black people were forced to listen to from their allies, as revolutionary fantasies (with blacks as the vanguard) combined with sexual fantasies for the international left in the thirties.

A History of the Essays

My first essay on racial fantasy was "Laughing at Leviticus." It wore, with some signs of strain, the presumptuous subtitle "*Nightwood* as Woman's Circus Epic." The crowding, and the effort to include everything in that mouthful, may be seen less as imitation of Djuna Barnes's style and more as overweening ambition to have the last word or to say it all. I have lightened the load of the title a little, as well as the notes. But the text of my essay accepts that it has a literary history of its own and must stand in relation to that history—of the arguments that flourished around and because of it, as Mary Lynn Broe and her pioneering colleagues sought to revive the reputation of Djuna Barnes.

"Laughing at Leviticus" is heavily rhetorical and obviously mine, but it is also the product of the modernist feminist ferment generated by Shari Benstock's *Women of the Left Bank*,[16] and so part of a feminist generation's work on modernism. The conversation has moved elsewhere. And perhaps I did overstate the case for *Nightwood* as an antifascist historical text, but the novel may continue to be read as a celebration of all the outsiders and outsider cultures that Hitler was about to wipe out. It still seems to me to make the case brilliantly for Jews as people, and against Jewish biblical prohibitive morality as it was internalized by European Christianity as an idea of order. That this is true whether or not biographers now "prove" that Djuna Barnes was a racist and an anti-Semite, does not need to be said. Despite the fact that T. S. Eliot was the novel's eventual publisher, I believe his introduction misreads it, for *Nightwood* openly celebrates disorder. Many years of reading *Nightwood* with students (along with Marguerite Yourcenar's disturbing *Coup de Grâce* and Klaus Theweleit's *Male Fantasies*) have convinced me that *Nightwood* might be called an Ur-text of European racial fantasies about Jews (and Gypsies, blacks, the mentally ill, and the crippled), depicting a virulent fascism that begins in Vienna and ends in New York. It is a death-driven fascism sexually charged by racial difference.

For the close-reading critic who loves allusive texts, *Nightwood* is a pleasure. Barnes is a great writer of the modernist dream of the primitive. Robin Vote is perhaps the prime example of the primeval woman. And the cast of outsider characters is queer and magnificent, as if Barnes were painting for posterity human types who would no longer exist after the triumph of fascism. *Nightwood* is also a grand fiction of racial and sexual fantasy that I read, as I do *The Waves,* as an antifascist protest. Both books are remarkable exposures of the fact that under the bare bones of the skeleton of realist novels are the diction and form of Shakespeare's dramatic soliloquy. Both novels announce the end of civilization, insisting that our art and our culture of talking aloud to ourselves is doomed. Who is listening? Is anybody listening?

This book is deeply concerned with the relationship of women and feminism to race and racism. I have been reading and teaching in the field of postcolonialism, though obviously my original Left-feminist perspective persists as I gather these readings into a volume. One of the issues at the forefront has been the relationship between white women and black men, caught in the struggle for their own rights and the rights of the other in the colonial context. I am also concerned with the crisis in masculinity that appears inherent in both the colonial order and postcolonial moves toward disorder, and the different ways these conflicts are worked out historically and represented in modernist writing about India and Africa.

Certainly Virginia Woolf's use of the metaphors of slavery to argue for the liberation of women in her feminist tract, *A Room of One's Own,* places Woolf within the nineteenth-century discourses of reform. But it also limits her capacity to see black women as women, or women from the colonies as Englishwomen. These issues of gender and race are discussed in "A Very Fine Negress." The essay has gathered about it a long oral tradition as a lecture, and so contains within it traces of the struggle with many audiences over certain difficult issues. That struggle has been to read Woolf carefully and critically with readers of color, while retaining my respect for her as the author of my own (and many others') awakening to issues of class and gender.

It is because I believe that the ability to *be seen* is key to identity as a speaking subject in the modern world that so much emphasis is put in this book on Woolf or her narrator's inability to see a "very fine negress" as a "human character." It is the negress's look of otherness that means that she cannot be recognized by the Englishwoman as a human character, let alone a sister Englishwoman. If she isn't seen to be a woman she doesn't exist historically. On the other hand the black woman's erotic exoticism in this text means that she is not going to be seen as an ordinary woman in struggle like the white feminist who uses metaphors about that struggle to make very poignant the arguments for white women's freedom. The denial of her social presence in a feminist text underscores the stake that feminists like

Virginia Woolf and we ourselves have had in fantasizing themselves as rescuers of these formidable, silent, obscure, inscrutable female victims in history. The black woman—like Virginia Woolf's cook—is a challenge to those sentiments that still reside in white hearts of darkness, sentiments that cast her only in the role of the relentlessly victimized and authentically oppressed subject. The colonizing eye is gendered, despite Woolf's claim that it is not colonizing the Negress. Surely she is not going to ask Mrs. Woolf's opinion about a hat. Her look is itself a symptom of Western scopic dominance.

On the cover of this book the black mother breast-feeding her child in a European city in a 1931 painting by Ernst Neuschul looks warily at the viewer and so does her child, as if to remind us that we have no right to look at her like that. In fact, I hear her saying calmly but firmly, "Don't look at me like that," asserting her claim to human character.

Two chapters concern the left-wing intellectual poet and publisher, Nancy Cunard. "Bonding and Bondage: Nancy Cunard and the Making of the *Negro* Anthology" was published in Mae Henderson's Harvard English Institute volume *Borders, Boundaries, and Frames: Essays in Cultural Criticism and Cultural Studies*. The photographs as well as the text of this essay have caused controversy. By publishing them in book form I hope to continue the discussion they have aroused. In "Laying Down the White Woman's Burden" I read Michael Arlen's popular romance novel *The Green Hat* and its Nancy Cunard figure as an icon of the Jazz Age, along with Mulk Raj Anand's unjustly neglected anti-imperialist novel *Coolie,* for its study of the white woman's relations with the colonized boy. In the romance novel and the protest novel, racial and sexual fantasies are evident because neither form forbids the acting out of desire.

Hearts of Darkness is an attempt to trace those fictions of racial fantasy that formed my own imagination and that, I believe, of many people of my generation. In this book the reader will find the author constantly at odds with herself, a condition that will change, I hope, as the conversation moves outward. Woolf and Barnes found in white feminist readers of my generation avid listeners. A modern multicultural audience challenges their new hegemony and hears in their voices certain hesitations and troubling sounds. Call it a buzz, a racist buzz. It is a sound that connects them to their age and their class. We could compare it to that hum the narrator of *A Room of One's Own* hears in poetry from before the war and the conversation of college men, quaint and romantic about the sexes—a poetry no longer possible after 1918. It may be a difficult challenge for white feminists, facing the problem of reading race in that revered classic of the rights of women *A Room of*

One's Own. Is the empire written there? Or, rather, how and why is the empire written there? Reading the buzz that hums along under our favorite feminist tract, we do not reject that conversation of women critics from the 1970s and 1980s about the text that inspired us. Lillian Robinson set the pace when she asked, "Who's Afraid of Virginia Woolf?" We listen to *A Room's* dissonances and disharmonies and begin to question the humming and buzzing of the culture behind the text.

The effort of these essays is toward an understanding of what marks the text in its context, to hear the humming noise whose rhythm alerts us to the time and place that produced it, as well as the edgy avant-garde tones of its projection into the modernist future. For modernism has had much more of a future than one could have imagined. In a new century the questions still before me concern the responsibility for writing those once vilified texts into classic status in a new social imaginary. If it was once the critic's role to argue the case for canonizing such works, perhaps it is now her role to question their status and explore their limits.

2

"A Very Fine Negress"

"It is one of the great advantages of being a woman that one can pass even a very fine negress without wishing to make an Englishwoman of her," Virginia Woolf wrote in *A Room of One's Own* in 1929[1].

Measuring the degrees of irony that raise the temperature of the debate about gender and colonialism, modernism and primitivism, race and nation, in this passage or in its individual words, as they traverse a particular modernist metropolitan passage/*flanerie,* cannot relieve it of the burden of racism. Even as an empty boast, it is full; as an alibi, it incriminates. If Virginia Woolf's negress recalls Baudelaire's poetic "negress," as well as the real Jeanne Duval and all the African women gazed at, written about, photographed, and measured by anthropologists and Western travelers and fantasized, fetishized, dreamed about, and demonized—as in the diaries of Michel Leiris or the paintings of Picasso—she is also very much the embodiment of Woolf's own anxiety about the limits of her double narrative of female emancipation and the history of women artists in England.[2]

However sharp the social pain the passage produces in the reader, we cannot make this particular subaltern speak. We can, however, undertake certain feminist historical rereadings to contextualize the specific procreative presence of the racialized other, the erotic and maternal Black woman at the intersection of low modernism and high, to think about the gender of the racialized gaze and the nature of this particular European vision of the heart of darkness. We can look at the way Woolf authorizes her portrait of the Englishwoman as a white slave ("she was the slave of any boy whose parents forced a ring upon her finger," 45) in the field of gender trouble in the scopic regime of the master/slave dialectic, by appropriating the history of bondage of the black body to tell the story of the white woman's oppression. The stillness of the figure of the fine negress signifies both bondage and otherness in the narrative of white women moving and struggling for freedom, a *passage* into national subjectivity that her *passage* from African identity to slavery has underwritten. *A Room's* specific status as a tract in the campaign for women's suffrage can be recalled, in which Woolf's polemical pamphlet employs the trope of interruption to acknowledge the historical moment in the suffrage movement when, under the leadership of the Pankhursts and their Women's Social and Political Union, Englishwomen broke their political silence and publicly interrupted men's debates.[3] We may challenge as well *A Room of One's Own*'s current status as fourth among the great English feminist emancipatory tracts. But, as Moira Ferguson makes clear in *Subject to Others,* white Englishwomen in the antislavery movement in the seventeenth and eighteenth centuries invented themselves as writers and politically conscious national subjects by portraying the slaves as oppressed and helpless objects. The strange presence of the "fine negress" in *A Room* may represent Woolf's unconscious recognition of an earlier pamphlet tradition in which white women "displaced anxieties about their own assumed powerlessness and inferiority onto their representations of slaves, . . . who in the process became more severely objectified and marginalized."[4]

FEMINISTS AND THE TROPE OF SLAVERY

If the figure of the "fine negress" is for Woolf and her readers in a sense locked into her role as the representation of slavery and racial terror, she cannot then be included in the figure "woman." The black woman's gender is there in Woolf's text, and in much of modernism, as what Homi Bhabha calls "the racial unchosen of cultural difference."[5] (It might be worth comparing the figure of the Jew and the Jewish woman in modernism, particularly in fascist writing and painting.)

"Indelible like the skin of the Black," William Thompson argued, the "brand of inferiority" was stamped on women from the beginning. And John Stuart Mill wrote: "I am far from pretending that wives are in general no better treated than slaves; but no slave is a slave to the same lengths, and in so full a sense of the word, as a wife is."[6] We may ask why English feminist rhetoric from Thompson through Mary Wollstonecraft and Mill relied so heavily on the metaphors of slavery.[7] An unsophisticated but rather logical answer appears to be that the situation of subjugation of married Englishwomen up through the nineteenth century, in their legal powerlessness to control their own lives, looked comparable to the situation of slaves. The *Appeal of One Half of the Human Race, Women, Against the Pretensions of the Other Half, Men, to Retain Them in Political, and Thence in Civil and Domestic, Slavery* (1825) by Thompson and Anna Wheeler, often considered the first feminist tract in England, set the tone by comparing the state of married women in England with that of West Indian slaves and declaring that slaves were better off: "A domestic, a civil, a political slave, in the plain unsophisticated sense of the word—in no metaphorical sense—is every married woman." Englishwomen, in their total subjugation to a husband's tryanny, lived the degraded lives of slaves: "Is there a female slave in the West Indies who would submit to such dictation from any male slave, if her companion, her equal, and no more than her equal, in degradation and misery?"[8] But Wollstonecraft's *Vindication of the Rights of Women* (1795) written at the same time as the protest against slavery was becoming very vocal, had compared the "uncivilised" nature of women, their ignorant and passionate behavior, to black slaves, both classes of people having the vices of the weak. When she called women slaves—and she did so often, not so much to evoke pity for their plight but as evidence of their debased irrationality—Wollstonecraft said, "I mean in a political and civil sense."[9] It was the domestic slavery of women in a political and civil sense that inspired Mill to write "the law of servitude in marriage is a monstrous contradiction to all the principles of the modern world, and to all the experience through which those principles have been worked out."[10] For Mill the continued historical containment of women in marriage after slavery had been abolished was due to its origins in their legal position as the property of their husbands. Women, like slaves, could not be allowed to own property since they *were* property.

Virginia Woolf's ideas appear to be situated in a similar ideological framework. Like Mill she is concerned in the extension of the quoted passage with imperialist colonialism as property owning, and anxious to attribute the desire to own human beings, trees, and dogs to men alone. Her extended and repeated evocation of the scene of a girl who refuses to marry her father's choice of a husband in the fifteenth century, as, like a slave, "locked up, beaten and flung about the room" is derived directly from George Macaulay Trevelyan's then recently published and now classic *History of England* (1926). But the savage scene of the abuse of a girl reaches back to all the other emancipatory feminisms that compared English marriage to slavery, and the outrage of the legal status of women as the property of husbands—Woolf, of course, imagines her white slave as daughter, and emphasizes the tyranny of fathers while sharing their analysis of marriage as England's "peculiar institution." She can then quite confidently, and with the example of powerful predecessors, (re)invoke the tropes of slavery in calling for the freedom of middle-class white women who want the vote in 1928 (an already classical polemical ploy in the culturally recognizable and mutually constitutive discourses of race and gender). What does it mean to be an Englishwoman and a citizen? is one of the questions asked by *A Room of One's Own*. What happened in the years between John Stuart Mill and Virginia Woolf—as Peter Freyer, Vron Ware, and Nancy Stepan point out in *The Idea of Race in Science* as an area for historical inquiry—was the development of scientific racism, anthropology, and the ideologies of colonialism, which rendered the legal abolition of slavery in 1833 practically moot in the face of theories of racial inferiority. What invites study is the changing relations between the concepts of gender and race in the nineteenth century. As Vron Ware writes:

> The existence of a popular movement against the slavery of blacks in the Caribbean and later in America provided a cornerstone for the buiding of a women's rights movement in Britain. Concepts of equality, legal and economic bondage, liberation and all the metaphors of servitude which were freely used by abolitionists were consistently borrowed by pioneers for women's rights to link their struggle to the wider one of human rights . . . As the movement for women's rights progressed, women were able to exploit the power of the slavery analogy in interpreting their own servitude but without needing any longer to refer to the slaves whose bondage had once outraged and inspired them.[11]

SLAVERY AND THE STEPHEN FAMILY

The colonial assemblies and courts . . . when they made a black or tawny skin a presumption of bondage, threw a convenient veil over the enormities of the slave trade and indulged their proud contempt of the African race.
James Stephen, *The Slavery of the British West India Colonies . . .*[12]

A Room of One's Own is linked to the English literature of female emancipation both historically and rhetorically. And Virginia Stephen Woolf is linked with both the antislavery campaign of her great-grandfather James Stephen, and the (reluctant but dutiful) writing and shepherding through Parliament of the Anti-Slavery Bill by his son, her more conservative grandfather, also named James Stephen (1789–1859), who was permanent undersecretary for the colonies. Feeling bowed by the ethical and political burden of the subject peoples of the British Empire, whose cause he claimed he had at heart, Woolf's grandfather is an interesting example of the installation of benevolent rhetoric in the service of the violence of empire. His career and writing would provide a fruitful source of knowledge on the relation between slavery and colonial oppression from the master's point of view. Known as "Mr. Mother-Country Stephen," he, too, had a genius for metaphors, and artfully and with great and lasting success, adopted the analogy of the family to frame extremely complex colonial relations around emotional questions of loyalty, love, and paternal care, relations that cast rebel nations as bad sons in a national oedipal drama.[13]

In the writings and political activities of her own family, Virginia Woolf found the polemic for racial freedom ready to hand as a model for arguing the freedom of her sex.[14] Family history cast Clapham Sect reformer James Stephen (1758–1832) as a hero moved to his efforts in the antislavery movement by the sight of a slave auction in the West Indies. Unlike many of his compatriots, James Stephen found that he could *indeed* pass "a very fine negress" without wanting to make an Englishwoman of her. Any "Englishwoman" of color was a slave. Unnerved by the fact that English law did not apply in the slave colonies, Woolf's great grandfather, unlike the narrator of *A Room of One's Own,* did indeed want to make an English citizen (legally), woman or man, of the wronged slave, for doing so would supposedly make her or him free.[15] But whether or not a black person or a former slave could be considered a person under English law was the subject of years of parliamentary debate (see Freyer for documented details). Stephen thought of England as *Enslaved by Her Own Slave Colonies,* as he titled one of his pamphlets (1826), anticipating Hegel's argument of the debasement of the master as well as the slave, and Virginia Woolf's similar argument later in *Three Guineas.* James Stephen's collected antislavery pamphlets, *The Slavery of the British West India Colonies Delineated* (1824–1830), obviously a model for his pamphleteering descendant, are concerned with the legal status of slaves in relation to British law, the relation of British law to West Indies governance, and the questions of whether slave ownership was legal in Britain and whether slaves who came to England had to be returned to their island masters. Stephen stands out among the antislavery agitators as deeply outraged at the racial basis of slavery. According to law and practice, all black people are slaves or potential slaves just because of their color; no white person can ever become a slave, as no black can ever escape from the condition. (364) Attributing the problem to its basis in protective legislation for property, Stephen argues that the legal position of slaves in British colonies is far worse than any other country. The escaped slaves had no recourse in English courts, but were sent back to their masters in the islands. In effect all black people in Britain could be kidnapped and pressed into slavery. "They have invented a cause of slavery, additional to all those which lawgivers, civil or barbarous, have elsewhere recognized, or rapacious avarice explored," Stephen argued, "namely having a black skin without a deed of manumission. They have thus contrived to effect what human despotism never attempted or imagined before. They have attached slavery in the abstract to a large portion of the human species; so that it is no longer a particular private relation, requiring the correlative of a master, but a quality inherent to the blood of that unfortunate race, and redounding to the benefit of the first man-stealer who reduces it into possession."

The first James Stephen's struggles with the concept of his own subjectivity as a British citizen and its relation to that of a slave, framed as they were by the ethics of Clapham Sect Christianity, make an interesting historical parallel to his great-granddaughter's struggles with the same question more than a century later. While Stephen stressed his (Christian) brotherhood with slaves, former slaves and black Englishmen, Woolf was was not so quick to claim equality or recognize a common humanity with her negress, and she seems nervous, too, about sisterhood under the skin. A century of ideological racism had taken its toll on the English radical tradition. She could use her great-grandfather's antislavery arguments and metaphors to articulate feminist claims for freedom and citizenship without relating racial subjectivity to gender. Her father, Leslie Stephen, keeping the faith, as it were, was among the supporters of the Jamaica Committee, formed by Thomas Huxley, Herbert Spencer, and Mill in response to Governor Edward John Eyre's outrages against a protest by Jamaican farmers at Morant Bay in 1865. According to Peter Freyer, 439 black people were killed in Eyre's "murderous 30-day rampage," 600 flogged; childrens' brains were dashed out, pregnant women's bellies ripped open, and one thousand homes of suspected rebels burned. They were unsuccessful in prosecuting Governor Eyre, whose defense committee included Matthew Arnold, Charles Dickens, Alfred Tennyson, Lord Thomas Carlyle, and John Ruskin, and he was retired with a pension.[16]

WHO WAS WOOLF'S NEGRESS?

Another contextualization of the problematic passage in *A Room of One's Own* would be thinking about it in connection to Leonard Woolf's major political work, *Empire and Commerce in Africa* (1920),[17] and Virginia Woolf's contribution to it. While I may consider this book to have been a major work, few readers of Leonard Woolf know of its existence, and he did not later claim its fiercely rational Marxist arguments as one of his important interventions in British politics. And I shall look at some moments in which Woolf herself may have gazed at "a very fine negress"—that is, when she went to see an exhibition of Negro art with Roger Fry. His subsequent claims for its genius, a notion he shared with modernism as a whole, are part of the theory of primitivism that animated the art-critical debates of the period. Virginia Woolf's visit to the enormous British Empire Exposition of

1924 at Wembley, where whole African villages were on view, complete with men and women of color imported especially to be gazed at by Europeans, is another source of Woolf's troubling encounter with "a very fine negress."

Despite Alice Walker's complaint in *In Search of Our Mothers' Gardens,* the book that became the bible of the Women's Studies movement in the United States and Europe, and the touchstone for activist and literary critical feminism, has inspired little discussion of its articulation of the categories "woman" and "nation." Nor has it provoked much speculation on why Virginia Woolf couldn't conceive of a woman (like herself) being both black and British, however (again like herself) uncomfortable the category. Perhaps it is because *A Room of One's Own* has been situated at the foundations of both a politics and an academic discipline that its racial problems have been largely ignored. Why didn't Alice Walker notice this passage?

WAS JUDITH SHAKESPEARE BLACK?

That a vision of a silent African specimen of womanhood ("a very *fine* negress") lies at the heart of arguably the most popular Western text of feminist emancipation, the text that gives us Judith Shakespeare as the archetypal victim of the oppression of women, merely underscores the claims made by black intellectuals Hazel Carby and Michele Wallace that gender is the stage on which race articulates itself.[18] Reading for the history of the "fine negress," we may be led, as Paul Gilroy would doubtless argue, to a reading of Judith Shakespeare's suicide/infanticide as an emancipatory act—as he reads the heroic tradition of slave suicides and the mother's desperate killing of her own child in Toni Morrison's *Beloved* and the real historical cases that inspired her. Death is read here as the liberator of the oppressed woman and the oppressed slave. Is Woolf aware of black culture's martyrs and murders as she creates her white victim as Judith Shakespeare?

What is it about the sight of a black woman that causes the European feminist intellectual to expose her anxieties about her own national identity, ethnicity, and color? Caught in the "freeze-frame" of the fetishizing gaze, she appears to be as fixated on the absent presence of the eroticized African maternal as the masters of modernism from Conrad to Matisse, from whose ranks her ethics and the uneven and uncanonical status of her work in England have hitherto kept her free. If the intellectual energy of Black Studies in the United States now makes possible such a critique as this one, Woolf's own internationalist pacifism and socialism as expressed in *Three Guineas* (1938) invite scrutiny of her earlier feminist polemic in terms of Paul Gilroy's cross- and intercultural concept of the "Black Atlantic"—itself a revision of the Pan-Africanism of many black intellectuals of the 1930s, especially evident in the work of George Padmore and Nancy Cunard in *Negro* and now replaced by Diaspora Studies, a field in which the *Negro* anthology may be one of the founding texts. If we are to detach the Negress from her textual niche as a monumental Madonna for white Western otherness, Peter Freyer's *Staying Power* provides in rich historical detail the extraordinary history of black people in Britain against which such statements as Woolf's may be read.[19]

Racial difference is at the heart of the constitution of the field of Women's Studies in the United States as well as the field on which its legitimation has been fought in both internal and external struggles. And it is sadly true that some white feminists, like Virginia Woolf's narrator, loudly protesting her innocence, have quite willingly passed blacks, Asians, chicanas, Native Americans, lesbians—without in the least wanting to make feminists of them, reserving the category as Woolf appears to do here.[20] Feminism's installation in the academy and the vexed field of feminist criticism and theory are haunted by the still, proud figure of the black woman caught in the white woman's gaze.[21]

Why does the sight of the black woman make the white woman so defensive and assertive about the limits of her own gender? Woolf's narrator's uneasiness at the sight of the black woman's body and insistence on her innocence of unnamed racial crimes are not strong enough for her to claim common womanhood, or even common nationality, with the object of her gaze. If she shared one category with the black woman, could she share two? Never entirely sure that she herself belonged to the category "woman" as it was socially constructed around motherhood and heterosexuality in Victorian-Edwardian England, Virginia Woolf was profoundly uncomfortable with socially limited notions of gender, as *Orlando* surely attests. But her fascination with the literature of exploration and travel, especially Richard Hakluyt and Captain James Cook, as well as with the prevailing late-nineteenth-century discourses of racial science, (filtered through Matthew Arnold, for example), appear in all her writing. Here we see it in the repetition of the words *savage* and *fetish* in a way the reader finds so highly charged in *A Room of One's Own*. Arnold's repetition of the word "fetish" to mean the worship of material objects in *Culture and Anarchy* reverberates behind her usage, as does his calling a rioting mob "savages."[22] She struggled with the definitions, and, perhaps because she had such difficulty placing herself, she may have found that placing the "negress" in relation to herself was almost impossible. This anxiety about identity is very different from the primitivism of most modernist artists, who found the racial Other a spur to the discovery of their own selves. If she was recently "made" into an

"Englishwoman" by virtue of getting the vote in 1928, Woolf saw the Negress neither as a fellow citizen of England nor as a possible member of her Society of Outsiders, one who might share the antinationalist ("white Atlantic"?) socialist pacifism of *Three Guineas*. Why does "she" (and here, of course, I mean the collective narrator of *A Room of One's Own*) rush to extricate herself from sharing the guilt of imperialism with white men? Her own relatives' stories made that complicity—or at least a certain level of it—clear. The text is marked by the guilty admission that the narrator's five hundred pounds a year comes from an aunt who died from a fall while taking the night air in Bombay. Woolf's generation of Englishwomen writers, she is saying, write with the blood of the nineteenth-century imperialists on their hands. The assumption that a negress must be a foreigner or colonial subject was an excuse for ignoring the presence in Britain of blacks in goodly numbers for centuries.

Following Gilroy, who asks that all modern literature and culture be "reconstructed from the slaves' point of view," we can work at resituating the text in relation to the history of slavery. The readings inspired by such a radical move are not interesting only in terms essential to the project of reading Woolf's text but to a complete revision of the study of culture. In behalf of such a project, I want to look at the relation between the figure of the silent black woman in *A Room* and its heroines. Judith Shakespeare is a case in point. If the words "a very fine negress" evoke the auction block and the slave bill of sale, then there is a clear connection to the abused and battered would-be artist, Judith Shakespeare. What if Judith Shakespeare were black?

A Room is narrated by those folk heroines the multiple Marys, an odd group of ghostly English martyrs to patriarchal insistence that women raise the children of rape. The sorrowful sisterhood is behind the narrative voice of the fourth Mary of the old ballad, singing her gallows song, in the text of *A Room*. In a sense it is she who is about to die (for having killed her own and the king's child) who passes the negress. There is a very complex derivation of identity for the speaker of *A Room of One's Own*. Perhaps the irony lies in her experience of a different kind of English slavery. In the case of the Negress we remember her role in the production of slave workers for white colonial masters.

OROONOKO AND RACIAL PORNOGRAPHY

Aphra Behn, praised extravagantly by Woolf as the first professional woman writer, and one of the heroines of *A Room of One's Own,* is clearly Woolf's predecessor in gazing at Negresses. Behn and her novel *Oroonoko* (1688), the story of a "royal slave," were revived and defended from scholars who claimed she had never been in Surinam, by Vita Sackville-West in her biography of Behn, part of Sackville-West's search for a tradition of her own. That Woolf should have adopted her friend's heroine as her own is strange, for Aphra Behn seems as unlike Virginia Woolf as a professional writer as she was like Vita Sackville-West: Tory, conservative, amorous, and adventurous, not to mention male identified. (Woolf's appropriation of Sackville-West's exact words about Aphra Behn without acknowledgment is part of a continuing refusal to acknowledge her pioneering but embarrassing work (1927) in the revival of Aphra Behn.[23] Woolf's concept of "the androgynous mind of the artist" seems to come as much from Vita's mysterious Mrs. Behn as from Coleridge, whose "female pen" and "masculine part, the poet in me" are cited by the ambitious author as part of a drama of self-creation. And Imoinda, the totally tattooed African princess of *Oroonoko*, may seriously serve as the origin of the figure of the "fine negress" who compels the gaze of the narrator of *A Room of One's Own*, as she is an exotic erotic object to Aphra Behn. Virginia's "very fine negress" may be simply another appropriation of Vita's heroine Aphra's "very fine negress," the visually spectacular Imoinda.

If Vita Sackville-West's search for her particular forerunners is the masked origin of Virginia Woolf's *A Room*, where victims are wanted rather than figures of the sexual and political dominatrix, Sackville-West's 1923 edition of *The Diary of the Lady Anne Clifford* (1590–1676) yields the name of Grace Robinson, "a Blackamoor" at the "laundry-Maid's Table," in the "Catalogue of Household and Family of Richard Earl of Dorset in 1613 to 1624 at Knole, Kent," Vita's ancestral home. The same list gives us "John Morockoe, a Blackamoor" in the "Kitchen and Scullery" and Mrs. Grimsditch at the "Parlour Table," sources, of course, for Woolf's *Orlando* of the previous year, based as it was on Knole and the Sackvilles, Vita herself, and including in passing the fantasy of "kissing a negress in the dark."[24] What is the relation between all these real and fictional Negresses, the laundress Grace Robinson, *Orlando*'s Negress and *A Room*'s Negress? At the very least this narrative tells us that Virginia Woolf knew there were black women in England from the sixteenth century on.

It is a commonplace in feminist critical recuperation of *Oroonoko* to argue that Aphra Behn earned her identity as a woman writer by telling the story of the Other, a "royal slave." And it seems logical to see Virginia Woolf installing that process as archetypal for women artists by situating Aphra Behn as the prototypical "woman writer." Her own *The Voyage Out* certainly bears comparison with *Oroonoko*, but is notable for having relegated the savage Other to the heroine's dreams.

At the risk of venturing beyond the limits of my field, I want to sketch here the outline of a theory of why race is at the heart of the English (woman's) novel, to share the results of a rereading of *Oroonoko* in the light of the present inquiry. As the inaugural text of women's writing in England (meaning middle-class fiction, and leaving aside the poems of the upper classes as Woolf does) the history of the "royal slave" does lock race and gender into the very conception of the novel but in a way that seems to benefit neither women nor blacks. Aphra Behn was an adventuress and a spy. If *Oroonoko* is a surveillance report, what does it tell her English Tory masters? Why is half the critical literature about whether or not Aphra Behn went to Surinam, how often, and when? As Vita Sackville-West wrote, if she wasn't an "eye-witness," she was a brilliant and original creator of fiction. It seems to me that the novel's message to an England worried about the prospects of the slave trade was that no slave rebellion would succeed. Even the best educated of the Africans could not organize and sustain the loyalty of the demoralized and spread-out plantation slaves; the activity of outlaw slave owners in putting down rebellions could not be countered by representatives of British law in the colonies. The slave leaders were naively moral and ethical by European standards, and could be deceived, betrayed, and murdered with impunity.

It seems to me that *Oroonoko* participates in a special brand of racial pornography concerned with representing the castration of the black male and disfiguring the black female. *Oroonoko* is a seventeenth-century *Story of O,* and its great sucess on the European stage in Thomas Southerne's version and in France in the eighteenth century as (supposedly) an antislavery appeal gives rise to the speculation that there was much in the depictions of torture in the literature of antislavery to appeal to the prurient mind. What was being staged was a European fantasy of black slaves in total submission to the knives of white people, cut down in their prime without struggle. *Oroonoko* is about cutting and writing, deforming and defacing the Other to create the self. If it is only a female pen Behn is brandishing, she uses its blade to cut her black characters to shreds. That is clearly why Vita Sackville-West admired it. Why does Virginia Woolf, otherwise holding her own in a battle with Vita about feminism, seem to condone her lover's sadistic racism?

Vita Sackville-West urged her readers to reject the theory that *Oroonoko* was "the first novel of emancipation." The narrative of freedom was not for her. She wanted to place it as a baroque fantasy and liked to think of the story as a costume drama with Aphra and her brother "dazzling the savages" with their clothes: "*Oroonoko* resembles those 17th century paintings of negroes in plumes and satins, rather than an actual slave on a practical plantation. She dresses him, it is true, in a suit of brown hollands, but none the less the plumes continue to wave in the breeze and the satins to glisten in the sun." (74) But Vita Sackville-West is drawn to the tale by her taste for cruelty. Like a fetishist gazing at a portrait of a bloody Saint Sebastian, pierced in martyrdom, she describes her pleasure in the text: "As it is, we must be content with the hope that Oroonoko and Imoinda, glistening, ebony, tortured figures that they are, running with little rivulets of blood, crowned with their martyrdom, bear little resemblance to life on the plantations, even in the seventeenth century, but rise as splendid evocations complete in themselves." (28) Somehow with the help of Vita Sackville-West's female pen the royal slave lovers have been reincarnated as a scupture by Bernini in an orgy of death, race, and sex. It is difficult for the reader to conceive of joining Virginia Woolf and Vita Sackville-West in laying flowers on the grave of the creator of such a bloody racial spectacle. Is the choice of a predecessor limited to Aphra Behn, the dominatrix, or Judith Shakespeare, the victim? Is the master/slave dichotomy the only way to conceive of a woman writer's relationship to the past?

"*Kissing a Negress in the dark,*" the phrase from the end of *Orlando,* published the previous year, that anticipates the one we are discussing here, also signals anxiety about national identity in terms of racial and sexual identity. Because that book is even more openly conceived as a tribute to Vita Sackville-West and the history of Knole, the presence of the names of black servants in the list of the contents of the house clearly inspired Woolf's fantasy of illicit sex, crossing race and class, in relation to the woman to whom she was so ambivalently attracted. Woolf regarded Sackville-West as in some sense quintessentially the Englishwoman because of her aristicratic pedigree, but also as a dark-mustachioed Other, with her exotic Spanish ancestress. Her sometime lover's promiscuity is as connected to her bloodlines as Orlando's final incarnation in the novel is as a male-identified woman who has sexual adventures with gypsies, servant girls, and prostitutes, under cover of marriage to the mostly absent Shelmerdine. This activity she and her husband call "kissing negresses in the dark," a reference to Vita's many lovers of both sexes and Harold Nicolson's male lovers. "In the dark" means on the side. But it also refers to the tradition at Knole of privileged liaisons with servants and dalliances with others, while maintaining the proper patriarchal passage of property and English identity in the white male bloodline. Lesbian and homosexual love in the biography/novel *Orlando* become naturalized as English, as Orlando's adventures are embedded in the history of England for five hundred years at home and abroad. What is necessary for an "Englishwoman's" identity, the subversive text says, is white skin and aristocratic blood. (The quintessential English couple, Orlando and Shelmerdine, despite the penchants of both for kissing Negresses in the dark, produce a male heir.)

Whether or not the Negresses give birth is not an issue. This was not, however, to prove true the next year for Radclyffe Hall's *The Well of Loneliness,* which became the subject of the obscenity trial that haunts the text of *A Room of One's Own.* But Stephen Gordon, the male-identified heroine of that belated "Condition of England" novel, wants, perversely, to reproduce lesbians, and that excludes her from English identity. It was tantamount to kissing her own "negresses" in the light, that is, at home. Could we speculate that *Orlando* was not banned because its heroine produces an heir? Could Orlando have become an English poet with becoming a mother? The two births are announced together. Where does that leave the childless lesbian writer? Woolf's text and her narrator's concern with exonerating herself from the historical guilt of imperialism (she doesn't want to "make an Englishwoman of her,") obsesses over the relation between sexuality, motherhood, and writing, invoking infanticide and battered daughterhood, in order to figure the gender of *The Poet* in terms of nationalism and race. Judith Shakespeare dies in childbirth, as a woman in the period in which Orlando pursues his adventures with Sasha and many other "negresses," if we use the word to mean forbidden lovers, as it does in *Orlando.* In her modern period Orlando's Negresses are female, if Other, and the possibility of illegitimacy is averted.

A POLITICAL FOOTBALL

Virginia Woolf's *Orlando,* her biography of literary history, addresses for us other issues apart from the problems involved in doing women's literary history and biography in the tradition of her own culture. As you will recall, the opening scene involves a little swordplay. Our eponymous hero, for surely Orlando is male in this moment of militant sportsplay that so indelibly marks the birth of western culture . . . "for there could be no doubt about his sex." Orlando is fencing with an opponent who cannot fight back, a scene of imperialism from India in the eighteenth-century to Iraq in the twenty-first. He is "slicing at the head of a moor." His harmless sparring partner is a "shrunken head:"

> It was the colour of an old football, and more or less the shape of one, save
> for the sunken teeth and a strand or two of coarse, dry hair, like the hair on
> a cocanut. Orlando's father, or perhaps his grandfather, had struck it from

the shoulders of a vast Pagan who had started up under the moon in the barbarian fields of Africa . . . Orlando's father had . . . struck many heads of many colours off many shoulders, and brought them back to hang from the rafters . . .

Woolf, *Orlando*

We may speculate about the function of this fetish in British culture and its relation to the concept of fair play. Orlando's solitary pastime, the equivalent of hitting a few balls, shooting a few baskets,—is a male ritual much practiced by the inhabitants of the British Isles and their descendants. The swinging target is the trophy head of a black man. English tribal chiefs have brought this object back from their wars of conquest in Africa. It represents the enemy, as dummies do on mock battlefields where soldiers practice killing. What does it mean that we are introduced to the quintessential English writer in an unguarded moment when he is practicing killing?

This opening scene is about the relationship of writers to violence, a subject that concerned Woolf deeply. It is about the connection between the production of culture and colonizing war and conquest. The question is still before us in ever more violent ways and war toys have been circulated beyond the elite military to mass markets. Orlando demonstrates a war game about the domination and destruction of the culture and people of another race. English Literature under the sign of the African's dead body, fetishized as a football.

Women are not to blame in Woolf's narrative of the origins of Englishness. Or are they? We need to take into account the fact that the rise of white women writers coincides with the destruction of African cultures, the plundering of its resources and people as slaves. The rise of the white woman is connected to the fall of the black man. Orlando's shrunken head is the family heritage. We cannot account for the flourishing of English culture, Woolf's novel says, without acknowledging the presence of the diminished, defeated, defaced black man at the scene of origins. The violent beheading and mutilation of the black man's body is the white woman's heritage as well. Orlando becomes a very fine Englishman as well as a very fine Englishwoman by fencing with the body of the other, the black.

The tension among and between the words *woman, Negress,* and *Englishwoman* in the passage in *A Room of One's Own* is electric. The word *fine* is similarly steeped in social significance, and also merits some attempts at explanation. I want to discuss the ways we make meaning out of text, and the problems we encounter when we do so.

It is a passage in which the narrator (and the narrator in *A Room of One's*

Own is painstakingly made of the collective voice of the Marys from the old ballad, a voice gendered specifically female, so that its relation to the author's "I" or "Virginia Woolf" is very distant) has been concerned with the "unsigned" nature of women's writing, with anonymity and the use of pseudonyms, with the veiled identity of the woman author, as I have argued in *Virginia Woolf and the Languages of Patriarchy.* The passage unveils itself as a boast that white women are morally better than men because they don't desire to mark, conquer, possess, or colonize the Negress.

Alf, Bert, and Chas, working-class hoodlums who boldly carve their names on tombstones and signposts, thus to deface public space, are invidiously compared (as men) to Currer Bell, George Eliot, and George Sand, great women authors who efface themselves. Let me make it perfectly clear that Virginia Woolf is not abusing the working class here. Her target is men in general, and they are all included under the names Mussolini or Napoleon. She is worrying about how the female signature can be produced without all the other evils that go with property and possession. Can a white (English) woman artist sign herself in the twentieth century without assuming complicity in the social sins of her male counterpart?

Identity is the issue, gender identity and national identity. Racial identity and citizenship. The speaker is both naming and blaming. The passage is deeply concerned with moving the woman artist out of the limbo of the unsigned, establishing a gendered subjectivity. To do it she signifies over the body of the racial Other. She earns her identity—Englishwoman—by appropriating the imperial gaze of the dominant male. Like Aphra Behn she appears to find a self or a writing identity by invoking the otherness of the slave. One of the questions to be addressed here is whether and why the feminist emancipatory text earns its energy at the expense of the racial Other. "All women," Woolf insisted, "together ought to let flowers fall upon the tomb of Aphra Behn, which is, most scandalously but rather appropriately, in Westminster Abbey, for it was she who earned them the right to speak." (69) "Shady and amorous as she was," (69) Aphra Behn "made, by working very hard, enough to live on. The importance of that fact outweighs anything that she actually wrote." (67) The tradition of women's writing with its "middle class" and "plebian virtues of humour, vitality and courage," which Woolf so cavalierly builds on the grave of Aphra Behn, like Behn's elusive sexuality and her politics as a Tory spy, is not a very sound structure. Suppose Aphra were originally Afra or Africa, and her lost history an erasure of racial identity? Did she work for her country as a spy to prove she was really an "Englishwoman?" Can we imagine the Negress kneeling in Westminster Abbey? Is she included in "all women"?

A Room of One's Own is, in terms of genre, a political pamphlet, a tract that has escaped from its category in terms of form, and arrived at classic status as what my students call "a novel." I have stopped arguing with them over the genre of A Room of One's Own. They are right. It is a novel. It has characters and plots. It has births and deaths and rebirths, along with all the diatribes and perorations that make it an extended lecture. If her "biography" Orlando is read as a novel, her pamphlet/speech A Room of One's Own may be read as a novel.

Beyond reading the text as a political pamphlet along with her great-grandfather's antislavery polemics, I want to look at the origins of the passage about passing a "very fine negress" in the discourse of art history and the recurrence of this figure for European modernism's similar identity crisis. The white woman's ethnographic voice is another low discourse currently under investigation by critics in Cultural Studies in which this passage participates. Woolf's (classed and gendered Englishwoman's) gaze at her "very fine negress" is part of a long tradition of white women's travel narratives and is clearly related to the young black women Lucie Duff-Gordon described to her husband in a letter from Thebes (Luxor) in 1863: "It is worth going to Nubia to see the girls," she wrote suggestively.

> Up to twelve or thirteen they are neatly dressed in a bead necklace and a leather fringe four inches wide round the loins, and anything so perfect as their shapes or so sweetly innocent as THEIR LOOK can't be conceived. My pilot's little girl came in the dress mentioned before carrying a present of cooked fish on her head and some fresh eggs. . . . I longed to steal her, she was such a darling. Two beautiful young Nubian women visited me in my boat, with hair in little plaits finished off with lumps of yellow clay, burnished like golden tags, soft, deep bronze skins, and lips and eyes fit for Isis and Hathor."[25]

A Room of One's Own continues to exist in the category of unofficial knowledge in some cultures, while it is canonized in others. Its origins as a suffrage pamphlet are obscured, as the feminist-historical discourse of "the struggle for the vote" fades from literary and cultural history. But even the reference to "Alf, Bert, or Chas." reworks the rhetoric of a particular suffrage poster that asked why lunatics and criminals had the vote when women didn't. Puzzlingly, then, it can be said to inhabit the category "classic" at the same time as it is relegated to the margins, depending on whether the culture in question has absorbed feminist practices, texts, and issues into its mainstream. Its shelf life is determined by the extent to which feminist methodologies and Women's Studies as a discipline have penetrated the universities.

Marked by its origins as a political pamphlet and not as a work of high literature, *A Room of One's Own* invites analysis, like all of Virginia Woolf's works, as a text that exhausts the limits of its genre. One might say that soliloquy itself collapses in exhaustion after it is worn to the ground in *The Waves,* and doesn't reappear until the French New Wave novel of the 1960s. Mocking its earlier existence as a series of lectures at the women's colleges, the speech-essay exults in its new status as antilecture, thumbing its nose at academic discourses of all sorts by adding characters and plot and all the attendant devices of fiction to its own form.

Saluting its oral origin, the text appears as a form of "printed voice," and it bows in tribute to Mrs. Pankhurst and the militant suffragettes by elevating their invention of a brilliant local political strategy to the status of literary trope. They had empowered a generation of fiercely trembling white British women to interrupt speakers at public meetings, to question from the floor or the balcony the men debating politics on platforms. These interruptions began as a nuisance and then enraged men who were used to the protection of their speech by formal rules privileging their debate with each other. Once women began to interrupt this male public discourse with their own questions, they quickly found their political voices. Rhetorically *A Room of One's Own,* when it interrupts itself over and over again in a series of digressions and asides that threaten to turn the narrative inside out, curtsies quite stylishly to the militant suffragettes and their insufferable and annoying tactics. It (im)prints the voice of English feminist protest, disruptive interruption, into a book from which the attentive reader may herself learn how to do it. She would not be surprised to learn that culture-making as a conversation between men is still a problem, so that the suffragettes' feminist technique of interruption is not yet obsolete as cultural praxis. But her own failure to give voice to the black woman is corrected by an emerging debate on the role and history of blacks in Britain and the diaspora, connecting national stories with stories of the passages from, to, and between Africa and the West Indies, the Americas, and Europe. The negress not only speaks, she speaks English. She *is* English.

"It is one of the great advantages of being a woman that one can pass," she asserts, "even a very fine negress without wanting to make an Englishwoman of her." (*A Room of One's Own,* 52) Woolf is here dissociating herself from nationalism and imperialism in its domestic or foreign aspects by attributing the desire to possess the Other to specifically European male "instinct, which murmers if it sees a fine woman go by, or even a dog, *Ce chien à moi."* "And, of course," she continues, "it may not be a dog, I thought, remembering Parliament Square, the *Sieges Allee* and other avenues; it may be a piece of land or a man with curly black hair." (52)

It is, of course, one of the great advantages of being a feminist literary critic that one cannot pass even a very fine example of registering objections without commenting on its self-serving racism and appallingly problematic assumptions. A white middle-class woman reader may assume that the passage is deeply and heavily ironic, since it is clear that the narrator has shown that there are in fact very few advantages to being a woman in England in the 1920s or before. For black readers it is a problem to pass over this passage in a primary feminist text.

Objecting first to the usage of those powerfully loaded words, *Negress* and *Englishwoman,* we might begin by examining some of the cultural freight they carry. Notice that both words are heavily gendered and exist as variants of the masculine normative nouns *Negro* and *Englishman.* Though both carry the burden of gender, it is not distributed equally. *Negress* is far more negatively marked than *Englishwoman* in its feminizing diminutive *-ess.* It seems to feminize the black woman but not to "womanize" her. The figure of race in the first is bound as tightly to gender as the figure of nation is bound to gender in the second. The unequal way in which each is marked as feminine, added to their already secondary status as exceptions to the male rule, makes it unlikely for these words to suggest alliance. Since *Negress* carries no national identity and *Englishwoman* carries no racial identity in Woolf's text, the effect implies that all the English are white and Negroes have no countries. (It is interesting that later, in an essay on words, Woolf merrily reveled in the cross-racial and cross-national adventures of "Mother English," celebrating liaisons unthinkable in the verbal impasse set up here against a discourse of sisterhood.)

But how was this passage to be read by the "negress" herself? Or did Virginia Woolf presume she couldn't read English, being illiterate, or wouldn't be likely to read a white feminist's polemical essay? Can we presume that the "negress" was an African national subject? How likely was this encounter in 1928 in England? As a colonial subject the black woman would have been deprived of national identity and politically disenfranchised. The "negress" may not have shared Woolf's impassioned pacifist rejection of "nation," her famous "As a woman I have no country; as a woman I want no country; as a woman my country is the whole world," from *Three Guineas.* If the Negress had no country, it was likely that it had been stolen from her or her ancestors by white European colonists. She may have experienced the loss of country, of national identity, of exile, displacement, and homelessness.

But her gender status might have been of more value in her native culture than Woolf's was in the England that had just that year, reluctantly and after a century of struggle, granted the vote to members of her sex. And, as the narrator makes sure to tell us, in keeping with the economic analysis of oppression that is a feature the text shares with Leonard Woolf's several studies of imperialism produced for the Labour Party in those years, the vote as a political weapon was of far less importance to her as a working woman than the money she received in a legacy.

If we track down the origins of the narrator's legacy in the text, we find that Woolf has provided us with a story. The white Englishwoman's economic freedom, the only freedom she thinks matters, has been earned at the expense of colonial expansion in the form of a legacy from an aunt. Her aunt died from a fall from her horse while taking the night air in Bombay. This confession that middle-class Englishwomen owe their freedom to the exploitation of the colonies in India and Africa is, I believe, a conscious move on Virginia Woolf's part. She is telling us that the five hundred pounds a year that frees the Englishwoman to write fiction, derives directly from the exploitation of her sisters in India and Africa. And that the aunt, who left her the legacy, was as implicated in colonialism as Woolf's real aunts and uncles were.[26] That precious "room of her own," so symbolic of feminist struggles in the early twentieth century, has been bought with blood money. The English woman reader is reminded of her fall, the original imperialist historical sin committed by her ancestress collecting butterflies in India or cataloging orchids in Africa, which funds the Edwardian freedom to write.

But if Woolf and her narrator are aware of these connections, how ironic is the narrator's claim that she has no wish to make an Englishwoman of the Negress? Does this signify a difference from the attitudes of her fore-aunts? Is she saying that she wouldn't colonize them or that she would not impose English language and culture on the already colonized? Was she concerned with the destruction and devaluing of native art forms and languages? Were they implicated in making Englishwomen out of Indian and African women, if only in the sense of bringing English culture to the colonies? If she tells us so clearly that gender did not exempt her aunt from responsibility, that there is indeed no feminist alibi for imperialism—is she signifying her own guilt as well? Is she not saying we have rooms of our own because they don't—our sisters in the former colonies on whose labor the "first" world largely functions? The answer is yes. And it is yes whether or not you attribute such an intention to the writer or the narrator of A Room of One's Own.

Perhaps we may undo some historical damage if we read *Room* with a black woman's text like Linda Brent's *Incidents in the Life of a Slave Girl,* which relates the confinement theme of *A Room of One's Own* to gender and race, suggesting the horror of the holds of slave ships in the narrator's seven-year confinement in a garret. We might then ask why Woolf claims such a small space for the woman artist's exercise of freedom, why she plays on the domestic locked-in/locked-out trope of the prison transformed into a private work space.

Though there were few black Britons at the time Woolf wrote, they were in fact there. But now the question of wanting or not wanting "to make an Englishwoman of her" is much more complicated. It obviously never entered Woolf's mind that the "very fine negress" could *be* an Englishwoman. And if she did not see her in terms of equality in national identity, she may not have seen her as a fellow woman either. In disclaiming the desire to colonize this fine figure of a Negress, doesn't she at the same time mark her out for colonization by her male counterpart? Certainly there is a large population of black Englishwomen at present who might be expected to be upset at the questioning of their right to such a national identity. They are legally *Englishwomen,* but Woolf's problem is still with us. The definition of Englishness is now being hotly contested in racial clashes, as is the definition of what it is to be German.[27]

How would this problematic passage be read now by a black woman? By any person of color? How will it be read and understood in a racially mixed classroom now?

Drawing on the literary and social insights about racial "passing" made by contemporary Black feminist critics Hortense Spillers, Mae Henderson, and Deborah McDowell, one senses here in Woolf's peripatetic narrator a classic figure of the "woman who passes" (walks by, overtakes) a Negress, that she is passing as a white male. If she has passed the Negress (literally) is she gazing at her back, her profile, or her face? Is she looking over her shoulder at this creature who captures her imagination? The reader at this point in the text is forced to recognize that the narrator not only has a gender, she has a color, and that color is white. She has a race as well as the person who is the object of her gaze, and that race colors her view. Could Mrs. Brown or Ms. Brown, as the case may be, gaze back at the pale, thin, popeyed, straggle-haired woman whose clothes are held together with safety pins—with impunity? What does Ms. Brown see? Not exactly a "very fine Englishwoman." Nothing to write home about. Not exactly the healthy pink-and-white finest-flower-of-her-race English rose, but a nervous, high-strung eccentric who draws the stares of people in the street.

The narrator's gaze is raced as well as gendered and powerfully erotic. Readers also stumble over the passage about "kissing a negress in the dark" in *Orlando*. What's the difference between passing and kissing? Was Woolf aware of the racial meaning of the word *pass*? One of Woolf's most charming personae is that of the *flâneuse*, the English version of the *flâneur*, the European male walker in the city, the dandy and artist-observer. Woolf resembles Walter Benjamin in the awkwardness of her insider/outsider position. She calls herself a street haunter and makes clear that she is breaking a gender taboo by her eccentric pattern of walking and looking, since those activities are usually reserved for men. As a woman she is supposed to be looked at, not to look herself. For that bold look of a woman is culturally assumed to belong to a prostitute. A lady's eyes are cast down in public. When she assumes the privileges of the gaze, as she looks at the Negress, is she any different from the men who make her so uncomfortable by staring at her as she walks the city streets?

Do her color and her class allow her to colonize city space in exactly the way that men do in regard to women? Ordinarily hesitant in gait (and often pathologically agoraphobic), does Virginia Woolf's fleeting passing as a man who gazes possessively on a woman in this passage, reproduce in her own gaze at a black woman the unequal power she observes in her critique of the male gaze at women, property, dogs, and unfamiliar (racially Other) men? (The "curly black hair" is presumably the Other of men with straight blond hair, or at least it is a sign of being possessed rather than possessing. It also reminds the reader of the difficult "hair of the Jew in the bath" passage in *The Years,* another problematic "racial" scene.)

The words that stop us short as we read the passage are those insolent ones, "very fine." Perhaps she did not think they were insolent words when she wrote them. Perhaps the whole passage is ironic, as listeners always tell me when I make this point in a talk. The word *fine* is also applied to a man's annexing attitudes in relation to the category "woman." But, as I have suggested, Woolf's usage here suggests that the category "woman" does not include any blacks, that a "negress" is altogether someone else. Either blacks are not women at all, or not women as the author defined them. What does it *mean* to say "a very fine negress"?

Woolf would have seldom passed black people of any kind, in the Oxford and Cambridge streets and quadrangles of her text. She may not often have encountered Africans or West Indians or African-Americans in the streets and public places she traversed in her daily walks in London or in Sussex in the 1920s. But she would have passed laundresses and waitresses and cleaners and cooks, white Englishwomen of the working class. She would not have been likely to be stopped in her tracks by "very fine" examples of their type, though it was class difference that made the telling distinctions in English culture. And it is not clear whether any of the black or Asian intellectuals, poets, and revolutionaries she encountered in the British Museum or the guests of her husband's whom she entertained at dinner, would have fitted the category "very fine negress."

Certainly Virginia Woolf's membership in the radical 1917 Club and her research and editing of her husband's position papers on imperialism placed her among the few white European intellectuals who were concerned about racial inequities in this period. But her youthful appearance in blackface in her brother's "Dreadnought Hoax" prank, impersonating a member of the Ethiopian ambassador's inspection party, calls her commitment into question. (In this context, of course, she could have seen an example of a "very fine negress" by looking in the mirror, though her disguise was probably meant to cross gender as well.)

That London in the twenties and thirties was not hospitable to blacks we know from Nancy Cunard's attempts to get hotel accommodations for her black friends (among whom were musicians, poets, and political leaders) and their experience of segregation in restaurants and public places. Both Cunard's pamphlet *Black Man, White Ladyship* (1931) ("How come, white man, is the rest of the world to be re-formed in your dreary and decadent image?" Ford, 108–109) and her monumental eight hundred-page anthology *Negro* (1934) exposed racism as they amassed an enormous body of important anthropological, historical and artistic work on global black culture(s).[28] Paul Robeson's biography, as well as those of other black artists, records the humiliations blacks underwent continually as they fell among the master race. However, as much as London oppressed people of color, Paris welcomed them.

We know that Virginia Woolf did a great deal of the research and fact gathering for Leonard Woolf's impressive anticolonial book *Empire and Commerce in Africa* (1920).[29] Surprisingly radical in its economic analysis of imperialism, it documents the annexation of territory by the European powers: "The British State in a few years added 26,000,000 square miles to its territory in order to supply its citizens with free markets." (9) He makes it a point not to discuss race, or, rather, as Paul Rich points out, like Hobson, he argued for enlightened trusteeship as English colonial policy, because Africa was a "continent inhabited by a population which belongs almost entirely to the non–adult races." (Rich, 77) "Only the sun, malaria and sleeping sickness have saved and will continue to save the African from extermination by the white man," he wrote (357). It could of course be argued that the revolutionary politics expressed by Leonard Woolf in this seldom-mentioned volume were a product of expiation of his guilt at having been a very successful colonial administrator in Ceylon. He was for nearly thirty years the secretary of the Labour Party Advisory Committee on Imperial Affairs, and drafted with Charles Buxton in 1926 "The Empire in Africa: Labour's Policy," which advocated "no economic exploitation of one class (native) by another class (white man.)" (78) He wrote as an ex-imperial administrator, seemingly without faith in revolutionary African nationalism to defeat colonial force. He analyzed race in terms of class.

But, as his work and that of Nancy Cunard make clear, there was a real, if small, liberal discourse (in Labour committees and left-wing journals) in England from 1917 through the thirties, which recognized imperialism and racism as part of English social history, even if it was marginal to the power of Trevelyan's narrative of national character in his *History of England* or *English Social History*. The production of knowledge about race by British Left intellectuals in this period (and especially the role of the Labour Party) deserves further study. Leonard and Virginia Woolf, as publishers at the Hogarth Press, produced many of the important British books on race and imperialism in both Africa and India.[30] Leonard Woolf's enlightened position papers did little to change government policy. Nancy Cunard's important research and publication of the history of black people internationally; her research trips to the United States, the West Indies, and Cuba to commission and write comparative histories of slavery for the *Negro* anthology; her fund-raising efforts in England on behalf of the Scottsboro Boys, as well as her writing and political work with George Padmore on racism and on the founding of Ghana, were the objects of surveillance by both the British and the U.S. intelligence agencies, and she has been systematically left out of all histories of the period.[31] There may be cultural forces at work to obscure the role of British Labour and the Left on racial questions. Certainly it is true that vested interests have prevented a clear account of the Labour and Left opposition to feminism and the struggle for women's rights in Britain becoming available. Certainly the Woolfs' friend Nancy Cunard's lifetime of radical effort in behalf of black liberation does not show a particular interest in black women. As a collector of African art, however, which she showed in her Paris shop for the Hours Press, Cunard exhibited and owned many "fine" examples of female fertility figures.

HEART OF DARKNESS

This figure of the "fine negress" haunts the history of modernism. Signifying the lost maternal primitive, the body of the heart of darkness, it haunts the writing, painting, and music of the period. It is ironic that it seems to function to obscure the history of real black women.

Dependent as European modernism is on the forms of African sculpture and on the theft or borrowing of African conceptions of the human figure in three-dimensional space, it is obvious now that the experience of colonial expansion into the space of Africa may have been the origin of what we call spatial modernism. The words *very fine* are not part of the discourse of political economy. They exist in the visual vocabularies of anthropology and art history. That the "woman" who calls the "negress" "very fine" can be constructed backwards as white and English and upper middle class but, above all, in possession of that very possessive, measuring, and judging gaze from which she herself suffered. Its racist ring also echoes the scientific discourse invoking the Victorian imperialist gaze of Mary Kingsley and the anthropologist-adventurers who photographed and took measurements of the natives of Africa and Asia and their flora and fauna as they "explored" their continents, rivers, and mountains.

Woolf's passage recalls the invocation of the word *fine* to refer to a particularly good example of a type. The "very fine negress" in this case might be a *specimen* collected and displayed for observation. Woolf's words participate in an old and well-established discourse of rational specimen collection and exhibition, part of the Western scientific will to know and name and own, to categorize, judge for beauty, size, color, and place in museums, zoos, or botanical gardens. This specimen-making gaze is deeply possessive and coldly judgmental, and if the Negress felt its colonizing sting, she may well have recoiled from its violent intrusion in horror or shame.

Steeped as she was in the Elizabethan literature of exploration and adventure, Woolf may have simply absorbed the language of the master race. "A very fine negress" might have been the words on a label for an ethnographic photograph mounted and on view in the Museum of Mankind or Musée de l'Homme or Museum of Natural History, or a sketched, carved, or sculpted figure in some scientific or anthropological volume or journal from Captain Cook to Malinowski or the *National Geographic*. The "fine" in this case may have indicated an especially interesting example of a racial type, a model of physical health or an example of extreme difference from Europeans. The further her look was from the Englishwoman, presumably, the finer the Negress.

It goes without saying that these figures were naked and that their most prominent features were the breasts. The eroticizing of the African woman's maternal qualities and the fetishizing of her breasts are common features of such ethnographic discourses, both written and photographic, from Michel Leiris to Margaret Mead. Toni Morrison unearths this history in the terrible version of a rape scene in *Beloved,* in which the slave Sethe, a nursing mother, is milked by her master's sons, who have been instructed in this racial "science" by Schoolteacher. When she kills her baby girl to keep her from slavery, she may also be invoking the figure of Shakespeare's sister, the pregnant suicide, from *A Room of One's Own,* who could be said to have killed her unborn child to keep her from gender slavery. (Morrison wrote an M.A. thesis on Woolf.)

An Englishwoman is Being Beaten

As I argued earlier, *A Room of One's Own,* like a good deal of feminist protest literature, uses the tropes of slavery to make the case for women's oppression. Woolf's Englishwoman, the fifteenth-century daughter who refused to marry the man of her father's choice (which she takes from Trevelyan's *History of England* [1926]), and who was "locked up, beaten and flung about the room" is created in her text as a slave, not a "freeborn Englishwoman," through the repetition of this scene throughout the text.[32] In staging the scene of women's history as *An Englishwoman Is Being Beaten,*[33] and calling on the historian George Macaulay Trevelyan as her authority in so doing, Woolf links the "very fine negress" and the "Englishwoman" as victims of male violence, as female bodies hurt and imprisoned against their will. She wants us to know how few the references are to women in the standard English histories. But she has other motives as well. By marking the scene of woman's oppression as such a scene of violence, she brilliantly links it with the scene of the slave being beaten. The words "locked up, beaten and flung about the room" come to signify the white woman's position in English national life. The rhetorical energy gathered in the repetition of the scene of an *Englishwoman* being beaten is used to fuel the feminist complaint. "Nation" and "Race" remain distinct categories. The rhetoric borrows from the literature of abolition and the antislavery movement of Woolf's Clapham Sect forebears to connect the victimized Englishwoman to victimized slaves. The repeated summoning up of the apparition of the battered white girl triggers in the reader the same response as mention of the Indian massacres did in previous generations. When Britons wanted to arouse racist feelings, they called up the figure of white women being raped and killed by Indians. Here Woolf turns the reader's anger toward the figure of the English father. In fact the whole text creates Englishmen with "Milton's Bogey" or God the father as the patriarchal enemy.

When Woolf appropriates the tropes of slavery for the cause of feminism, we are shocked and moved despite ourselves. Surely women were not as badly treated as slaves, we think. But the repetition of this drama, in which a father abuses his daughter, as constitutive of the English national character, is almost intolerable. She doesn't allow any other picture of an English-woman's life to intrude on this performance. If this is the case, why would a Negress want to be an Englishwoman, since an Englishwoman is a slave?

Woolf's portrait of an Englishwoman as a slave girl is dependant on her portrait of an Englishman as a tyrant father. But her construction of free-dom is in the choice of a lover or husband, not of work or a room of one's own. Yet marriage is just a continuation of the daughter's enslavement. She really pushes the point on the difference between empowered women in fiction and imprisoned women in history or real life: "[I]n fact she was the slave of any boy whose parents forced a ring upon her finger." (45)

(We can see a similar commandeering of another rhetoric of freedom (on a different scale) in Afro-American historical recycling of the Old Testa-ment to create the liberatory culture of black Christianity.)

"It was certainly," she writes, "an odd monster that one made up by reading the historians first and the poets afterwards—a worm winged like an eagle." (46) Putting white Englishwomen in the monster/slave category leaves no room for the Negress as victim. By repeatedly focusing the reader's eye on the picture of a white woman being beaten, Woolf incites a feminist narrative desire to rescue the victim, or the daughter in oneself. She also blocks any movement of the text toward linear closure. If history cannot change woman's position over time, the reader and the narrator can collab-orate to liberate a space, a room into which she cannot be locked; one in which she cannot be beaten and flung about.

The word *fine* also means pure, perfect, delicate, and precious, or smartly dressed, and the *OED* points out that it is often used ironically. (There may be an echo of class hostility behind the ironic usage.) But here Woolf seems to mean that the Negress is an object of art of superior quality, an exquisite or rare piece of sculpture to be seen, admired, and acquired by the collec-tor. The "woman" is moving past the still figure of the Negress, looking at her body as an art object (and sexual object?). Is the erotic charge Woolf herself teaches us to see in the male gaze there in her own exploitive eye-balling of the Other? Is the Negress she passes perhaps a polished figurine the viewer conflates with the African woman it resembles? (Here we need a chorus of the popular song "You're So Fine," a selection of instances of black English usages of the word *fine* in the United States, the West Indies, England, and English-speaking Africa, and a picture of Virginia Woolf from the black woman's point of view. Similarly the passage's association of the Negress with a dog [as wild creatures to be tamed and domesticated] reminds one of Woolf's citation of Dr. Johnson's comparison of a woman preaching to a dog dancing. Since so much of the literature of protest on the issue of women's liberation continues to be written in terms of the metaphors of slavery, and Woolf herself certainly called on this tradition, it is unfortunate that this passage implicates her so firmly in the culture she wished to abjure.)[34]

But we may imagine another scenario. When Roger Fry took Virginia Woolf to the Chelsea Book Club exhibition of Negro art in April 1920, she found it both "dismal and impressive," she told her sister Vanessa (*Letters,* vol. 1, 429).[35] Fry's essay championing Negro art appeared in the *Athenaeum* and formed part of his influential book *Vision and Design.*[36] The whole-hearted embrace of African forms for their purely aesthetic qualities, which Fry espoused, along with other primitivist modernists like Matisse and Picasso, shocked the art world and began to change public attitudes. Arguing that African sculpture was the closest thing there is to "pure art," without any romantic associations with real life or representation, his essay suggests that Woolf's Negress may have been derived from the remembered Yoruba figure that so captivated Fry, that her "fine" was an echo of his "pure." Of course, it was only pure in the sense that Fry was looking at these elegant plastic forms out of context. They had of course cultural "meaning" in Africa, but he was even less likely to want to make a specifically African woman out of the image of a "very fine negress" than Virginia Woolf was to make an Englishwoman of her. According to Mariana Torgovnik, Fry's obsession with an African figure led to the suicide of a Frenchwoman who was his lover, it having threatened her sense of her own womanhood.[37]

Since Virginia Woolf's statement comes at the end of a long paragraph in the text bemoaning the effects of the *fetish* of the cult of chastity on women's lives in the course of English history, it suggests that she may have been applying anthropological methods to her own culture. It is possible that she was making an effort to escape the ethnographic gaze and trying *not* to see the figures as fetishes. The effort of seeing outside of the familiar frameworks of her own culture, which Fry required of her, may have been so difficult and exhausting that she came to think of a Negress not as a woman but as a work of art, a statue with pronounced female genitals. Fry's attribution of aesthetic purity to African carvings of the female form (when to the prurient eye they were sexually provocative) may have lead Woolf later to reflect on the social concept of chastity and its restriction of women's bodies in Western societies. Woolf may have associated the formal purity of the sculpture Fry celebrated with a similar social and political freedom for women in African societies. Her use of the word *fetish* to refer to barbaric English customs regarding women is certainly ironic here, mocking the anthropologist's tone in regard to supposedly backward cultures. It is her own culture that is barbaric in its treatment of the "religious importance" of chastity in women's lives. She may be thinking that to make an English-woman out of such a free and pure creature would be to restrict her free-dom and power. But I doubt it.

Roger Fry's interest in Negro art was lodged in the visual and the spatial. Since the power to create expressive plastic form is one of the greatest of hu-man achievements, he wrote, it was difficult "to admit that certain nameless savages have possessed this power not only in a higher degree than we at this moment, but than we as a nation ever possessed it. . . . They have indeed complete plastic freedom . . . these African artists really conceive form in three dimensions." Speaking of the maker of the Yoruba sculpture, Fry says that "he actually underlines, as it were, the three-dimensionalness of his forms." But great artists do not great culture make. Negro cultures are un-civilized because they have produced no critics. "It is for want of a conscious critical sense and the intellectual powers of comparison and classification that the negro has failed to create one of the great cultures of the world, and not from any lack of the creative aesthetic impulse, nor from lack of the most exquisite sensibility and the finest taste" (*Vision and Design,* 70–73). It is the power of the critical gaze, the discerning eye, that decides whether the Negress is fine or coarse, that determines what is civilized. And yet he has already told us that the "savage" eye sees better than the civilized. Appar-ently it can see only to make, not to judge.

Roger Fry is completely mystified by a culture that produces artists of such power who do not sign their work. He implies that if they had signed their sculptures he would accept African societies as cultures in their own right. But the missing signatures consign them to the dustheap of history (and of course silently justify the theft of these objects to be preserved in ap-preciative museums and private collections in the West). When Woolf claims that anonymity runs in women's blood is her passage building on his as well as collating race and gender oppressions? She puts down to chastity anonymous cultural production by women, even as late as the use of male pseudonyms by Western women writers in the nineteenth century. The great unsigned artists of the past are what she claims as her female heritage of anonymous artists. They didn't even write Alf, Bert, or Chas on the trees. The *unsigned* nature of the woman artist's work links it to Fry's valuation of African anonymous work as the "purest" forms there are. Is Woolf claim-ing a similar status to that of the anonymous African sculptors for her un-signed women? Is Africa romanticized by a certain Modernism as the place where the chastity of women is not fetishized, hence women are free and artists are free to render that freedom in pure form? Woolf's language de-

scribing the woman artist in sixteenth-century England is about confinement, "tortured and pulled asunder," "thwarted and hindered," ending her
days "in some lonely cottage outside the village, half witch, half wizard."
There is a reversal here of language that was then being applied to the culture of the Other in anthropological discourse; witches and wizards along
with fetishes are being attributed to her own culture.

In marrying Leonard Woolf and associating herself with radical ideas and
ideals, Woolf shed many of the beliefs and prejudices of her family and class.
But one could argue nonetheless that she has robbed her "very fine negress"
of subjectivity in much the same way as men appropriated hers. The white
female upper-middle-class gaze of the art collector or connoisseur reduces
the black woman to a beautiful object to be "appreciated" or consumed.
When Roger Fry celebrated the African artist's aesthetic emphasis on the
protuberant parts of the body, he must have been aware that European
viewers would see savage sexuality where he saw vision and design. It was
perhaps a struggle for someone like Virginia Woolf to use the word *fine* and
the discourse of art appreciation to refer to a naked black female body.
Britons' notions of themselves as the "imperial race" fostered a problematic
of gendered social purity, setting the white woman against the native, which
anticipated Roger Fry's artistic fascination with "purity" of forms.

Helen Calloway writes, following Homi Bhabha, that the notion of purity emerged as a powerful signifier for the production of difference in the
discourses of imperialism and English national identity, justifying repressive
laws and "ruthless violence against incipient insurgencies."[38] At the same
time that art critics like Roger Fry and artists like Picasso and Matisse were
collecting, exhibiting, and celebrating (as well as copying or translating into
Western art forms) the arts of African peoples, especially carvings of the female body, imperialist administrators and missionaries were attempting to
impose Victorian gender roles as a way of controlling women's independence in Africa. Presumably one of the ways in which Fry's vision of a
Yoruba wooden carving of a woman was "fine" in Western terms was its
representation of a proud and free female body.

UNDER AFRICAN EYES

Although I cannot yet place a negress or even an ordinary black woman at
the scene of the exhibition of Negro Art in London in 1920, I am sure she
was there. The work of Peter Fryer and Gretchen Gerzina has shown how
strong a black presence there has been in England since the beginning of

slavery. And now, Josh Gosciak's work shows that the West Indian writer Claude McKay was in England from 1919 until 1922 working with C. K. Ogden, the linguistic philosopher, pacifist, feminist and publisher of McKay's poems in The Cambridge Review. McKay also worked as a journalist for Sylvia Pankhurst's paper the *Workers' Dreadnought,* a left wing journal that published his poetry as well. Ogden felt that the magazine had scored a coup in publishing a black artist. He enthused:

> . . . here was no ordinary set of verses. From an academic point of view, the emergence of a remarkable personality, the first of his race to express himself in such a medium might alone have secured him attention. Are we not ethnologists? Do we not send expeditions to strange parts to hunt for the dusky, bosky art-products of Hoo-Doo and Voo-Doo? Are there not literary critics in universities who maintain that without a knowledge of the classics our noble English language cannot be writ? Have we not Schools of English to show that three years on top of ten are necessary for the acquisition of a style? Yet here was the mountain come to Mohamet, a Daniel come to the lion's den for judgment.
>
> [*Cambridge Magazine* Jan—March, 1921]

Ogden's words are not remarkable in a period white primitivist discourse that often claims the blacks it discovers as "the first," to do something with no evidence, often accompanied by what became a cliché—an invented pedigree of "pure African" blood. But Ogden was elated to find in McKay's poems proof of his own theories of Basic English, believing he had found the key to a world language in McKay's easy mastery of the structures and rhythms of English poetry and adaptation of the forms for his own use. This meant that language and culture could be separated from racial origin.

McKay was more than a living display of the claims of the "Basic English" group to Ogden. Soon they were sampling all the cultural delights of London in the twenties. They went to classical concerts, to the Negro Art show and to the controversial Post-Impressionists, writing avidly to each other their opinions and critiques. If Virginia Woolf passed Claude McKay at the exhibition of Negro Art, it is possible that their companions, Ogden and Roger Fry, recognized each other. The Woolfs would not have frequented the International Club, where McKay brought Ogden to meet foreign intellectuals, blacks, radicals, and Bolsheviks, but he might have been noticeable at the 1917 Club, which Woolf visited immediately after seeing the Negro Art Show, and the scene of racist attacks on McKay by British leftists. While the 1917 Club was a political haven for the Woolfs and other socialist members of Bloomsbury, it was not mixed racially and had none of the international camaraderie of the colored clubs McKay enjoyed. Claude McKay was very handsome, in addition to his qualities as artist and writer. He might fit the description of a "very fine Negro." Can we imagine Virginia Woolf observing the attack on him in the 1917 Club that he described to Ogden? Can we imagine what distinction she made between the African statues she saw at the exhibition and the West Indian poet who claimed equality with her and her culture?

In his Soho flat, Ogden kept a collection of African masks that later inspired some passages in McKay's novel, *Banana Bottom*. They met frequently at the British Museum, where McKay was doing research for his Dutch mentor, J.L.J.F.E. Ezerman, for a book to be called *The Negro*. McKay was awed by the Benin bronzes. "I've been looking at the girl's head you spoke about," he wrote to Ogden. "I suppose it is the one with the elaborate horn-like headdress. It is great indeed, the cheeks, chin, and forehead are exquisite." He noted the tremendous difference between African art objects. Some seem "Greek," and others, like a Congo woman's head in the shape of a vessel, seem too primitive. He told Ogden that his responses were often personal; as a West-Indian:

"They make me think of medicine gods and charms to frighten evil spirits. In the islands among the natives it is the reptile world that the obeahmen use to inspire fear in their clients—snakes, frogs, lizards, etc. We have a weird superstition about a salamander which I will tell you of sometime. Naturally in all Negroes, at least the West Indians, where there is no real fear there is a great aversion to reptiles. And I sense the atmosphere of fear in the images, Indeed the limbs make me think of reptiles. There is no repose, grace or dignity in them, They are disturbing. I shouldn't care to live among them."[39]

In his novel *Banana Bottom* (1933) Claude McKay raises the question of European fascination with primitive art. The emancipated feminist who adopts Bita Plant and sends her to England to be educated as an "exhibit" to the native Jamaicans, is partly based on Sylvia Pankhurst, his English left wing feminist mentor who was devoted to the cause of African liberation. Unlike the heroine of his novel, McKay never returned to Jamaica. Recalling his London experience of the fashionable explosion of interest in African art in the twenties, in *Banana Bottom* McKay brilliantly describes Mrs. Craig's visit to a missionary collection of African art. The powerful scene combines elements of his own surprise and fear at first sight of these objects with a portrait of the overwhelming elemental physical response and rising sexual tension he imagined white women to feel when they encountered certain African images. The missionaries have "a striking collection of savage craftsmanship which they were exhibiting as heathen idols with lectures on 'The Customs and Superstitions of the Primitive African'." For her the masks and statues are obscene: "For those small statues with important points exaggerated and others minimized the word that came to her lips was 'grotesque.' . . . they seemed to take on a forbidden actuality and potency, as if they were immortal . . . The objects were so positively real. Surely they possessed some elemental force representing more than mere idol-making. She was troubled to think they might have their origin in some genuine belief . . . that the night-wrapped creatures of Africa might also have had there in the jungle their own vision of life." Mrs. Craig is overwhelmed with terror at what she feels are 'satanic' forces. When she reaches out to touch the eye of a grinning mask: ". . . the mocking thing suddenly detached itself and began dancing around her. Others followed the first and Priscilla found herself surrounded by a grinning dancing fury. [She] remained transfixed, deprived of voice to shriek her utter terror among those bodiless barbaric faces circling and darting towards her and bobbing up and down with that mad grinning . . . suddenly she too was in motion and madly whirling round and round with the weird dancing masks."

McKay's phantasmagoric scene of the white woman confronted by primitive African art (and her own demons) is profoundly disquieting. It suggests the scenes in films of the period of Africans dancing in violent sexualized or cannibalistic fury aimed at whites. The passage is much like a dream related by Nancy Cunard in which she finds that she unconsciously "knows the steps" of the dance and joyfully joins the Africans. Mrs. Craig is more reluctant, but she, too, joins the Africans and dances all night in a private orgy. McKay's vision in this extraordinary scene imagines what happens if the tables are turned and African eyes are upon those who had the power to look at them, returning the gaze of the white westerner. Does Priscilla Craig experience the powerlessness blacks have felt at being seen without being allowed to look back? She touches the eyes behind the masks to see if they are real. The disembodied eyes (and somehow their disembodiedness is crucial to the "uncanny" being evoked here), set her feet to dancing as if unlocking her own primitive feelings. McKay's brilliant scene challenges the imperialist fetishism of the white gaze.

Can we read the African eyes in this passage as McKay's call for African art to liberate white viewers into a new kind of seeing that would allow black people to gaze back, to exchange glances with those who "pass" and look at them with impunity?

I imagine Claude McKay outside the British Museum as he was often during his sojourn in London, waiting for his friend, C. K. Ogden. He is clearly what Virginia Woolf would call a very fine Negro. He has the sensibility of his heroine Bita Plant and the verbal power of the Jamaican poet. What does he think as Virginia Woolf walks past? Does the black writer know who the white writer is? Has the white writer read the black writer's poems in *The Cambridge Review*? Would it occur to him to think of *her* as an art object, fine or not so fine? The emerging black intellectual raises his eyes to hers, trying out his new powers. Does she look back? Lower her eyes? Turn away? Let us imagine that their eyes lock together for a moment, then turn slowly and respectfully back to their objectives.

The fragile boundaries of Woolf's self-conscious role as *flâneuse,* her vacillation between safety and danger in looking at the black woman's body, and perhaps trying to erase difference by regarding the figure as an art object rather than a woman like herself, a sister subject to the same white male gaze that wants to possess "a fine woman," do not disappear from *A Room.* There is no bonding at the level of gender, however much she may possibly, to give her the benefit of the doubt, regard real African women and their representations as superior to their Western counterparts, one could argue that she still remains a "cold stranger" to the object of her gaze. Is it that under the Western woman's eye the Negress becomes merely a racial subject, and that whiteness is not yet a racial category for Woolf herself (although it will certainly become one in *The Waves)?*[40] John MacKenzie has documented the British popular cult of spectacles of imperialism in pageantry, propaganda, film, photography, and theater.[41] Woolf's eye and that of her narrator may be indulging that European visual lust to see and categorize the Other. As Ian Jeffrey puts it, "[T]he camera became a coloniser," "Through photography Europe could provide itself with a visual representation of the remodelling of the world through economic and political control."[42] The power and widespread circulation of images of "savages" in a discourse of visual imperialism may have prevented the English public from seeing what Roger Fry could see in "a very fine negress," the *beauty of pure form.* But Virginia Woolf was perhaps more likely to have passed "a very fine negress" in the flesh outside the confines of the exhibit at the Chelsea Book Club or the pages of Roger Fry or Clive Bell's formal theories of beauty.

It was a standard feature of Victorian and modern exhibitions to display "primitive" villages, complete with human villagers, and we know that Virginia Woolf was among the twenty seven million people who went to the great exhibition at Wembley in 1924–1925.[43] Images of the Indian Pavilion appear in *The Waves,* and that novel re-creates Indians as Africans— savages, cannibals with assegais—in the imagination of the white Londoners who are its characters. MacKenzie points out that the colonial exhibitions were very popular and that the practice of bringing peoples from overseas began in 1867 in the Paris exhibitions where exotic foods were served by exotic peoples in reproductions of the streets of Cairo complete with belly dancers and camel rides. And French "explorers" traveled around Europe with Senegalese and Dahomean villagers. Wembley's enormous spatial displays of imperial power in the colonies included an anthropological section, whose offical guide referred to such "native customs" as "human sacrifice and cannibalism," sensational propaganda that prompted a group calling itself Students of Black Descent to complain to the Colonial Office about the way Africans were "held up to public ridicule" in Wembley (110). The overwhelming spatial expansion and dominance of the exhibition grounds themselves, often requiring maps and guides and transportation for the crowds of viewers, themselves mimicked imperial expansion and enforced its naturalization as exploration and modernization.

If indeed Virginia Woolf (or the narrator of *A Room of One's Own*) passed "a very fine negress" in the context of such a colonial exhibition, it is understandable that her instinct would have responded to the degradation and exoticizing of the Other by protesting in shame and embarrassment that she had had nothing to do with the colonizing efforts of her fellow Englishmen or the imperialism which set before the eyes of metropolitan citizens the raw and naked "primitive" villages and people that were the sources of their own material wealth and well-being.

Locked up in the Victorian house by the spatial limits on a young lady's experience, we assume she had already seen more than one "very fine negress" in her imagination and in the pictures of the travellers. Perhaps some of the ambivalence we feel expressed in Woolf's spatialization of race, gender, gaze, imperialism, and nationalism in this passage from *A Room of One's Own* has its source in the conflicts between her own upbringing and the Bloomsbury socialist and liberal anti-imperialist values she shared with her friends and her husband, if not with the Negress she passed in the street. Certainly her very British room of her own is a space in which one can escape being the object of the gaze of others, of being judged by gender as fine or not so fine according to Victorian standards of what a woman should be or do, if not by race. But the freedom being sought, the space imagined—is merely for privacy in confinement, to police one's own prison, as it were, not to stretch into unbounded space. The three-dimensional figures of African women which modernism admired and appropriated suggest a history and experience of physical freedom in immense spatial terms, far beyond the imagination of confined Western women. It is hard to imagine Ms. Brown, the contemporary version of the "very fine negress," content in such confinement, or wanting only a room rather than a country or a planet of her own, though perhaps that romanticizes an antiurban Africanity.

Politically and ethically, critics and anthropologists may rob the writers of subjecthood by isolating them as objects to be studied, a problem that has drawn much serious critical attention. But this question also raises the vexed one of whether one may write across gender, class, race, or ethnic lines, as well as the question of just who may write safely about whom. Let us continue to search for the places where the negress in London or Paris wrote about the European woman or spoke back to that gaze, as Claude McKay does in *Banana Bottom*.

3

Britannia Rules *The Waves*

What has made it impossible for us to live in time like fish in water, like birds in air, like children? It is the fault of Empire! Empire has created the time of history. Empire has located its existence not in the smooth recurrent spinning time of the cycle of the seasons but in the jagged time of rise and fall, of beginning and end, of catastrophe. Empire dooms itself to live in history and plot against history. One thought alone preoccupies the submerged mind of Empire: how not to end, how not to die, how to prolong its era. By day it pursues its enemies. . . . By night it feeds on images of disaster.

J. M. Coetzee *Waiting for the Barbarians*

The waves drummed on the shore, like turbaned warriors, like turbaned men with poisoned assegais who, whirling their arms on high, advance upon the feeding flocks, the white sheep.

The Waves (77)

OTHER PEOPLE'S EYES

Virginia Woolf's novel *The Waves* has consistently been read as a work of high modernism, a novel of the thirties that is not a thirties novel.[1] Its canonical status has been based on a series of misreadings of Woolf's lyrical text as synonymous with and celebratory of upper-class genteel British culture. A look at its structure and time frames, however, makes clear that the italicized interludes take the form of a set of Hindu prayers to the sun, marking its course during a single day and that these (Eastern) episodes surround a (Western) narrative in Coetzee's "jagged time" of "rise and fall," a phrase repeated throughout the novel, as a sign of the "fall" of British imperialism. It is true that imperialist history is divided into chapters called "the rise of . . ." or "the fall of . . . ." In *The Waves* Woolf explores the way in which fiction imitates the wavelike motion just then declared by scientists to be a key to the universe. But her interest is also in the relation of class (and race and gender) to culture, and the novel explores the way in which the cultural narrative "England" is created by an Eton/Cambridge elite who (re)produce (the national) epic ("the rise of . . .") and elegy ("the fall of . . .") in praise of the hero.

When a text like *The Waves* situates itself in the oppositional framework of minority discourse but is refused a place among the countercanonical classics of the thirties by a certain set of cultural guardians, one senses their fear of "poetic" language and experimental structure as vehicles for radical politics. The interpretive history of the reception of the text, particularly its rejection by those Left critics whose ideology it presumably shares, exposes an awkward gender and class bias, a certain paternalism in British Left criticism from F. R. Leavis to Raymond Williams, which cannot come to terms with a "Marxist" novel that is not realist, an anti-imperialist novel that is not (I am sorry to say) written by a man.[2] The failure of the text to reach its contemporary intended audience and its subsequent status as "difficult," or only available to an elite, has ensured its relegation to the "unread" except in formalist or philosophical terms and has operated as a cultural imperative that continues to deprive Virginia Woolf of readers of color or the working class.

Why, one may ask, have left-wing guardians of English culture steered such readers to Lawrence and Orwell for their moral and political heritage, rather than to the radicalism of Virginia Woolf? What a different narrative of modernism might have emerged if Frederic Jameson had read *The Waves* with Conrad's *Lord Jim* as exposing the ideology of the British ruling class. Perhaps he would have been forced to question his privileging of *Lord Jim*. Edward Said's praise of *Kim* and Jameson's exploration of fascist modernism are moves that seem deliberately to avoid reading or acknowledging the profound critque of imperialism and the class system in Virginia Woolf's work. Some very astute critics are unable to accept Woolf's irony about an author figure so like herself in the portrait of Bernard, and they seem to ignore the antipatriotic and anti-imperialistic outbursts in the text as inconsistent with an incorrect notion of the author's politics based on her gender and class. The interpretive history of *The Waves* for a socialist feminist critic then, is largely a negative burden, for *The Waves* simply does not exist as a cultural icon of the thirties, as part of the discourse about ("the rise of . . .") fascism, war and imperialism in which it was written. The critical act of replacing it in this discourse is an aggressive cultural move made possible now, I would argue, by the legitimation of "Cultural Studies" and the combined methodologies of feminism, Marxism, and Post-Colonialism.

In offering a reading of a modernist classic, one is usually faced with a series of prior interpretations, a critical discourse into which one extends one's own reading. There is also an oral and sometimes written parallel pedagogical history of the life of the text in the classroom, strategies for teaching, a kind of praxis regarding students' responses and its relation to other texts in a course, as well as the relation of the text to other works in the writer's canon, which is also historically absent.

The Waves exists only in the other cultural narrative of the "high," where its presence is muted by misreading and underreading. To what extent it is possible to undo an interpretive history at the ideological level is unclear. What we know is that Virginia Woolf, the self-proclaimed outsider, has been appropriated by insiders but not valorized, taught, or much written about except as a minor figure while excluded from outsider status altogether. The "rescue" of the text I here attempt is, of course, addressed to those deeply indoctrinated by a Leavisite legacy in which a mythical "Virginia Woolf" was created to stand for an elite, effete English culture against which a democratic "Great Tradition" strenuously struggled. Adena Rosmarin has theorized the cultural process of recuperative reading: "[T]he argument that best accounts for the work is coincident with the argument that best accounts for the manifold histories of its reworkings," (21) an idea that moves me to say that it is the project of Cultural Studies that allows one now to read *The Waves* as a narrative about culture making. Exploring the relations between race, class, and gender in the text and in the history of its production allows us to see those forces at work in criticism as well. Bernard in *The Waves* authorizes his role as "inheritor" of civilization by a recurring vision of a "lady at a table writing, the gardeners with their great brooms sweeping," a vision in which English culture is represented as an aristocratic female figure in a grand country house, leisure for creativity provided by the security of the fixed class position of servants. He insists that the two figures are inseparable, that you cannot have one without the other. Once the reader pries apart Bernard's pairing, and questions the inevitableness of Elvedon as a figure for art, it is possible to read the novel as a critique of the culture-making process, especially as a feminist's exploration of the representation of woman as culture while excluding women artists from the canon. But in order to read this way one has to be open to irony in Woolf's voice and aware of her critique of class and empire. Bernard is a parody of authorship; his words are a postmodern pastiche of quotation from the "master" texts of English literature as part of Woolf's exploration of the nature of subjectivity.

Woolf's "biographeme" was Desmond MacCarthy, her model for the character of Bernard, the "man-of-letters," editor of *Life and Letters,* prominent reviewer and arbiter of taste, writing as "Affable Hawk" a series of judgments of literary value in which he claims that there is no such thing as a "great" woman artist (Woolf argued with him in "The Intellectual Status of Women," but he never wavered.) This process by which the actual Desmond and the fictional Bernard figure woman as culture while denying either women or the working class the chance to create culture, to follow Rosmarin again, can be plotted in both the formalist and the materialist versions of modernism, interpretations of *The Waves* and the problematic scapegoating of Virginia Woolf herself. She may represent culture, but she may not create it. Insofar as Elvedon *is* Bloomsbury in the novel and Bloomsbury/Virginia Woolf is an enormous inflated straw woman against whom both the Left and Right may (and did) fulminate from the thirties to the present, we notice that the figure of woman-as-culture in *The Waves* is constructed as demanding the continued oppression of the working class, a move which allows both certain marxisms to continue misreading. Such interpretations of the author's class and gender as "lady" denied feminism a founding place in modernism or in English Left criticism by insisting on its inability to ally with the working class. It deprived socialist women of a model critic and founding mother, and it foreclosed the possibility of inserting gender (and race) into a predominantly class-centered oppositional narrative at an earlier historical date.

Other cultural narratives about Virginia Woolf were invented and circulated around this master narrative of the lady — Quentin Bell's biography constructed backwards from the suicide, which produced versions of madwoman and victim, feminist narratives of the survivor of child abuse, American feminist revival of *A Room of One's Own* as a founding text for Women's Studies as a field, a practice that sometimes ignored the class narrative in the text. Also problematic was the explicit rejection of Woolf as the origin of modern socialist feminist critical practice by American empiricist feminists, responding, it appears, to the demand of English Left cultural authority. It is not my purpose to claim "subaltern" status for Woolf or *The Waves,* or even that my reading of its politics is a restoration of a lost original text. Woolf alienated a contemporary Left audience in "The Leaning Tower" by exposing the way Left intellectuals romanticized the working class and neglected the political education of their own class. (Their heroizing of Lawrence is as problematic as the demonizing of Woolf.) Her fiction relentlessly connects imperialism to patriarchy, and *Three Guineas* insists that the origin of fascism is in the patriarchal family, not in Italian or German nationalism, a politics recuperated by certain seventies feminisms but certainly not by the British Left.

While the development of minority discourse makes possible a rereading of *The Waves* as cultural critique, theories of the postmodern have redefined modernisms in such a way as to suggest a modernist avant-garde's discomfort with a text that acknowledges its implication in a dominant culture. By Linda Hutcheon's definitions *The Waves* is a postmodern novel. It undermines humanist faith in the coherent subject; it challenges the idea of the artist's integrity. Its parody and irony mock the complicity of the hero and the poet in the creation of a collective national subject through an elegy for imperialism without a modernist rejection of social responsibility. The intertextuality of *The Waves* with Romantic poetry clearly places it in the postmodern camp; politically, it recalls by allusion to Shelley's earlier Orientalism another historical moment of English fetishization of selfhood and individualism as the struggle against death. It questions the white man's anxiety about identity as universal. Amid modernism's rage for order, it revels in oscillation. *The Waves* not only welcomes science into art but actually creates "the quantum self" in incorporating the new physics and wave theory into the reader's perception of a set of six characters who merge into one, and a kind of "quantum text" presenting the relativity of time in a doubled temporal structure in which the reader is expected to collate the simultaneous rise and setting of the sun in one day, in the "Interludes," with the experience of "listening in" on several minds thinking at once and over a lifetime in the text itself. I am making some major claims about the text, but it certainly is a remarkable literary feat. Read against the cosmic oscillations of light waves and ocean waves of an indifferent universe, the words of the soliloquies of human struggle and striving are experienced through the ear, the rhythm carrying the meaning in waves of sound.[3]

The route by which this reading emerged is explicitly charged with cultural meaning, and marks a historical moment in which one may introduce gender into cultural studies partly because Said's theory of orientalism (but not necessarily his practice) demands it. A student challenged me to "recuperate *The Waves* for feminism," and simultaneously I began to teach the novel to students at the City College of New York, trying to articulate a reading strategy for those explicitly excluded by race and class from a "high" cultural narrative of inheritance. What became apparent is Woolf's provision of such reading strategies in the text through Bernard's demand as an artist for an audience of "other people's eyes" (I's, ayes), ways I shall call reading simultaneously as a "Greek" and as a "barbarian." Prying open this difference as readers allows us to enter into the racial/colonial narrative in the way that opening the lady/sweepers pairing assists in the interrogation of class. It is also a comic postmodern "play-poem," as she called it, calling into question the pretensions of the artist, and it is this point at which many readers resist her mockery of mastery.

I will argue here that *The Waves* (1931) is a thirties novel, that the issues it is concerned with are race, class, colonialism, and the cultural politics of canonicity itself. *The Waves* is about imperialism. In it Virginia Woolf interrogates the color problem, setting a British metropolitan *whiteness* against the colored colonial world as a vast desert against which an intellectual elite like the Bloomsbury group creates itself as culture. *The Waves* might have been called *Waiting for the Barbarians* because of its emotional evocation of white fear and guilt for colonial and class oppression, the collective dream ("white sheep") of being assailed by the assegais of the savage enemy. But fifty years of readings are difficult to displace—just as readers of Edith Sitwell's *Facade* have been prevented from hearing its profound critique of British naval power because of a narrow notion that the political is foreign to a performative aesthetic emphasizing sound, dance, and children's nonsense rhymes. Postmodern performance art may allow us to recuperate Sitwell's text, music, and megaphone as well as its mockery of English maritime power, which she shared with Virginia Woolf. We might think Woolf's youthful participation in the "Dreadnought Hoax" in 1910—a prank in which she and her friends, posing as the emperor of Abyssinia and his court, boarded a formidable secret man-of-war of which her cousin, William Fisher, was flag commander, and got away with it—as a kind of rehearsal for *The Waves*.

Consistent with the socialist politics and antifascist ethics of *The Years* and *Three Guineas,* which explore the relation of the patriarchal family and state institutions to fascism, *The Waves* investigates the origin of cultural power in the generation or group formed by the British public school and its values. Woolf mocks snobbish, eternally adolescent male bonding around the ethos of "the playing fields of Eton," and exposes the cult of the hero and the complicity of the poet in the making of of culture as he exudes cultural glue (in the form of an elegy for the dead hero) as a source of social cohesion, the grounding for nationalism, war, and, eventually, fascism. I want to claim here that Woolf in 1931, despite her personal privilege in class terms, prophesied the doom of the insular "civilization" that produced her, by specifically problematizing *whiteness* as an issue. If, as I have argued, *A Room of One's Own* is an elegy for all the lives of women left out of history, *The Waves* deconstructs the politics of the elegy as an instrument of social control. In the process of inventing a new name for her fictions, Woolf thought "elegy" might do. But in exploring its function she revealed the ethical problems to be faced in using this patriarchal genre. *The Waves* insists that we see that the modernist epic-elegy is a melodrama for beset imperialists.(*The Waste Land, Ulysses,* and so on, might be read in the same way.) *The*

Waves marks the end of empire, but to read it this way, as part of the post-colonial carnivalesque, one must be willing to read the comic and ironic and perhaps even regard with relief the death of the author it enacts. The study of the silenced colonial Other, and the search for the subaltern voice, while not articulated in Woolf's text, do lead us to recognize the power of the white woman's critique of herself and her social system, the complicity of English literature with imperialism and class oppression, especially when such a critique is not to be found in the writing of modernist men. The gardeners and the natives do not speak in *The Waves;* they are pictures taken under Bernard's imaginary Western eyes. But their presence and that of Mrs. Moffat, the charwoman, and Bernard's nanny-muse suggest that we ask whose interest it served to mark this text apolitical for five decades? For Virginia Woolf self-consciously creates here a literature of color, and that color is white, a literature written under the protection of the "white arm" of imperialism and defining itself by the brown and black of colonized peoples, ideologically asserting itself even in the unconscious of oppressed and silenced women in Rhoda's fantasy of her white flower fleet. *The Waves* is about the ideology of white British colonialism and the romantic literature that sustains it. There are 117 instances of the word *white* or *whiteness* in this very short text reported in the Haule-Smith *Concordance,* evidence of Woolf's effort to interrogate the color problem of whiteness as ideology.[4] A "barbarian" reading notices *The Waves* as a white book, as Toni Morrison's recent provocative reading of Melville recalls the moment in American history "when whiteness became ideology. And if the white whale is the ideology of race, what Ahab has lost to it is personal dismemberment and family and society and his own place as a human in the world. The trauma of racism is, for the racist and the victim, the severe fragmentation of self." Bernard's "world without a self" is the white postcolonial world. The fragmented selves of the "civilized" characters in *The Waves* are directly related to the politics of British imperialism. If Bernard is an Ahab figure, the vision of a "fin in a waste of waters" may belong to his own white whale, his obsession with Percival and India. (We know that Woolf read *Moby Dick* on February 14, 1922, and again on September 10, 1928; her centenary article on Melville, for which she read all his work, appeared in the *Times Literary Supplement* of August 7, 1919. Her diary mentions *Moby-Dick* in connection with Desmond MacCarthy (Diary vol. 3, 195), and she also jokes about Moby-Dick's whiteness.)

This Occidental tribe of alienated characters, so often read as figures in a *roman á clef* of Bloomsbury intellectuals, collectively inscribe their class and race superiority only by imagining a world of the savage Other in India and Africa, where their representative, Percival (a Siegfried, a superman, the strong silent bully who will by the end of the decade be a fascist idol), secures their privilege by violent exertions of brute force. As *Orlando* writes the history of English literature based on a founding gesture of violence and conquest, Orlando's slicing at the shrunken head of a Moor, the trophy of a violent British adventure against African blacks, *The Waves* writes the death of the (white Western) author in Bernard's assumption of literary hegemony by absorbing the voices of his marginalized peers into his own— he needs "other people's eyes" to read his and other people's I's, their lives and selves, to make his stories. We are forced as Bernard's captive audience to see that the primal narrative of British culture is the (imperialist) quest, and he and his friends idolize Percival, the violent last of the British imperialists, as his (imagined) life and death in India becomes the story of their generation. Percival embodies their history, and Bernard, the man of letters, ensures by his elegies to Percival that this tale, the romance of the dead brother/lover in India is inscribed as the story of modern Britain. My reading of the novel goes against the grain of its reception as ahistorical and abstract by insisting that it records a precise historical moment—what I am calling *the postcolonial carnivalesque*—in Percival's quixotic ride on a fleabitten mare and fall from a donkey, of England's fall from imperial glory and the upper-class *angst* of the intellectuals, their primal terror in imagining the "assegais" of subject peoples turned against them, their agony at contact with the masses and the classes at home, who threaten the order of their whiteness with blood and dirt.[5] The success of Woolf's postmodern practice is evident in her own ambivalence about the "fall," unless she was joking when she wrote to Quentin Bell in 1935 that she shed a tear at the film *Lives of the Bengal Lancers:* "[T]hat's what comes of being one generation nearer to Uncle Fitzy" (*Letters,* vol. 5, 383).

In its loving misquotation and textual appropriation of Romantic poetry, *The Waves* may participate more fully in postmodernism as Linda Hutcheon defines it than it does in a modernism in which its tenuous canonical place was earned by praise for technical difficulty and apparent antirealism as a representation of consciousness. The Western valorization of individual selfhood is mocked by Woolf in her exhaustion of the form of soliloquy, and the notion of individual literary genius is disposed of by an overdetermined intertextuality with Romantic poetry, which simultaneously pokes fun at Romantic diction and ideology and demonstrates how powerful certain phrases and images are in the invocation of patriotism and nationalist claims for English "genius."

The waves that interest me here are those called up in the English (almost) national anthem, "Brittania Rules the . . . ," waves that surround an island imperialist culture defining itself as civilization against the perceived savagery of those whom it has conquered across the seas, specifically in this text, India. The children of empire, the British ruling class of the thirties, six characters lacking patronymics, fixed forever in their first names by an absent authority, fixate on the seventh, Percival, the hero, the man of action, the figure whose body they all identify with England. (Since they only address themselves and not each other, and the women don't even call themselves by name, Woolf is enacting a discursive infantalization that is emphasized by the use of the pure present: "I come; I go.") Woolf's authorial hand has torn these characters out of the bosoms of their families as if to isolate for scientific study the peer group as carrier of ideology. While *To the Lighthouse* and *The Years* provide acute social critiques of marriage and the family, *The Waves* examines the role of childhood friendships and schooling in the formation of individual, group, and national identity, and the group's production of the figures of hero and poet to consolidate cultural hegemony. The school scenes are in fact an indictment of the British public school system, exposing the barbarism and cruelty by which upper class boys learn to be "Greeks," inheritors of culture—what Woolf's cousin J. K. Stephen first called "the intellectual aristocracy."

We may note that to claim anti-imperialism as Woolf's aim in this text is not to assert its difference from her other novels. For India figures just as powerfully in *Mrs. Dalloway,* and the song of the caretaker's children in *The Years,* as I have argued elsewhere, is a reminder of the pidgins and creoles of the colonized peoples who will, she prophesies, return to the mother country and populate the London of the future. Peter Walsh, in the mode of Brantlinger's "Imperial Gothic," sees himself as "an adventurer, reckless, he thought, swift, daring, indeed (landed as he was last night from India) a romantic buccaneer," (*Mrs. Dalloway,* 80) as opposed to the crowds of returned Anglo-Indians "in the Oriental Club biliously summing up the ruin of the world." (246) "Fresh from the centre," in this case, India, not London, Peter is sought out by Lady Bruton at the party where the Prime Minister discusses what the government means to do about the crisis in India (244, 274). Why is Peter's role as failed colonial administrator figured in fantasy "inventions" of the conquest of strange women he follows and seduces? Even though he "disliked India, and empire, and army," (82) he admires the statue of Gordon and imagines a mythical "Grey Nurse," a sinister matriarchal figure combining Mrs. Dalloway and Queen Victoria as England, fantasy representations of female figures in whose name he acts. Mrs. Dalloway

serves as symbolic mother country for the colonials, and as a figure of the
Home Front willingly accepting the belated war death of Septimus Smith
as her due. The patriarchal mythologizing of woman as a figure to mask or
take the blame for imperialism explodes in the description of Conversion
"even now engaged—in the heat and sands of India, the mud and swamp
of Africa, the purlieus of London . . . even now engaged in dashing down
shrines, smashing idols, and setting up in their place her own stern counte-
nance" (151). Mrs. Dalloway herself and the novel bearing her name become Britannia.

Jacob, like Bernard, in *Jacob's Room,* is named an "inheritor," related to
the gentlemen who are "manfully determined" "to impose some coherency
upon Rajahs and kaisers and the muttering in bazaars," and make wars based
on "the statistics of rice fields, the growling of hundreds of work people"
(*Jacob's Room,* 172). Recent theoretical work on colonial discourse by Said,
Spivak, Homi Bhabha, Abdul JanMohamed, and Benita Parry—has raised
several problems about colonial and anticolonial discourse, the dichotomies
of master–slave relations and the question of the silenced subaltern subject.
My project here intersects with these studies by pointing out Virginia
Woolf's early and brilliant deconstruction of the relation between imperialism and English culture, and by asking why what now seems so obvious
in the text was ignored by readers and critics as *The Waves* was canonized
because in its abstract and poetic way it was thought to embody a celebration of the ideology it so defiantly condemns. Edward Said in particular has
asked why modernist writers do not deal with colonialism. Gender is clearly
an important issue here, and we may note that Said is not alone turning away
from the radical critique of colonialism in Virginia Woolf for a more com-
fortable recuperation of *Kim.* Raymond Williams's Cultural Studies bashes
Bloomsbury (and Woolf) to keep Marxism macho. Within Woolf studies,
readings of *The Waves* as a novel of consciousness have become so en-
trenched that it is as awkward to insist on Woolf's ironic and comic portrait
of the artist as a colonialist clown as it once was to argue that *To the Lighthouse* is a critique of Victorian marriage. The resistance, one suspects, is due
to the cultural Left's unexamined acceptance of the Leavises' rejection of the
possibility of radicalism in a woman of Woolf's class. *The Waves,* of course,
is a devastating study of just how such cultural elites (and antielites) establish themselves. Recent work in Cultural Studies, however, recognizes, as
Woolf did, the primacy of patriarchal ideology in British imperialism and
class consciousness, and that gender is often the site of both discourses, the
place of articulation of the fear of difference. This is why, it seems to me,
Aziz is not figured as an Indian nationalist until very late in E. M. Forster's
A Passage to India, but as a widower in the land of *sati,* or widow burning,

a superfluous husband whose political cause is the education of women. In *Mrs. Dalloway* Septimus Smith is assaulted by the words "women burnt alive" on the streets of London—does Woolf mean to suggest that his colonization as a member of the working class is related to British men envisioning themselves as the saviors of Indian women? Forster explains the failure of interracial friendship not by invoking the history of the master-slave relationship between men, but by denying the patriarchal element in British imperialism and blaming the women, Adela and Mrs. Moore, for the collapse of England's civilizing mission in India. What in fact he is working out is his difficulty with the feminist movement in England, displacing his anger at English women suffragettes on to his characters in India. Similarly Woolf figures colonialism as radical-liberal womanizing in her portrait of Peter Walsh in *Mrs. Dalloway.* The empire is run by this marginal day-dreaming anxious ladies' man with the assistance of women like old Miss Parry, one of the seemingly harmless amateur anthropologists and naturalists who catalog exotic orchids (to establish difference even among the animals and plants?), so that the sins of the spinster aunts and the lady travelers are on the heads of the nieces and daughters of empire. White women are complicit in colonialism. Miss Parry is one of the army of surveillance experts in information retrieval, satisfying the imperialist urge to know, the lust to set eyes on everything under the sun.

But, to return to *The Waves* as a modernist canonical text. *The Waves,* much to the chagrin of C. H. Sisson, who called it "trivial" in the *Times Literary Supplement,* was among the first four volumes in a new Cambridge Landmarks of World Literature Series begun in 1986 with *The Iliad,* the *Divine Comedy,* and *Faust.* I suspect that the novel appears on this list because like the other texts, it clearly explicates the cosmology of its time, Einstein's theory of relativity, the lack of correspondence between human life and the workings of the universe: "I reflect now that the earth is only a pebble flicked off accidentally from the face of the sun . . ." (159) and because it engages explicitly with wave theory and the principle of oscillation in the universe—"rise and fall and fall and rise again." It is ironic that a novel that critiques the canon-making process itself, mocking Bernard as self-appointed inheritor of the Romantic tradition of genius, should occupy, however tentatively and uncomfortably, such a position.

Harold Bloom has found a way to fit Woolf and *The Waves* into his oedipal narrative of literary history by infantalizing her position in *The Waves* and especially Bernard's last speech (which I read as comic) as a "feminization of the Paterian aesthetic stance." He sees *The Waves* as belated Romanticism, denying the politics of Woolf's incessant intertextuality with the Romantics as a merciless parody of the English culture-making machinery

in which one genius succeeds another. Aside from Paterizing the unpatriar-
chal Pater, this canonical move places Woolf in an eternally "belated" position as daughter of a minor and "weak" figure, when, if one were to take his
oedipal narrative of literary history seriously, one would have to take account, surely, of her sense of herself as Shakespeare's sister. If Left cultural criticism ignores Woolf's critique of class, gender, and imperialism, and formalist
literary history returns her text to Quentin Bell's biographical role of "Victorian spinster," feminist readings often argue that Bernard's fluency depends
on the suppression of Rhoda, that her silence is necessary for his speech.

But to answer my student's question, I do not think that *The Waves* can
be recuperated for feminism. Correctly, I believe, Woolf exposes here the
way each of the white women in their Foucauldian roles as sexualized social beings, Rhoda the hysteric, Ginny the prostitute, and Susan the mother,
collaborate in Bernard's plot to canonize the physical and verbal brutality,
class arrogance, and racial intolerance of Percival.[6] In their roles as victims,
silenced subjects, the women still participate in imperialist practice. Only
the indifferent listener to Bernard's tale—the unnamed someone met before on a ship going to Africa, who is collared on Shaftesbury Avenue as
captive audience for Bernard's autobiography, the story of a man of letters
and his coterie, a belated defense of Western culture and its obsession with
death—is innocent of complicity, offering the reader a model of refusal and
resistance. What Bernard tells him is the story of the poet's obsession with
the hero, the story of how the genre of elegy encourages patriotism, nationalism, and imperialism. He tells of his haunting early vision of Britannia, "the lady at a table writing and the gardeners with their great brooms
sweeping," at Elvedon, the classical country house of English history. He
cannot, he says, separate one image from the other. Great art depends on le-
siure, he believes. The sweeping classes and the writing classes are eternal
verities, and he, himself, as "inheritor," will always have a "Mrs. Moffat" to
"sweep it all up." As an artist, "He do the police in many voices," stealing
the subjectivities of his friends, their marginalized voices and silences, their
images of disaster and the meaninglessness of the universe.

THE MYTH OF THE FALL

India (and often Africa) is a haunting presence in all of Woolf's fiction. Imperialism is figured as a "fall" that casts an immoral pall on all of English culture, certainly as the founding figure for her own family's "rise" to power
in English social life. And oscillation, Bernard's observation of "rise and fall
and fall and rise again," as the principle of the universe, is a major part of a

feminist's writing of patriarchy's participation in imperialism and her project of dismantling binary oppositions. While Bernard comforts himself with the claim that "[t]he Oriental problem is solved," the reader recognizes that the Occidental problem is being posed in a mass delusion of grandeur and racial and class superiority shared even by homosexuals and hysterics when they participate in the national self Woolf wanted to portray as it imagined Others of the Empire in India or Africa. While *The Waves* does present the making of the London metropolis as civilization out of a common dream of the disorder, silence, and immobilization of Indian natives as an explicitly patriarchal act of Cambridge intellectuals (fueled by a common homoeroticism shared by heterosexual men and women), it does not avoid showing white women's complicity in the process. Rather, each specific type of white alienated speaking subject is shown to contribute to Bernard's modernist making of a discourse for his generation—the postcolonial carnivalesque. Yet the reader overhears each soliloquizing speaker as if to remind us that what seems like a hegemonic discourse of the center/metropolis was made of many dissenting uncentered voices, like the marginalized voices that make the "voice" of *The Waste Land*."

The Waves is about canon formation. Its theme is the creation of the (nationalist and imperialist) culture bearer in Bernard's assumption of the role of poet of his generation. He names himself "the inheritor" in great exhilaration. But it is precisely the role of inheritor of class privilege and Stephen family history—her concern for the sins of the fathers as makers of imperialism and patriarchy—that allows Virginia Woolf to critique the system from within. As I have argued in "Liberty, Sorority, Misogyny," the Stephen family in the nineteenth century were the great professionalizers who consolidated the power of the rising middle class in British institutions. They were also great reformers. The Stephen dynasty escaped its poor Scottish origins and began with the first James Stephen writing his way out of debtors' prison by claiming that such imprisonment was against the Magna Carta. His son was educated by money earned by his uncle in the West Indies, and the second James Stephen was made into an abolitionist by witnessing a slave auction in St. Kitts in 1783 and, on his return from the West Indies, joined forces with Bishop Wilberforce and the Clapham Sect. Beginning with her great-grandfather, who wrote the Anti-Slavery Bill (though it was her paternal grandfather, James Stephen, permanent under secretary for the colonies, who got it passsed), the Stephen family shaped British ideology, especially in relation to colonial policy in India. A patriarchal tyrant at home, Mr. Mother-Country Stephen, as he was called by the press, brilliantly invented the family metaphors that locked colonial subjects into the roles of infantalized bad children in relation to a benevolent "Mother Country."

All the Stephens were conscious makers of ideology, but the mother-country metaphor made an impact in shaping colonialism British-style in behind-the-scenes bureaucracy by creating the colonial subject as a child and displacing the patriarchal power that fueled colonialism onto a less threatening female figure, ensuring that any revolt of the colonized could be constituted as a crime against the sacred institution of motherhood, Queen Victoria growing into the role of imperial mother as the nineteenth century progressed. Stephen invested the philosophy of imperialism with the theology of the patriarchal family, rewarding their complicitous women with power over servants in a replication of the master-servant relationship, which, James Fitzjames Stephen argued as a political philosophy, was the model for a man's relation to wife and children. James Stephen implemented a policy of making the conquered colonies British, members of a family. His son, Fitzjames, was one of the chief codifiers of Indian law, a major feat of cultural hegemony, for it was through the rigorous application of law and a system of courts and judges that the British were able to govern and to create a native governing class. This classification and centralizing of disparate systems of law was a rehearsal for similar work in England, a centralizing and professionalizing activity that standardized the law according to an Old Testament evangelical obsession with punishment. Often the colonies served as testing grounds for policies later implemented at home. It is clear that this codification of disparate practices into a single system lay the groundwork for certain narratives of nationalism in both India and England. Leslie Stephen in his monumental *Dictionary of National Biography* created a master cultural narrative of England as a history of the lives of great men, and his sister, Caroline, in her youth wrote a history of sisterhoods, nuns, and nurses, which argued that all such separate organizations of women were a threat to the patriarchal family.

Fitzjames's daughter Katherine (1856–1924) was principal of Newnham College, Cambridge, and her sister, Dorothea, spent many years in India studying Indian religions, publishing *Studies in Early Indian Thought* in 1918. This work done by the Stephen family was all cultural anthropology—classifying information. Their brother, J. K. Stephen, the model for Percival in *The Waves*, "bard of Eton and of boyhood," misogynist poet and parodist, studied law and edited a journal called *The Reflector* before his strange death at age thirty-three, related to a fall from his horse (the origin of the tragic and culturally unifying scene in *The Waves*). Julia Stephen, Woolf's mother, wrote on two subjects, the power of the nurse over her patient and the responsibility of upper-class women to discipline and control their servants. Virginia Woolf's insistence in her work on the relation of patriarchy to imperialism and both to class and fascism comes from careful study of her family's legacy and her refusal (guilt?) to be the "inheritor" of the class privilege and power over servants with which such women were bought off to serve the interests of patriarchal state institutions and colonialism.

Imperialism in India and the exploitation of servants in England thus fused in her imagination with her own revolt as a feminist and, as I have argued elsewhere, the charwoman appears as a major figure in each novel, marking her concern with class, along with barbed references to India and other colonies, marking her concern with race. Middle-class white women in England traded their own freedom for a power over servants (or natives in the colonies), which replicated the master/slave relationship of husbands and wives. That these markers in Virginia Woolf's writing have generally been ignored or misread by critics does not diminish their signifying power. Even that classic text of feminist emancipatory literature, *A Room of One's Own,* clearly indicates that literary freedom for the white middle-class English woman writer is bought at the expense of complicity in colonialism. The narrator dissociates herself from the racism of her family and class by announcing that she could pass even "a very fine negress" without wanting to "make an Englishwoman of her." She will not participate in the social mission of "civilizing" the natives in the manner of her family. Yet the word *fine* suggests that she is not wholly free, for it is a word used to describe an object not a fellow subject, as if the Negress were an exotic work of art displayed for a collector. (Here, of course, one may see Woolf's part in the "orientalism" of modernism, from Picasso's appropriation of African sculpture for his painting to the cult of black American jazz and dance in Paris and other European capitals.) Woolf had a double legacy regarding race. While her great-grandfather had devoted his life to the emancipation of slaves (in recognition that his own rise in status had been paid for by exploitation of the colonies), her grandfather had introduced a different system of exploitation by making a certain colonial subject "English."

The narrator of *A Room of One's Own* owes her freedom and five-hundred pounds a year to a legacy from an aunt who died after a fall from her horse in Bombay. This fall recurs in Woolf's writing as the sign of the sins of the fathers. It anticipates Bernard's carnivalized fall from a donkey while racing in India (obviously a reference to Forster's *A Passage to India* as well), the move from horse to donkey signifying the decline of the Raj in the comic end of British colonialism. Her cousin J. K. Stephen's quixotic fall from a horse and his early death, the various versions of this event that circulated as family mythology, and Desmond MacCarthy's elegy for this ferocious figure in *Portraits,* invest the fall with literary and political resonance in Woolf's work. She often used figures of horses and donkeys to describe her own work as an artist. Neville, in *The Waves,* constructs his whole worldview around the opposition between the rider and the reader, the hero and the poet, marking again the complicity between culture and colonialism. Woolf problematizes the figure of fall–rise as the basic binary of class, race, and gender by turning it into a figure of oscillation, the continous wave motion of the universe. In *The Waves* she criticizes the twentieth-century colonial and postcolonial discourse that replaced her grandfather's nineteenth-century myth of the mother-country and her childish colonies as Imperial Family Romance. The new myth for twentieth-century colonialism was an imperialist *Boy's Own* story, the adventure of brotherly love, a homoerotic adoration of the strong, silent violent hero conquering the desert alone. All the characters in *The Waves* participate in this drama of Percival riding against the spears of the enemy, and they gain a national identity by mythologizing the hero. Reflecting on their common feeling, one may understand the rise of fascism.

Leonard Woolf, Virginia Woolf's husband, veteran of seven years in the Ceylon Civil Service and author of *The Village in the Jungle* (1913, reprinted by the Hogarth Press in 1931, the year of publication of *The Waves*), always associated his years in Hambantota with the image of himself on horseback among natives on foot. In his letters to Lytton Strachey in the Harry Ransome Humanities Research Center at the University of Texas, he reveals his desire on coming down from Cambridge to teach in a British public school. When he found that Jews were never hired for these positions, he chose the civil service but agonized at length to Strachey about his difficulties learning to ride, a necessity for such a post.

His memoirs trace the "innocent, unconscious imperialist" to his rejection of the role of "imperial proconsul." Accused by a native lawyer of whipping him in the street, Woolf rejected the accusation as false on the literal level but symbolically true, realizing that the people of Jaffna were "right in feeling that my sitting on a horse arrogantly in the main street of their town was as good as a slap in the face." (Leonard Woolf, *Growing,* 1961, 113–114). Later, as secretary of the Labour Party's Advisory Committee on Imperial Affairs, he advocated self-government for India, espousing advanced but not revolutionary views. His novel is bold in its narrative rejection of the notion of the possibility of justice in the application of British law in Ceylon, but its diction participates in the portrayal of the jungle and its people as savage, cruel, and sinister by the repetition of the words *evil* and *obscene.*

This scene, the raising of the cart, resonates with the scene of the hero's fall from his donkey, also mythologized by Bernard as the death of the Christian knight in pursuit of the Holy Grail as part of his vision of the "rise and fall and fall and rise again" of the narrative of colonialism. "He would have done justice. He would have protected. About the age of forty he would have shocked the authorities. No lullaby has ever occurred to me capable of singing him to rest." (243) (These are the very words used by his friends on the death of Woolf's brother Thoby, and by Desmond Mac-Carthy on the death of her cousin, J. K. Stephen.) Neville opposes the rider to the reader, sees Percival as Alcibiades, Ajax, and Hector. His fall from a donkey while racing becomes history. Critics have remarked here on Woolf's memorial to her dead brother, Thoby. But the mention of Ajax and the ignominious nature of his fall reminds this reader of Woolf's cousin, J. K. Stephen, whom she compared to Ajax, and the strange and contradictory reports of his fall, which led to madness and early death. Leslie Stephen and Quentin Bell tell of a stone thrown from a train, which hit his head and knocked him off his horse, and again of his riding into a windmill—the stuff of legends. He was a violent man made into a hero by all the Cambridge men who wrote about him. Woolf's version of the fall and the poet's mythologizing of violence is a critique of family history as well as cultural history.

"THE WAVE THAT NEVER BREAKS"

J. K. Stephen, whose violent misogynist poetry and strange early death plays a part in some contemporary claims that he was Jack the Ripper, either alone or with the duke of Clarence, whose tutor he was at Cambridge, makes an interesting source, not only for Percival but for the whole hero-poet narrative that is British culture. As I have shown elsewhere, Woolf read Wortham's 1927 biography of Oscar Browning, which described her cousin as a hero, and more importantly, Desmond MacCarthy's sketch of him in *Portraits* (Macmillan, 1932).

There seems to be some justification for reading Bernard as a Desmond MacCarthy figure. "The Affable Hawk," as he signed himself as literary editor of the *New Statesman,* had been a Cambridge Apostle and friend for many years, despite her battle with him over gender and writing (see "The Intellectual Status of Women" reprinted in *Diary,* vol. 2, Woolf's response to MacCarthy's claim that women are inferior to men in intellectual power, and that women's "desire to be dominated is . . . a proof of intellectual inferiority"). The amiable but heated exchange between MacCarthy and Woolf in the *New Statesman* in 1920 ended with Woolf's argument that men

controlled culture, which she called "a condition of half-civilized barbarism. At least that is how I define an eternity of dominion on the one
hand and servility on the other. For the degradation of being a slave is only
equalled by the degradation of being a master" (*Diary*, vol. 2, 342). Her diary records many instances of having to "work off the intense depression left
by Desmond." She was furious at his description of the "butterfly lightness"
of an essay she published in his journal (197). In one case she worked off the
depressing influence of the Man of Letters as master of British culture with
"a beautiful image": "[H]ow he is like a wave that never breaks, but lollops
one this way & that way & the sail hangs on one's mast & the sun beats
down" (*Diary*, vol. 3, 27). The beautiful image of 1925 returned in 1928
when she first conceived of *The Waves*, then called *The Moths*, as an "abstract mystical eyeless book." In the same diary entry for November 7, she
fantasizes writing a history of Newnham or the women's movement, plans
The Waves as a "playpoem," and complains at length about Desmond, "the
wave that never breaks," finding him more than ever "depressing, . . .
mouldy, . . . rather sodden rather creased and jumbled," with a hole in his
blue sock:

> [H]e is resolute & determined –thats what I find so depressing. He seems to
> be sure that it is his view that is the right one; ours vagaries, deviations. And
> if his view is the right one, God knows there is nothing to live for: not a
> greasy biscuit. And the egotism of men surprises & shocks me even now. Is
> there a woman of my acquaintance who could sit in my armchair from
> 3 to 6.30 without the semblance of a suspicion that I might be busy, or
> tired, or bored; & so sitting could talk, grumbling and grudging, of her
> difficulties, worries; then eat chocolates, then read a book, & go at last,
> apparently self-complacent & wrapped in a kind of blubber of misty self-
> satisfaction? (Diary, vol. 3, 204)

She saw, I believe, the Bernard-Percival relationship acted out in
Desmond's memoir of J. K. Stephen in *Portraits* as "our real laureate,"
mooning as Neville and Bernard do over Percival, over the giant who was
"violently masculine, a lover of law and abstract argument," the "Philis-
tine," "Bard of Eton and of boyhood." MacCarthy praises the "prowess of
that wild-looking man with rolling but abstracted eye and path-clearing
gait, whom I can just remember, hatless and slovenly, mouching round the
Playing Fields." This is the origin of Woolf's "Eton" scenes in *The Waves*,
where Percival mooches around the same playing fields. Much of Oscar
Browning's obituary for J. K. S. is concerned with Stephen's Eton poems,

but MacCarthy remembers his parodies best (and they are still praised and collected in volumes of satire. In the parody of Byron (recall Bernard's obsession with Byron, an obsession shared by Desmond MacCarthy), Stephen writes: "Whoever will may write a nations's songs/As long as I'm allowed to right its wrongs."

and the parody of Wordsworth reads:

> Two voices are there: one is of the deep;
> It learns the storm-cloud's thunderous melody,
> Now roars, now murmurs with the changing sea,
> Now bird-like pipes, now closes soft in sleep;
> And one is of an old half-witted sheep
> Which bleats articulate monotony,
> And indicates that two and one are three,
> That grass is green, lakes damp and mountains steep;
> And Wordsworth, both are thine: at certain times
> Forth from the heart of thy melodious rhymes,
> The form and pressure of high thoughts will burst:
> At other times—good Lord! I'd rather be
> Quite unacquainted with the A B C
> Than write such hopeless rubbish as thy worst.

While MacCarthy calls Stephen a "Hallam without a Tennyson," he may have had too many Tennysons for Woolf's taste—her father in his biography of Fitzjames Stephen, Oscar Browning and Browning's biographer, and Desmond MacCarthy. All these apostrophes to the dead hero add up to "culture," what Bernard does to re-create England by memorializing Percival. MacCarthy moaned about being a failure and overpraised his male peers while ignoring or despising women artists. He does create J. K. Stephen as Percival. His book of portraits dedicated to himself at age twenty-two is the tidal wave that never breaks that Woolf parodies in *The Waves*. "It is curious," MacCarthy wrote, "how nearly every group of young men, some of whom afterwards became famous, has had its inconspicuous hero to whom, while the world was looking up at them, they looked up to." Bernard is Desmond and Percival is J. K. Stephen, the patriarchal imperialist makers of British culture.

Parodies of the Romantics enforce their canonical power. Stephen also attacked Kipling and Rider Haggard, longing for the day "When there stands a muzzled stripling-Mute, beside a muzzled bore-When the Rudyards cease from Kipling-And the Haggards ride no more." J. K. Stephen was painted as Ajax, and Woolf remembers his violence. Bernard's memories of Percival repeat the figure of oscillation ("rise and fall and fall and rise again") of the force of cultural inheritance as a wave that drowns alternative voices. The story of Percival's fall is countered by the story of how he raised the bullock cart and imposed his Western values on the lazy and incompetent "native." For Woolf this recurring fall is a primal scene of the fall, England's fall from heroic history, her family's fall from ethical purity, her culture's fall into colonialism and its angst. In *The Waves* Woolf uses the case of her cousin (conflated with her dead brother, Thoby, who was said to look like Jem) to explain the deadlock embrace of violence and poetry in the English male cultural script.

Mrs. Moffat Will Sweep It All Up

The most powerful undertow in *The Waves* is class. The ruling-class characters define themselves as clean, free, and dominant against the dirt and ugly squalor of the masses. Bernard is bound to the big house by strong narrative ties. Elvedon and its lady at a table writing, its gardeners with their great brooms sweeping, the haunting memory that fuels his sense of himself as a writer, is *not* a fixed and eternal figure for writing. Not only do the characters imagine their racial superiority by conjuring up the peoples of Asia and Africa as the enemy whose assegais are poised against them, they build their class superiority by hating and despising the working class. Rhoda is afraid of the "squalid" people in the Tube; Neville "cannot endure" that shopgirls should exist next to beautiful buildings; Susan sees country folk living like animals on a dungheap; and even Bernard composes little stories that all betray his class and gender bias. He plots the greengrocer's Saturday night dream as an oscillation between the thought of having mailed his letter to the lottery and killing a rabbit, a projection of his own obsessions with chance and violent death onto Mrs. Thatcher's parents' class, and this story makes life "tolerable" for him. The lady-gardener aesthetic is surely being mocked by the author of "The Leaning Tower," who urged the thirties poets to convert members of their own class to divest themselves of privilege rather than becoming missionaries to the lower classes. This aesthetic, which figures English culture as a lady, not a woman, and insists on the unalterable relationship between the gardeners and the lady, the working class and the writing class, is historically specific to Bernard in England in the early thirties and certainly not in any way an aesthetic Woolf endorses.

To read *The Waves* in this way, as an indictment of Woolf's own class and culture (it is, of course, equally clear that Woolf acknowledges her own complicity in and sentimental attachment to Bernard's values), is to read against the accumulated critical readings that valorize this novel over her other works as a celebration of the English artist as Cambridge intellectual. But I want to argue that *The Waves* is the swan song of the white Western male author with his romantic notions of individual genius, his Cartesian confidence in the unitary self and its identity. *The Waves* is about the death of the author, and it anticipates poststructuralist debates about subjectivity, as it articulates the problem of the postmodern artist and his anxieties. Byronic man, the romantic artist–hero, sings his last aria against death. Make no mistake—I too am moved by this aria, the swan song of the single self. But I am also, as a woman and a socialist, very much relieved. I confess that I feel like the character in Djuna Barnes's *Nightwood* in the audience for a performance of Wagner's *Parsifal* in the thirties—"Oh, my God, they have shot the Holy Grail." Virginia Woolf shoots the Holy Grail in *The Waves*. Her Percival is the last shabby chivalric imperialist whose death English culture can claim as a pretext for a coherent unified cultural and social text, as she documents the replacement of the patriarchal family by the peer group or generation as the agent of social cohesion. If those readers who despise Woolf for her supposed class loyalty and snobbish membership in the Bloomsbury group were to read the novel without its critical history as a canonical text, they might see that it deconstructs both the idea of individual genius (which she already attacked brilliantly in *A Room of One's Own* by asserting that Shakespeare was only the product of his age), and also the idea of a cultural elite, showing that their power is derived from sex, class, and racial privilege.

The boundaries between self and Other, between classes and sexes, between the colonizers and the colonized that Woolf maps here are perhaps best expressed in Neville's appalling vision of "death among the apple trees," the doom of the "unintelligible obstacle," his version of the "immitigable" Wordsworthian tree (24) that literally stops him in his tracks, and figures the dilemma of the postwar intellectual dealing with the pastoral myth of "England's green and pleasant land." The origin of the "story" for which Bernard and his friends search is in the burbling of blood from a cut throat, the wars and imperialist adventures on which their power was built. The violence of Woolf's subject, the dominance of monologic male voices over culture, is clear in the language of blood she uses in discussing revisions in her diary: "And I am getting my blood up." She wants to avoid chapters and run all her scenes together "so as to make the blood run like a torrent from end to end." She views her achievement as if she had created in the novel a living body "done without spilling a drop" (343). The body of her text, *The*

Waves, is the corpse of the literary canon, the mausoleum of white, male English culture.

Bernard figures himself as the "continuer" of a dead tradition with a "devastating sense of grey ashes in a burnt-out grate" (80). The poet, like T. S. Eliot, in this modernist "Waste Land" is he who now takes the poker and rattles the cinders so that they fall in showers through the grate" (81). The ashes and cinders that haunt this novel as an aftermath of World War I and—for the modern reader—prophecy of the Holocaust, invoke dirt and disorder as the artist's inspiration, marking his own urban civilized dependence on the slum. The ash gray dawn of the opening prelude pictures the canvas of sea and sky as a wrinkled gray blanket, a smoky woolen cloth over a bonfire, a kind of blank page "barred with thick strokes moving" (7), where birds sing "their blank melody." Like Bernard's "dead fire" in a burned-out grate, this ominous opening scene suggests the end of writing and the end of a certain kind of culture, Bernard's dependence on servants like Mrs. Moffat to reinforce his image of himself as "chosen." *The Waves* may be read as a thirties text that is visualized as a blurred and smudged prison narrative—a kind of barred writing. This "picture" of barred writing is also a visual representation of the writing of music on barred manuscript pages, as part of Woolf's obsession with her competition with Dame Ethel Smyth's composition of an opera-oratorio about the necessity for the dissolution of the individual self, *The Prison,* while she was writing *The Waves.*

In the opening scene the arm of the lady with the lamp clarifies the light until "the dark stripes were almost wiped out," (7) recalling the traditional representation of Britannia ruling the waves. It seems to me that this opening passage as a hymn to dawn also invokes the Indian text, the *Rig Veda,* as Virginia Woolf's cousin Dorothea Stephen explained it in *Studies in Early Indian Thought,* to call up Indian philosophy and its emphasis on astronomy and the randomness of the universe, a major subject of *The Waves* as it incorporates relativity theory and the new physics into fiction.[7] According to Stephen, Indian thought emphasizes that personal character is not important in the scheme of the universe: "In early Indian thought we have the boldest and the most consistent effort that the human mind has ever made to show that it is nothing" (172). Is it too much to suppose that Virginia Woolf used an Indian religious text in writing the death of a particular form of white Western culture? When she called *The Waves* "mystical" did she mean Eastern mysticism? [The Vedas are in fact mentioned on page 186 as texts Bernard will never read, though Louis, the white colonial returned to the mother country, the T. S. Eliot figure, is familiar with them.] The specific uncanniness of the poetic language of *The Waves,* its ecstasies of apostrophe, are common to both the Romantic lyrics of Shelley and Keats and to prayer—in this case the mode of Hindu religious texts. While popular sentiment might declare that the sun never sets on the British empire, *The Waves* emphatically dramatizes the very historical moment in which the sun *does* set. If we read the opening sections, the interludes, as a Western imitation of or homage to the Hindu Gayatri, or prayers on the course of the sun, we may see that Woolf surrounds the text of the decline and fall of the West (the transcendental self striving and struggling against death) with the text of the East, random natural recurrence.

But the narrative of violent struggle bleeds into the interludes; they are not entirely passive and innocent—assegais appear even here. While no native of the Subcontinent actually speaks in *The Waves,* Hindu philosophy, which embraces death is invoked in an ironic reading of the ending with Bernard's famous ride against death as "the enemy." He sees himself "with my spear couched and my hair flying back like a young man's, like Percival's" (297), galloping in India. In fact Percival was riding a donkey, not "galloping," and this longhaired rider seems to be not Percival but a reincarnation of Shiva, in what may be read as a new dawn "kindling" in the East as Western "civilization is burnt out" (296). (This Eastern dawn also ends *The Years.*) W. B. Yeats recognized Woolf's incorporation of Eastern philosophy in her text, linking it with *Ulysses* and Pound's *Cantos,* which "suggest a philosophy like that of the Samkara school of ancient India, mental and physical objects alike material, a deluge of experience breaking over us and within us, melting limits whether of line or tint; man no hard bright mirror dawdling by the dry sticks of a hedge, but a swimmer, or rather the waves themselves" (64–65).

Aurora in the opening of *The Waves* is a giant eraser in the sky, dividing night from day, destroying Ginny's dream of fluid time—"the week should be all one day without divisions" (54)—another resistance to the "jagged time" of imperialist histories in the rise-and-fall mode. She may be a symbolic version of Woolf's recurring charwoman, working on a universal scale. She is Chaos and Mrs. Moffat in her human incarnation. It is here that Woolf exposes the poet's identification of the one who cleans up pollution as the *origin* of disorder. Bernard is aware that he needs someone to clean up his mess: "'Mrs. Moffat will come and sweep it all up—' I fancy I shall often repeat to myself that phrase, as I rattle and bang through life. . . . 'Oh, yes, Mrs. Moffat will come and sweep it all up'" (81).

Already the gardeners were laying down their brooms as Woolf wrote in the early thirties, and certain writers were having to do without servants.

Certainly there were those in India who reformulated Bernard's "The Oriental problem is solved" into articulations of a British "problem." Bernard always feels "powerless" to alter these fixed class relations between the lady at a table writing and the gardeners with their great brooms sweeping, between art and work; he cannot "stop" or "dislodge" the permanence of their relations, he tells us. In her other novels Woolf has figured class in the (privileged) voices of her charwomen. Whether this is a romantic fetishization by a bourgeois writer is a matter for discussion. But here it is a lady who writes and male gardeners sweeping, as if her focus has shifted to expose very clearly the complicity between the artist and class inequity (as in her essay "The Leaning Tower"). Louise De Salvo points out that the drafts of *The Waves* originally included mention of working-class children who were "washing up plates" as the upper-class children sat at their desks, and "Florrie" who went out as a kitchen maid when the others went off to school in Switzerland (183).

But in *The Waves* English culture is based on both class differences and imperialism with Bernard as its "continuer, . . . the person miraculously appointed to carry it on." He reveres his "masters," buys a picture of Beethoven in a silver frame, discusses "What is to be done about India, Ireland or Morocco?" with old gentlemen under chandeliers in rooms where power is so pervasive that they even decide on the disposition of the very days of the week, Friday or Saturday (255). He fantasizes that his training as a member of the ruling class will allow him to behave with dignity when a telephone call comes asking him "to assume command of the British Empire."

"Our English past—one inch of light" (227), Bernard's vision, is more pessimistically viewed by Louis, the Australian T. S. Eliot figure, who thinks that "the lighted strip of history is past and our Kings and Queens; we are gone; our civilization; the Nile; and all life . . . we are extinct" (225). As an ex-colonial subject Louis is most afraid of the dissolution of empire. He hears the great beast of revolution stamping on the shore. He commutes between a garret where he can observe sordid sights of poverty and degradation, and a mahogany desk in a posh office where he plans for swimming pools on luxury liners: "I pick my way over broken glass, among blistered tiles, and see only vile and famished faces" (202). (Doubtless it is on one of his company's ships going to Africa and ruling the waves that Bernard has met the unnamed person to whom he tells his life story in the last section of the book, the only "dialogue"—such as it is when the Other is a reluctant listener—in this monologic text.) In Louis's soliloquy Woolf connects the British businessman, spreading commerce and colonialism, militarism and patriarchy, with Napoleon, Plato, and Sir Robert Peel: "I like to hear . . . the heavy male tread of responsible feet down the corridors. The weight of the world is on our shoulders" (169). His identity is so insecure that he needs the continual reinforcement of his class position by walking the slums. Louis participates in what Stallybrass and White call the nineteenth-century "construction of subjectivity through totally ambivalent internalizations of the city slum." (21)

Bernard constructs his subjectivity by internalizing the second of the figures pointed out by Stallybrass and White—the nurse or the nanny. Using the work of Jim Swan and Jane Gallop, Stallybrass and White look at Freud's obsession with his own and his patients' nurses or nannies during the time that he was working on the theory of the Oedipus complex. The critical role of the nurse in initiating the child sexually while engaged in hygiene by bathing children of the middle and upper classes, is displaced when Freud claims this role for the mother of the male child. Both mothers and fathers are absent in *The Waves,* but Bernard remembers his nurse, Mrs. Constable, for his whole life. She is his muse, and the primal scene of writing is for him the memory of her turning the pages of a picture book and naming the objects. But his recurrent dream of her squeezing the sponge over his naked body, releasing "arrows of sensation" (239), is so fearful a moment that he wishes to save other newborns from the experience. Are we to see that his rigid Tory politics, imperialistic hero worship, and barely repressed homosexuality are all derived from this childhood experience? He does have an image of his appetitive self as a "hairy ape" who lives inside his body, a self he despises and also projects onto the "savages" Percival is taming in India. One could say that his life is circumscribed by his nurse and his charwoman, Mrs. Constable and Mrs. Moffat. Woolf is laying out a psychological trail to explain Bernard's origin as the self-appointed arbiter of British culture.

The clearest exposition of the politics of the novel is in the scene at an expensive restaurant, where the six young white "inheritors," sleek and well fed, eat roast duck and think of themselves as the center of civilization. They create themselves as civilized only by imagining Britain's colonies as savage. The Greeks define themselves against the barbarians. (There are nineteen direct references to India in the novel and several indirect ones.) And they each fantasize India as dark, dirty, disordered, and directly threatening their own deaths. The language of their dreams of Percival in India is thoroughly racist and colonialist—"incompetent . . . natives in loincloths," "strange sour smells," "remote provinces are fetched out of darkness," "muddy roads," "twisted jungle," "the vulture that feeds on some bloated carcass," "the dancing and drumming of naked men with assegais," "ruthless," "flap-ping bladders," "painted faces," "bleeding limbs which they have torn from the living body" (136, 137, 140). India silently becomes Africa. The "Ori-ental problem" becomes the "African problem." Woolf's white British characters see the colonized as cannibals. Neville says, "We are walled in here. But India lies outside" (135). The following passage with its mythol-ogizing of Percival as a hero in his righting of the bullock cart (a rewriting of the classic scene with a bullock cart in Kipling's *Kim*), exposes Bernard's complicity with imperialism, how necessary his mythmaking capacity is to the maintenance of domination and submission, master and slave:

> "I see India," said Bernard. "I see the low, long shore; I see the tortuous lanes of stamped mud that lead in and out among ramshackle pagodas; I see the gilt and crenellated buildings which have an air of fragility and decay as if they were temporarily run up buldings in some Oriental exhibition. I see a pair of bullocks who drag a low cart along the sun-baked road. The cart sways incompetently from side to side. Now one wheel sticks in the rut, and at once innumerable natives in loincloths swarm round it, chattering excitedly. But they do nothing. Time seems endless, ambition vain. Over all broods a sense of the uselessness of human exertion. There are strange sour smells. An old man in a ditch continues to chew betel and to contem-plate his navel. But now, behold, Percival advances; Percival rides a flea-bitten mare, and wears a sun-helmet. By applying the standards of the West, by using the violent language that is natural to him, the bullock-cart is righted in less than five minutes. The Oriental problem is solved. He rides on; the multitude cluster round him, regarding him as if he were—what indeed he is—a God." (135–36)

This scene is a carnivalization of racism's master plot, a scene created again in many films and fictions in which the white man brings order and reason to the natives and is made a god. But Woolf's grammar is strangely off kilter here—the incompetent cart—the absent Percival as the subject of the bullock-cart-righting—why is there a passive construction? Bernard's colonialist fantasy contains all the elements of a textbook study of the oper-ations of racism, imperialism, and colonialism—and yet there is something comical in the fleabitten mare, the sun helmet. (This resembles a scene from a colonial exhibition or a film like *The African Queen*. There was in fact a colonial exhibition in Paris in 1931, and Josephine Baker, the black exotic dancer, was chosen queen until it was pointed out that she was in fact an American.) It seems possible also that Woolf's image of the overturned cart invoked in some readers the figure of the juggernaut, Krishna's cart, under whose wheels the faithful would throw themselves, to the British, along with sati, or widow burning, evidence of the savagery of India. Rhoda sees "beyond India," imagining "pilgrimages" from her peers into a landscape where a "white arm . . . makes no sign, it does not beckon, it does not see us" (139). One could imagine that Rhoda alone sees the "white arm" of the mysterious woman with a lamp who brings the dawn, a Britannia in endless surveillance of conquerable lands. But it seems important that the arm is white, and that it forms a triangle when resting upon the figure's knee, then a column, then a fountain. The mighty white arm of empire and "civilization."

Andreas Huyssen argues that the mark of modernism is fear of contamination. This is Bernard's fear (Mrs. Moffat will sweep it all up). Rhoda fears the puddle and all human beings; Neville fears the recurrence of murder; Louis fears the "great Beast stamping" in the East; Susan hates Ginny all her life for having kissed Louis. The contamination of kisses and classes; the fear of dirt, disorder, and dying; the fear of Africa and India, is the recurring theme of the speakers' monologues. Neville says, "We must oppose the waste and deformity of the world, its crowds eddying round and round disgorged and trampling. One must slip paper-knives, even, exactly through the pages of novels, and tie up packets of letters neatly with green silk, and brush up the cinders with a hearth broom. Everything must be done to rebuke the horror of deformity" (180). How dark their hearts are, writer and character surveying the end of empire.

4

Laughing at Leviticus

Nightwood as Woman's Circus Epic

Lion and woman and the Lord knows what

W. B. Yeats

O monsters, do not leave me alone. . . . I do not confide in you except to tell you about my fear of being alone, you are the most human people I know, the most reassuring in the world. If I call you monsters, then what name can I give to the so-called normal conditions that were foisted upon me? Look there, on the wall, the shadow of that frightful shoulder, the expression of that vast back and neck swollen with blood. . . . O monsters, do not leave me alone."

Colette, *The Pure and the Impure*

Djuna Barnes's great Rabelaisian comic epic novel, *Nightwood* (1936), now excites the critical attention it deserves. As a contribution to the effort to revive it this essay is a feminist interpretation that argues, among other readings, that *Nightwood* is a brilliant and hilarious feminist critique of Freudian psychoanalysis and a parody of the *discourse of diagnosis* of female hysteria. Using Julia Kristeva's *Powers of Horror,* I argue that *Nightwood* in its original title of "Bow Down" and its continual reference to submission and bowing, or lowering of the self, is a study in *abjection,* and that by its concentration on the figure of the "One Who Is Slapped," the downtrodden victim, it figures by absence the authoritarian dominators of Europe in the thirties, the sexual and political fascists. While Kristeva studies abjection as a pathology, I maintain that Barnes's portraits of the abject constitute a political case, a kind of feminist-anarchist call for freedom from fascism. Looking at Nikka's tattoo as a defiance of the Levitical taboo against writing on the body, I see the body of the Other—the black, lesbian, transvestite, or Jew—presented as a text in the novel, a book of communal resistances of underworld outsiders to domination. Its weapon is laughter, a form of folk grotesque derived from Rabelais and surviving in circus.

With Bakhtin's *Rabelais* as model methodology, I see *Nightwood's* extravagant language and imagery as a direct descendant of medieval "grotesque realism" (as the *Ladies Almanack* is certainly a descendant of the Rabelaisian almanac hawked about at Paris street fairs). In this "reversible world," or "world turned upside down," Barnes moves from high to low culture, from opera to circus, and even expands Bakhtin's categories from their body-base in the material to include the mystical and mental grotesqueries he excluded.

I would also argue that the status of *Nightwood* as a lesbian novel or a cult text of high modernism has obscured the ways in which it is a French novel, indebted as much to Victor Hugo and Eugène Sue as it is to Rabelais. My purpose in reviving *Nightwood* is political. Strangely canonized and unread, it cannot function as a critique of fascism. The revision of modernism in which this essay participates is an effort to read race, class, and gender back into the discussion. Unlike most expatriate writing from this period, *Nightwood* paints the Paris underworld and demimonde with its own colors, not a specifically American palette. Its characters are her modern "*misérables*," brothers and sisters to the "hunchback of Notre Dame." *Nightwood,* like modernism itself, begins in Vienna in the 1880s. Freud, fascism, Hitler, "high art," and the *Lumpenproletariat* haunt the text as a potent "political unconscious." *Nightwood's* hysterical heteroglossia is a perverse and almost postmodern folk text in which language and its possibility for figuration is as potent and explosive as in Shakespeare or Joyce.

TATTOO AS TABOO

Ye shall not make any cuttings in your flesh for the dead, nor print any marks upon you.
Leviticus 19:27–28

In order to be pure and symbolic, Kristeva argues, the patriarchal body may have only one mark, the circumcision, which cut duplicates in the symbolic order the natural cut of the umbilical cord that separates mother and son. The ritual cut replaces the natural cut—"the identity of the speaking being (with his God) is based on the separation of the son from the mother."[1] In political terms patriarchal identity is established by marking the body to distinguish it not only from the unclean mother but from the polytheistic worshippers of the mother goddess, who threaten the tribe. The establishment of marked sexual difference with rigid boundaries differentiates the people

of the Bible from other religious cults, such the worship of Dionysos in
Greece, where the *erasure* of sexual difference was the point of ritual activity. (However, the Jews were neither the first nor the only people to use
circumcision, a practice some anthropologists see as a form of menstrua-
tion envy.)

Writing on the body, I believe, is breaking a powerful patriarchal taboo
for the inheritors of the Judeo-Christian ethos, in which the possession of
the Logos is indicated by writing on the holy tablets. Making human skin
into a page or a text violates the symbolic order. A body covered with marks
is too close to the natural "unclean" state of the newborn's body, with the
marks of the "unclean" placenta, the traces of its mother's blood on it. A tattoo, then, is not only taboo but the birthmark of the born-again—the self-
created person who denies his/her birth identity. This "monster" is a
carnivalesque figure who revels in the taboo-shattering act of making the
body a book, dissolving the difference between spirit and matter. (The
Levitical taboos, which include incest and homosexuality, mark out any
aberrant or physically blemished person as unpleasing to God. While the
prohibition extends to prevent the union of same with same or human with
animal, it also extends to the mixing of things: Seeds or breeds of cattle
should not be mingled; clothing should not be made of linen *and* wool.)[2]

In this context Djuna Barnes's *Nightwood* might be called "The Lamen-
tations of the Levitically Impure." Leviticus is about separation. *Nightwood*
is about merging, dissolution, and, above all, hybridization—mixed
metaphors, mixed genres, mixed levels of discourse from the lofty to the
low, mixed "languages" from medical practice and circus argot, church
dogma and homosexual slang. Barnes's revision of the Old Testament parallels Joyce's revision of Homer in *Ulysses*. By making hybrids of the sacred
texts of Western culture, both writers revitalize "high" culture by carnival-
izing the dead bodies of the old texts, engorging them in a sacred/profane
cannibalism. *Nightwood* is also a *dangerous* novel, if we use Mary Douglas's
concept of "purity and danger" for the whole social order of this novel is
"impure."[3] The world is turned upside down for carnival; it is the reversible
world of the circus, the night world of lesbian, homosexual, and transvestite
Paris. Leviticus writes the rules for purity of blood. Ironically, it is Felix, the
wandering Jew, marked as impure by a world that has incorporated his culture's ethic of purity and named the Jew himself as impure, who searches
hopelessly for a "pure" aristocratic European bloodline: "With the fury of
a fanatic, he hunted down his own disqualification" (9).[4] *Nightwood* makes
a modernism of marginality. Its "danger" is that the excluded object of its

rage, the white Christian male, might read it. The Aryan superman is absent from the text, but his "uprightness" is the ethic which the characters' abjection opposes.

At a party in Vienna in the twenties, echoing act 2 of *Die Fledermaus,* the characters of *Nightwood* meet. Count Onatorio Altamonte is entertaining "the living statues," collecting for his amusement, as some European aristocrats did, circus people, Jews, transvestites, exiled Americans. I take one passage as my example here, but the whole novel encourages close reading. Dr. Matthew O'Connor tells Felix the story of "Nikka the nigger," whose name not only mimics the obscenity of the word, like a Middle European mispronunciation of the American racist epithet, but has a feminine ending. He "used to fight the bear at the Cirque de Paris." His role is savage primitive male battling the beast for the thrill of an effete audience. But O'Connor exposes the myth of the fascist projection of savage sexuality onto the black man:

"There he was, crouching all over the arena without a stitch on, except an ill-concealed loin-cloth all abulge as if with a deep-sea catch, tattooed from head to heel with all the *ameublement* of depravity! Garlanded with rosebuds and hack-word of the devil—was he a sight to see! Though he couldn't have done a thing (and I know what I am talking about in spite of all that has been said about the black boys) if you had stood him in a gig-mill for a week, though (it's said) at a stretch it spelled Desdemona. Well, then, over his belly was an angel from Chartres; on each buttock, half public, half private, a quotation from the book of magic, a confirmation of the Jansenist theory, I'm sorry to say and here to say it. Across his knees, I give you my word, 'I' on one and on the other, 'can,' put those together! Across his chest, beneath a beautiful caravel in full sail, two clasped hands, the wrist bones fretted with point lace. On each bosom an arrow-speared heart, each with different initials but with equal drops of blood. . . ."

"The legs," said Doctor O'Connor, "were devoted to vine work, topped by the swart rambler rose copied from the coping of the Hamburg house of Rothschild. Over his *dos,* believe it or not and I shouldn't, a terse account in early monkish script—called by some people indecent, by others Gothic—of the really deplorable condition of Paris before hygiene was introduced, and nature had its way up to the knees. And just above what you mustn't mention, a bird flew carrying a streamer on which was incised, '*Garde tout!*' I asked him why all this barbarity; he answered he loved beauty and would have it about him." (16–17)

O'Connor exposes in his tale ("at a stretch it spelled Desdemona") the white man's projection of desire for the white woman onto the black man, the white's naming of the black's genitals as "rapist," the white man's desire to rape and kill woman. The pun on the word *spell* suggests that his penis is *named* Desdemona, as O'Connor's penis is *named* Tiny O'Toole, but "spell" could also be read sexually as "to satisfy" Desdemona or, in another meaning, to take someone's place. The name concealed by Nikka's knickers is Verdi's Desdemona more than Shakespeare's, as Nikka acts an operatic Othello. The miscegenation and murder suggested by "Desdemona" are also in the tattoo's "confirmation of the Jansenist theory," defined by the *OED*. as the heresy of belief in the eternal battle of good and evil, the belief in the "perverseness and inability for good of the natural human will." Nikka's tattooed body is like one of Lambroso's drawings of criminals or Djuna Barnes's drawings for *Ryder* or *Ladies Almanack*. There are no margins; the margins devour the page; every inch of space is covered with drawings and text, breaking both the Levitical taboo of writing on the body and the taboo on mixing objects, for text and drawings clash with one another, mixing the sacred and the profane, the vulgar and the reverenced, the popular and the learned. The texts of each breast and buttock contradict one another as the ferociously oxymoronic frenzy of Barnes's prose style as well as her painting style continually yoke opposites together in violent opposition, mocking Levitical prohibitions in an endless play at dissolving and reconstituting difference.

The length of the name Desdemona suggests a gigantic penis and is part of an age-old tradition of sexual jokes. But it also suggests Othello and "savage" jealousy and murder. The reference to Victor Hugo's *Nôtre Dame de Paris,* with its famous digression on the criminal underworld and the sewers, is in the line "Paris before hygiene was introduced." [5] Hugo's earlier novel *Bug-Jargal* (1818, 1826) was, like Aphra Behn's *Oroonoko,* a study of a figure of "the royal slave." [6] This figure is a projection of a "phallic Negro" and is the white man's archetypal erotic animalization of the black. The white's spelling of desire on the black's penis, the pricking of the "prick" in what must have been a very painful procedure, renders him impotent as a man while it mythologizes him as savage maleness. The black man's body is a text of Western culture's historical projections and myths about race. The angel from Chartres represents the myth of the black as angelic, innocent, and childlike during the early days of slavery; the book of magic refers to Europeans' fears of African religions. The Rothschild rose from Hamburg may suggest money made in the slave trade. The "caravel" suggests a slave ship, and the elegant wrists the ladies who benefited from slavery. In a further description of the tattoo, O'Connor claims that an obscene word runs down one side into the armpit, a word uttered by Prince Arthur Tudor on his wedding night, "one word so wholly epigrammatic and in no way befitting the great and noble British Empire." (16) We may assume that that word, *merde,* is the doctor's favorite and the author's too, since the text is as full of references to bird droppings as Paris itself.

We know from Barnes's long response to Emily Coleman's essay on *Nightwood* that she expected readers to understand the references to Victor Hugo in the novel and to see it as part of the comic tradition of grotesque realism reaching back through Hugo to Rabelais.[7] In *Les Misérables* Jean Valjean's fellow convict, Cochepaille, is tattooed with the date of the defeat at Waterloo, 1815. In *Nightwood* Robin wanders from church "monstrously unfulfilled," with her large monk's feet, and the nuns at the Convent of Perpetual Adoration give her a sprig from their rosebush and show her "where Jean Valjean had kept his rakes." (46) Hugo describes the way in which the basest word in the French language, *merde,* became the finest word, as General Cambronne hurled it at his enemy on the battlefield. Hugo says that the expression of the excremental equals the soul, and in a note about the novel he claimed that *merde* was the *"misérable de mot,"* the outcast word, as his *misérables* were outcast people.[8] The fecal motif in Hugo's sewer chapters is continued in Barnes's *pissoir* passages and her description of O'Connor's chamber pot.[9] For Hugo the person who says *"merde"* is Prometheus, expressing the obscene laughter of the oppressed. The language of the latrine, which O'Connor speaks in the novel, is regenerative and Rabelaisian, as voiding is cleansing. Gutter language, *fex urbis,* is the voice of outcast people. In these chapters Hugo explores the argot of the underworld, its special culture, and defines it as *"verbe devenu forçat,"* the word become a convict.[10]

Similar convict words are chained together in Dr. O'Connor's speeches, his stories of grotesque and painful suffering, the intensely overdetermined figures banging against the bars of the prison-house of language. His swearing, the mixture of prayer, oath, and profanity, the inclusion of the Virgin Mary and shit in the same sentence, go back to Rabelais, reminding us of Gargantua arriving in Paris and drenching the crowd with urine, his *"Mère de . . . merde . . .* shit, Mother of God." Dung and defecation in the Rabelaisian tradition described by Bakhtin are part of carnival's reversal of authoritarian values, the eruption of folk humor in a bawdy acceptance of decay as renewal, of death as part of life. The language of this irrepressible force, as Bakhtin says, privileges the lower parts of the body. Critics who have described *Nightwood* as modernist decadence or the product of perversity have missed its deep roots in folk culture, via Hugo and Rabelais. For Barnes is the female Rabelais, the articulator of woman's body/bawdy language. Like Hugo and Rabelais before her, Barnes writes scatology as ontology. She affirms being by celebrating the Below, the belly, the bowels, the big feet of Robin Vote and Nikka, who is a natural black man only to the knees.

Nikka's tattooed body, to return to the text, is a cabalistic ritual object put on display at the circus. He fights the bear and reminds us of Eugène Sue's Morok and Hugo's bizarre *L'Homme qui rit,* whose monstrous and maimed characters resemble *Nightwood*'s. The friendship between the bear-like man, Ursus, and the civilized wolf, Homo, reminds us of Robin Vote as "the beast turning human," and the novel's controversial last scene with the dog; and Hugo's circus wagon as a universe of human, animal, and divine monsters, is an earlier version of the circus world of *Nightwood.* "Garlanded with rosebuds and hack-work of the devil," Nikka's body is also a journalist's page (hack; Barnes as a brilliant journalist and "hack" writer; printer's devil). The tattoos, with their combination of text, vines, flowers, gothic script, and so on are an exact version of the early definition of the grotesque. In *Rabelais* Bakhtin described the bold infringement of borders in early grotesque art, in which forms "seemed to be interwoven as if giving birth to each other" and the uncanny passing of animal, vegetable, and human into one another. (*Rabelais,* 32) Nikka's body is like one of Djuna Barnes's drawings for *Ryder,* which I describe as "Pennsylvania Dutch surrealism," to capture its combination of primitive folk naiveté and vitality with mythical beasts, texts, human figures, and grotesque vines.

But the art of tattooing is also a kind of bloody needlework. Thelma Wood, Djuna Barnes's lover and the model for the character of Robin Vote in the novel, was an artist who did silverpoint etchings, an art form one might call, with its dangerous uncorrectable pinpricks, a "high art" form of tattoo. These etchings are also tabooed objects, studies of cannibalistic flowers and fetishistic shoes. (Thelma Wood's Berlin sketchbook is in the McKeldin Library, University of Delaware.)

In the body of Nikka, Barnes creates an aesthetic of the modernist grotesque, a delicate and exotic refinement of the gross Rabelaisian realistic grotesque and the romantic intellectual grotesque of E.T.A. Hoffmann. Nikka's body as ritual object asserts the unalterable real grotesquerie of the human body. In *The Painted Body* Michael Thévoz follows Lacan in seeing marking the body as primitive human grappling with the mirror stage of development and identity-formation, so that human skin is humanity's "first ground and surface of sign-making." [11] In other words, the body is our first

book, the primal blank page on which our ancestors wrote. Anthropological evidence places the most ancient tattoos on the genitals, a tattooed or
decorated phallus or voluptuous female body decorated on breast, buttocks,
and genital areas among the first human artifacts. Our own bodies were our
first works of art, a remaking of the self. *Nightwood*'s project is a remaking of
gender and race categories of selfhood and it is preoccupied with skin as a
blank page. In Nikka's case the tattoo so graphically described is another of
Barnes's reversals, for Africans seldom used tattoos to mark the body. They
used scarification or body painting, while light-skinned peoples, notably
Asians, used tattoos. Marking the body seems to enact opposite meanings, a
symbolic separation from the mother as in Kristeva's use of the terms "semiotic" and "symbolic," where "semiotic" means all that Plato excluded from
art—circus, carnival, festival, music, laughter, and dance. But it also marks
the return of the repressed savage and unconscious desire. *Nightwood*'s language is a perfect example of this "semiotic" in practice.

Thévoz sees the original tattoo as a symbolic mark of the human being's
social relation to culture, and circumcision as a representation of the taboo
against incest with the mother. In Western culture, tattoo has been used to
mark the subject as a slave or a convict and has lost its ritual social origins in
inclusion rather than exclusion from culture. The modern tattoo is like the
mark of Cain, a sign of exclusion. But it also identifies the body with a certain class or group. The meaning of tattoo has changed historically from
embodying symbolic law in "primitive" societies to marking the outlaw in
modern societies. Hence the figure of the lesbian in the modern novel feeling she has the mark of Cain on her forehead. (Cain seems to survive as a
figure for the prepatriarchal. He is driven out because he will not slaughter
an animal for a patriarchal god.) Nikka in *Nightwood* is like a convict in
Kafka's *In the Penal Colony,* whose body has been tattooed by the infernal
machine which tattoos each criminal with the text of the law he has in-
fringed. French soldiers in the nineteenth century often tattooed the side of
the hand with the word *shit* so that it would deliver a message when they
saluted their superiors.

Djuna Barnes was fascinated with *maquillage.* Body painting, makeup,
extravagant costuming and cross-dressing were part of the style of what
Shari Benstock calls "Sapphic Modernism." Figuring Nikka as abjection,
his skin a text on which the dominant culture writes him as Other, Barnes
writes from the place of exclusion as woman, exile, and lesbian, juggling the
double message of the memory of body marking as beautiful and social
and its present meaning as sinister and shameful. Thévoz relates the angry
or erotic tattoos of modern convicts and mental patients as the outcasts'

defiance of logocentric society's exclusion of him, hence the body and hair painting of contemporary "punk" culture. The answer to the question raised by Nikka's tattoos in *Nightwood* may be found in the barbaric Ilse Koch's collection of tattoos cut from the skin of victims of Nazi persecutions at Buchenwald. Given the Levitical prohibition of writing on the body, these "works of art" were not taken from the bodies of Jews but from those of other outsiders; when does Barnes cease to laugh at Leviticus and begin to shudder?

Since so many readings of *Nightwood* situate the reader as "normal" and the characters as perverse and "damned," reading against the grain of the text's privileging of the oppressed as "us," I propose this reading as a sisterhood under the skin with the victimized, as the "fluid blue" under Robin's skin allies her with Nikka. In a similar way many studies of the Nazis (aside from the brilliant film *Our Hitler*) emphasize the perversity of individual sadists rather than the complicity of a whole nation in genocide. Such readings deny not only history and reality but the power of art, in fiction like *Nightwood,* to change us.

Modernism, then, if we take *Nightwood* as its most representative text, is a tattoo on the backside of a black homosexual circus performer. The non-Aryan, nonheterosexual body is a book in which the modern failure to understand or assimilate the difference of race, class, and gender is inscribed. Sexuality, liminality, and color are textualities written on the body in thousands of pinpricks, little dots which make a language of bloody ellipses, a dot-dot-dot or code of absences as presence. The representation of taboo in tattoo is a fierce example of the display of the body as Other, a ritual hieroglyphics of pleasure and pain, an invitation to read the body of the Other as a book. What is absent is the Nazi who will burn this book.

If Joyce in *Ulysses* writes ancient and modern patriarchy, mythologizes woman, and others the mother, Djuna Barnes in *Nightwood* laughs at Leviticus, brings all the wandering Jews, blacks, lesbians, outsiders, and transvestites together in a narrative that mothers the Other. While Joyce privileges the fertility of the modern mother goddess and her private parts, Barnes privileges the penis. It is the nonphallic penis she celebrates, the limp member of the transvestite, Dr. O'Connor—who masturbates in church like the Jongleur of Nôtre Dame doing tricks for the Virgin Mary—and the black man's impotent genitals that bear the white man's sexual burden.

The symbolic phallus as law is absent from *Nightwood,* replaced by the wayward penis of the outlaw and transvestite. But its presence is brilliantly conveyed in the person of a woman, Hedvig Volkbein, Felix's mother, who dies in childbirth, not quite convinced by Guido, an Italian Jew masquerading as a German aristocrat, that his blood is untainted. Hedvig represents German militarism. With her "massive chic," her goose step, her "hand, patterned on seizure," she dances in "a tactical maneuver" with shoulders conscious of braid and a turn of head that holds "the cold vigilance of a sentry." Like Lina Wertmüller's daring representation of a Nazi concentration camp commandant as a woman in her powerful film *Seven Beauties,* Barnes breaks taboo by representing absent Aryan patriarchal power in the person of a woman. In the film Italy is to Germany as woman is to man, the Other. So the Italian male is Other to the German woman, feminized by fascism.

Kenneth Burke says *Nightwood* is not political, that it has nothing to do with the Nazis.[12] Burke's discomfort with the seeming anti-Semitism of *Nightwood* is understandable. The scholar working on the text is confronted with T. S. Eliot's editorial cuts of passages that seem overtly homosexual or questionably anti-Semitic. But Djuna Barnes identifies with all outsiders. She was originally named Djalma, after Eugène Sue's *The Wandering Jew.* Sue's Djalma is tattooed by a "thug" in Java during his sleep. His killing of the panther onstage in chapter 14 is surely a source for Robin's scene with the lion in *Nightwood.*[13] But I would argue that the "political unconscious" of *Nightwood* is located in its supposedly irrelevant first chapter, meant to disguise its existence as a lesbian novel.

As *Nightwood* is not only a lesbian novel, its antifascism is apparent only when it triumphs over its own anti-Semitism, when we realize that its characters—Jews, homosexuals, lesbians, transvestites Gypsies, blacks, and circus performers—were all to perish in the Holocaust. Felix Volkbein is named for his role as wandering Jew (and the Yiddish Theater in New York?) his Middle-European sadness contradicting the happiness of the Italian (Latin) "Felix." As "Volkbein" he is the foot soldier of history, the portable slave, the leg man of disaster, the unofficial advance man of the Paris circus, as Nora Flood is in reality the leg woman of the Denckman Circus. Like the Roman fragment of a runner's leg in his parent's plush Vienna flat, Felix is "dissociated" from his past. As his ancestor's black and yellow handkerchief reminds him of the medieval Roman circus in which Jews were forced to run around the arena with ropes around their necks, his restless search for "pure" racial nobility to which to "bow down" signifies his internalization of racial difference while underscoring the reality of a Europe in which racial purity has been obscured by mixed marriages and false credentials. The dismemberment and fragmentation of the Roman statues, the runner's leg, the "chilly half-turned head of a matron stricken at the bosom" recall early Roman circuses, which sacrificed outcast Christians to the lions, medieval circuses where outcast Jews were terrorized, and prophesy with chilling accuracy the Nazi destruction of millions of Jews and other outcasts, devoured by their modern technological lions, the gas chambers and ovens of the concentration camps.

The blond Aryan beast slouching toward Buchenwald is present in this novel only in Hedvig's resemblance to him in 1880, but Felix's uneasiness, his attraction to the Catholic Church, his scholarly labors and devotion to the past, to his sick child, and to the topsy-turvy world of the circus are reminders of what was destroyed by fascism's ugly fist. Felix is *literally* the foot of the folk, the embodiment of Bakhtin's carnivalesque, the preserver of circus culture and history.

Joyce's Night Town, with cross-dressed Bella-Bello played against Bloom in a corset, like Tiresias in Eliot's *Waste Land,* suggests emasculation, not the ancient powerful life force of mythical transvestite figures. Barnes's doctor-transvestite is only posing as a gynecologist, and he identifies with the maternal principle. He lampoons all the male sex doctors whose own sexual identities were so troubled, from the mad Otto Weininger to Havelock Ellis (who was aroused only by women urinating) to the Freud of the Fliess letters. Unlike Joyce's Night Town, Barnes's *Nightwood* privileges the female world of night, magic, and ritual in the last scene in the chapel in the forest (Dante's dark wood), suggesting that "culture," in the primitive figure of Robin as racial memory, survives in America as Europe is destroyed by fascism.

The exiled Felix with his monocle reminds one of Djuna Barnes's sketches of Joyce as *Nightwood* in its static structure reflects Stephen Dedalus's aesthetic of stasis and proves it wrong, for fiction can be just as "impure" standing still as it can be while wandering. Joyce is recalled in O'Connor's chamber pot, in the naming of Nora, in her flat in the rue de Cherche-Midi, the location of the eye clinic where Barnes visited Joyce after his many operations. Did he give the manuscript of *Ulysses* to the author of *Nightwood* in tribute to a writer of one of the few modernist texts to rival his phallogocentricism? Or, by giving the logos to a woman-identified man, does Barnes rob it of patriarchal privilege? Since O'Connor, "the Old Woman who lives in the closet," defines the female as only the maternal and womb centered, his is a matriarchal phallogocentrism, a gynologos, not a cliterologos. Molly's yes is answered by Robin Vote's no to marriage, no to motherhood, no to monogamous lesbianism. Robin's no is a preverbal, prepatriarchal primitive bark—as the novel ends in the United States and she ritually acts the bear before her Madonna-Artemis, goddess of autonomous sexuality, owner of her body and her self. As Europe bows down to fascism, O'Connor asks, "Why doesn't anyone know when everything is over, except me? . . . I've not only lived my life for nothing, but I've told it for nothing—abominable among the filthy people" (165).

Despite Burke's denial of its political awareness I believe *Nightwood* is the representative modernist text, a prose poem of abjection, tracing the political unconscious of the rise of fascism, as lesbians, blacks, circus people, Jews and transvestites—outsiders all—*bow down,* as the text repeats, before Hitler's truly perverted Levitical prescriptions for racial purity.

We might also see the "political unconscious"[14] at work in the other meanings of tattoo. After the doctor finishes telling the story of Nikka, Felix asks him about Vienna's "military superiority." For a tattoo is also a military drum signal or alarm call, as well as a symbolic drama or masque performed before a battle by soldiers by torchlight, to act out the victory of valor over the forces of the night. The rosy-faced German boys the doctor recalls will soon be at the gates of the night world of Paris. The drumbeats of racial "purity" will sound against Nikka, O'Connor, and Volkbein. The evening of the "living statues" and outcasts at the count's is a museum of soon-to-be exterminated human types, like Hitler's Jewish Museum in Prague, meant to be all that was left of Jewish culture after the Holocaust. As Hugo's *Nôtre Dame de Paris* is an "antihistorical" novel prefiguring the Revolution, *Nightwood* is an "ahistorical" novel anticipating the Holocaust.

When the "living statues" are expelled from the party, the scene anticipates uncannily all the "expulsions from the party" of modern European history. Their refuge is a café on Berlin's Unter den Linden, the traditional meeting place of homosexuals and political aliens. O'Connor explains the count's action as fear of impotence, he "suspected that he had come upon his last erection" (25). The erection is a signifier of order and uprightness. And the remark is uncanny in the light of subsequent political events, as is Frau Mann's lament, "I've an album of my own . . . and everyone in it looks like a soldier—even though they are dead" (27). The narrator may say with Doctor O'Connor: "'Oh, *papalero,* have I not summed up my time! I shall rest myself someday by the brim of Saxon-les-Bains and drink it dry, or go to pieces in Hamburg at the gambling table, or end up like Madame de Staël—with an affinity for Germany'" (126).

RITUAL AS INSTRUCTION: BARNES CRITIQUES FREUD

My voice cracked on the word 'difference'; soaring up divinely.

Nightwood

Nightwood is problematic for the woman reader and unusual for modernism because it is such tightly closed text, and the narration is so distant and detached. Its heteroglossia resides in the doctor's multivoiced stories of abjection; its carnivalesque is not open to the audience but stylized and ritualized in the performative mode. The intimacy of a Colette or Woolf novel, in which narration is shared with the reader, so that she feels cocreative in the making of the text, is avoided. The narrative voice seems to have no gender except in the vitriolic description of Jenny, which privileges Nora's pain. Jenny Petherbridge, as the most abject character (because her author hates her) might be Barnes's portrait of the voyeuristic reader or literary critic, collecting other women's clothes and cast-off loves. Strictly limited to this role of "audience," the reader is is forced to "bow down" to the text, to replicate the anxiety of abjection. The reader reads at the site of what the late Naomi Schor calls the "bisextuality" of female fetishism. As a lesbian novel *Nightwood* dramatizes illicit love in patriarchy, and some readers may find Nora's possessive infantilization of Robin as patriarchal as Hedvig's militarism or Felix's fixation on Germany. Despite the fact that its plot is a lesbian love story, *Nightwood* does not write the lesbian body as *Ladies Almanack* does, nor does it dramatize female desire, except insofar as it voices victimization, sets the alienated subjectivity of all outsiders, and flaunts bourgeois concepts of normality by privileging the private pain of a panoply of "monsters." The indeterminate desire of transvestite, Jew, lesbian, and black makes the forbidden erotic into a political cry for freedom. Mlle. Basquette, raped on her wheeled board, is the archetypal sexual victim as "basket case," humiliated and used by male sadism as Nikka is abused by male masochism. Racism, sexism, anti–Semitism, and homophobia are challenged by this text. The desire of the disabled, like Mlle. Basquette, "a girl without legs, built like a medieval abuse," (26) for love and freedom *as they are,* rather than to be made "normal," cannot be made into a universal principle of natural law. As Hans Mayer writes in *Outsiders,* "The light of the categorical imperative does not shine for them." [15] As O'Connor says, "even the greatest generality has a little particular" (89). Mlle. Basquette looks like the figurehead of a ship and is raped by a sailor. She is the disabled woman, hostage to men, of Hans Christian Andersen's "The Little Mermaid," as brilliantly analyzed by Nina Auerbach in *Women and the Demon.* There is always another Other.

Such a spectacle of human bondage as *Nightwood* provides by centering the marginal, articulates the angst of the abject so well that the absent upright, the pillars of society, are experienced unconsciously by the reader as the enemies of the human spirit. Figuring plot as plight in the tradition of the great nineteenth century French realist fictions of Hugo and Sue, Barnes modernizes the story of the oppressed hunchback or Jew to include sexual outcasts. As a melodrama of beset "perverts," *Nightwood* transcends its models by its refusal to play on the reader's pity. The human dignity of the aberrant is maintained by the narrator's objectivity, the irrepressible comic carnivalesque tone and the exuberant vitality of obscene language.

The linguistic richness of *Nightwood,* its choked abundance of puns and plays on words, its fierce allusiveness to medieval and Jacobean high and low art, the extraordinary range of its learned reach across the history of Western culture, marks it as the logos-loving match of *Ulysses.* We are not accustomed to thinking of Djuna Barnes as a learned woman, a scholar as well as a writer. Nor does *Nightwood* arrange itself neatly next to other modernist experimental women's writing in an antilogocentric act. Gertrude Stein robs words of meaning, objectifies them, empties them, and fills them again out of her own ego. Woolf and Colette experiment with an intimate and flexible female sentence. The narratives of Jean Rhys, H. D., or Elizabeth Bowen are inescapably women's novels. If we place *Nightwood* among female antifascist fiction of the thirties, Christina Stead's *The House of All Nations,* Virginia Woolf's *The Years,* and Marguerite Yourcenar's *Coup de Grâce,* it fits thematically. Woolf's novel traces the rise of fascism from the 1880s to the 1930s by concentrating on the origin of fascism in the patriarchal family. Stead condemns capitalism for its collaboration with fascism. Yourcenar brilliantly exposes German militarism and its patriarchal code of honor by privileging the ruthless and ethically bankrupt officer-narrator, leaving the reader the work of judging his self-serving narrative. In light of these antifascist texts, *Nightwood*'s project is to expose the collaboration of Freudian psychoanalysis with fascism in its desire to "civilize" and make "normal" the sexually aberrant misfit. *Nightwood* asserts that the outcast is normal and truly human. Freud and fascism, by labeling deviance, politically and medically, expose the inhumanity of the madness for order in every denial of difference from Leviticus to the sex doctors, Kraft-Ebbing, Ellis, Weininger, to Freud himself. Barnes makes us all misfits, claiming that in human misery we can find the animal and the divine in ourselves.

In this reading Nora is the archetypal Dora or female hysteric, and Dr. Freud is brilliantly parodied in the figure of Dr. Matthew-mighty-grain-of-salt-Dante-O'Connor. The lesbian patient chooses as doctor a transvestite whose most passionate desire is to be a woman, whose womb envy is so strong that it parodies Freudian penis envy mercilessly. The psychoanalyst's office is a filthy bedroom with a reeking chamber pot. Freud's famous totems, the sacred objects from ancient cultures that people his shelves and tables in H. D.'s famous tribute, are mocked by O'Connor's rusty forceps, broken scalpel, perfume bottles, ladies' underclothing, and abdominal brace. The psychoanalytic structure is ruptured as the patient asks the question and the doctor answers. The doctor sits in bed in a granny nightgown and wig, powdered and rouged, and the patient stands by his bed; it is three in the morning, not three in the afternoon. The patient is rational, puritanical, and analytical; the doctor is mad. When Nora complains of heartbreak at the loss of Robin, Matthew mocks her: "A broken heart have you! I have falling arches, flying dandruff, a floating kidney, shattered nerves *and* a broken heart! But do I scream that an eagle has me by the balls or has dropped his oyster on my heart?" (154)

But he proves to be a brilliant feminist psychoanalyst as he devastatingly deconstructs her dream. Floating in a Chagall-like dreamscape, her grandmother, "whom I loved more than anyone," is in a glass coffin, with her father circling the grave struggling with her death. In the dream she watches, unable to do anything; then her father's body stops circling and drifts immobile beside the grandmother's body.

O'Connor detects the absence of the mother in Nora's dream. "'It's my mother without argument I want!' And then in his loudest voice he roared: 'Mother of God! I wanted to be your son—the unknown beloved second would have done!'" (149–150) The two grandmother-incest dreams constitute a revisionary psychological constitution of the female self, which we may call a *nonnology*. The *nonna,* or grandmother, may well become a young woman's role model and beloved in cases of real or imagined incest, when the mother has not protected the daughter from the father's assaults. Nora refuses to deal with the relationship between her love for Robin and her own role as daughter in the family. She begs the doctor to tell Robin never to forget her. O'Connor's psychological advice to the upright Nora is that she must bend, bow down, experience the body, and get out of herself in ritual or carnival, let herself go, deal with the animal in herself:

> "Tell her yourself," said the doctor, "or sit in your own trouble silently if you like; it's the same with ermines—those fine yellow ermines that women pay such a great price for—how did they get that valuable colour? By sitting in bed and pissing the sheets, or weeping in their own way. It's the same with persons; they are only of value when they have laid themselves open to 'nuisance'—their own and the world's. *Ritual itself constitutes an instruction* [emphasis added]. So we come back to the place from which I set out; pray to the good God; she will keep you. Personally, I call her 'she' because of the way she made me; it somehow balances the mistake. . . . That

priceless galaxy of misinformation called the mind, harnessed to that stu-
pendous and threadbare glomerate compulsion called the soul, ambling
down the almost obliterated bridle path of Well and Ill, fortuitously
planned—is the holy Habeas Corpus, the manner in which the body is
brought before the judge." (150)

The doctor continually points out to Nora that the rigidity of her American Protestant consciousness; her fear of the body; of drink, promiscuity,
and dirt; make her love for Robin destructive, possessive, and patriarchal in
its insistence on monogamy and control of the beloved. He mocks her romantic possessiveness: "[T]here you were sitting up high and fine, with a
rose-bush up your arse" (151).

Like Freud, O'Connor has an inexhaustible fund of case histories of
aberrant behavior, and he has a great deal to say about the art of writing. "I
have a narrative, but you will be put to it to find it," (97) he tells his "patient." He begs Nora to stop writing letters tormenting Robin: "Can't you
rest now, lay down the pen?" Since he has no one to write to, he takes in
"a little light laundry known as the Wash of the World" (126), the psychoanalyst as Irish washerwoman, the writer as producer of dirty linen.
"Haven't I eaten a book too? Like the angels and prophets? And wasn't it a
bitter book to eat? . . . And didn't I eat a page and tear a page and stamp on
others and flay some and toss some into the toilet for relief's sake—then
think of Jenny without a comma to eat, and Robin with nothing but a pet
name—your pet name to sustain her . . . " (127). Telling one of his homosexual stories, in which he claims that he can tell the district and nationality of every penis he encounters like a gourmet, he says "must I, perchance,
like careful writers, guard myself against the conclusions of my readers?"
(94) He rails against American cleanliness, praising "the good dirt"; because
a European bathes in "true dust," he can trace the history of his actions.
His body is his page. "*L'Echo de Paris* and his bed sheets were run off the
same press. One may read in both the travail life has had with him—he
reeks with the essential wit necessary to the 'sale' of both editions, night
edition and day" (89).

Nora's problem is the body/mind split. "The Anglo-Saxon has made the
literal error; using water, he has washed away his page" (90). The doctor
wants Nora to recognize her animality, to face her desire for Robin as physical, and to stop seeing herself as "saving" a lost soul.

The great writer writes from the body. The dirty bedsheet is the writer's
page. Patriarchal culture has traditionally seen woman as a blank page on
which to write. So Nora sees Robin, and projects herself on to that page.

Djuna Barnes's genius lies in her ability to overcome Nora's anxieties, and she is one of the few women writers whose novel was run off the same press as her bed sheets. Contemporary novels, such as Gabriel García Marquez's *A Hundred Years of Solitude* or Günther Grass's *The Flounder,* owe a great deal to the "fantastic realism" of *Nightwood.* Feminist fantastic realism has its own as yet critically uncharted history, but certainly *Nightwood* may be read in the context of Sylvia Townsend Warner's *Lolly Willowes,* Rebecca West's *Harriet Hume,* Joanna Russ's *The Female Man,* and their brilliant successor, Angela Carter's *Nights at the Circus* (1985). I have argued in "A Wilderness of One's Own" that these novels often appear after a period of realism in fiction reflecting political activism on the part of women, like Woolf's *Orlando* and *Flush,* in which the writer is frustrated by the failure of struggle to change the power structure.

Nightwood differs from its sister texts in its anticipation of historical horror, its proleptic impulse. Women writers have traditionally been forced to wash away from their page any mention of desire. It is as if Djuna Barnes had decided to include in *Nightwood* every word, image, and story women have never been able to tell, to flaunting every possible taboo from the excretory to the sexual, and to invent, in Nora's grandmother-incest dreams, her *nonnology,* taboos uncataloged even by Freud. Her boldness is remarkable. Even H. D., in her *Tribute to Freud,* was sly and subtle in her critique of "the master." She undermines his authority by greeting his dog first, by getting him to complain that she won't love him, by pretending that he treats her as an equal, by claiming that he approves of her relationship with Bryher, by describing him as a fellow student of myth and the collective unconscious. In short H. D. fictionalizes Freud as Jung. Her "tribute" is really to woman's power to make the analyst collaborate with her, to save her "abnormality" for her art.

Djuna Barnes's critique of Freud is less directly personal than H. D.'s, but both are part of a modernist feminist insistence on woman-centeredness and partnership between doctor and patient. *Nightwood* challenges not only Freud, but the whole history of the treatment of female hysteria. Dr. O'Connor's lies seem to Felix "to be the framework of a forgotten but imposing plan" (30). "[T]he great doctor, he's a divine idiot and a wise man" (31). Matthew says "the only people who really *know* anything about medical science are the nurses, and they never tell; they'd get slapped if they did" (31). (The nurse is a major icon of European modernism. See Barnes's friend Antonia White's brilliant story "The House of Clouds," and one of many novels about nursing in World War I, Irene Rathbone's *We That Were Young* [rpt. 1989, Feminist Press].)

O'Connor claims that he is "not neurasthenic," and pronounces, "No man needs curing of his individual sickness; his universal malady is what he should look to" (32). These remarks are part of the slapstick dialogue, with Felix as "straight man," which introduces "La Somnambule." Stage Irishman and stage Jew mock each other's racial traits as liars and meddlers and make fun of doctors. The comic pair then wake sleeping beauty, in the person of Robin Vote, "meet of child and desperado" (35). In keeping with the carnival spirit of their "act," O'Connor plays magician or "dumbfounder" at a street fair and turns his back on the patient to make up his hairy face with her powder and rouge and steal a hundred-franc note. The reader "watches" this scene as a cabaret act, and "reads" it as a pantomime of Sleeping Beauty woken by the wrong prince, as well as a classic crooked apothecary or quack doctor joke.

The narrator tells us that "the woman who presents herself to the spectator as a 'picture' forever arranged is, for the contemplative mind, the chiefest danger" (37). The "picture" of the disheveled Robin flung like a dancer on the bed in a scene like Rousseau's "jungle trapped in a drawing room," emphasizes her legs and feet in men's white flannel trousers and dancing pumps. Extraordinarily cinematic, the scene reverses the reader's picture of Marlene Dietrich in thirties vamp films like *The Blue Angel* or *Blonde Venus* (which even has a gorilla, a "beast turning human"). We remember Dietrich "transvested" from the waist up in male top hat and tails, pointing the contrast to very feminine legs. In a famous essay Kenneth Tynan wrote of Dietrich what might be said of Robin Vote: "She has sex but no particular gender. They say . . . that she was the only woman allowed to attend the annual ball for male transvestites in pre-Hitler Berlin. . . . [T]his Marlene lives in a sexual no man's land—and no woman's either. . . . [S]he is every man's mistress and mother, every woman's lover and aunt." [16] In the context of *Nightwood,* one would say, every woman's lover and grandmother.

Lesbian subculture in Paris in the twenties and thirties affords many examples of the woman in a tuxedo. (Rebecca West once described Radclyffe Hall and Una Troubridge as looking in their male attire and cropped hair like "a distant prospect of Eton College." [17]) As tattoo is a form of the general Levitical taboo against transvestism, Robin's appearance in men's trousers is another version of writing on the body, or rewriting the body. The carnival of cross-dressing destabilizes identity, keeping bisexuality from being anchored to one pole and acting out a "female fetishism," denying Freud's assumption the fetishism is exclusively male. Naomi Schor's argument "that ultimately *female travesty,* in the sense of women dressing up as or impersonating other women, constitutes by far the most disruptive form of *bisextuality*," applies more fully to *Nightwood* than any other novel I can think of, though it is characteristic of the lives and work of the whole movement of "Sapphic Modernism." If "female fetishism is an oxymoron," then one may argue that Djuna Barnes's style itself is a form of fetishism that allows the reader free play in the riddle of sexuality.

Even Robin's skin participates in tattoo and links her to Nikka and to Nora's obsession with her as "purity's black backside." Consoling Felix for the loss of Robin, O'Connor later compares her to a horse whose "hide was a river of sorrow. . . . Her eyelashes were gray-black, like the eyelashes of a nigger, and at her buttocks' soft centre a pulse throbbed like a fiddle. . . . Yes, oh God, Robin was beautiful. . . . Sort of fluid blue under her skin, as if the hide of time had been stripped from her." Robin's "hide," her "flayed body," is "the infected carrier of the past"; she is "eaten death returning" (37), exactly Bakhtin's construction of the material body as the memory of culture. The "fluid blue" under Robin's skin is like Nikka's tattoo. The scene at the circus, when Robin is lionized by the lion's eyes, reminds us of Mae West's brilliant articulation of female animal desire in the classic thirties film *I'm No Angel*. As a heroine Robin rescues libido from the exclusive possession of men. The agency of her desire and its refusal to be fixed as the desired object of lesbian lovers, husband, contained in motherhood, or controlled by T. S. Eliot's or other critics' reading of her as doomed, damned or pathologically placed as a medical case study, is a textual triumph. Even Robin's voice (reported, for she speaks only twice) resembles Marlene Dietrich's: "In the tones of this girl's voice was the pitch of one enchanted with the gift of postponed abandon: the low drawling 'aside' voice of the actor who, in the soft usury of his speech, withholds a vocabulary until the profitable moment when he shall be facing his audience" (38).

It is precisely that pitch of postponed abandon that characterizes the art of Dietrich. The "low drawl," the slight catch in the phrasing, the way she sings the sensual as if it were a lullaby, and, above all, the sense that every song is sung as if she were remembering it from a long time ago—these are the things that constitute her appeal. So Robin's "soft usury" of speech is related to her archetypal resemblance to the ancient past. There is a non-threatening animal growl to this voice—O'Connor would call it the voice of the dream prince, the "uninhabited angel," the genderless or empty sign of her body in which child and desperado meet. Robin is a speechless picture for much of the novel, but her outburst at Nora (the fetish talks back?) when she is drunk in the street, is telling: "You are a devil! You make everything dirty! . . . You make me feel dirty and tired and old!" (143) She makes

Nora give money to an old prostitute: "'These women—they are all like her,' she said with fury. 'They are all good—they want to save us!'" (144) Robin's sisterhood with the downtrodden, crawling in the gutter with outcasts, is the way in which "ritual constitutes an instruction" for her. Her abjection is the reverse of Nora's uprightness, and it is privileged in the novel as the more *humane condition*. She doesn't want to be saved; she wants to be free.

There is an ironic message for Nora in Matthew's tale of the London "Tupenny Upright:"

> ladies of the *haute* sewer . . . holding up their badgered flounces, or standing still, letting you do it, silent and indifferent as the dead . . . their poor damned dresses hiked up and falling away over the rump, all gathers and braid, like a Crusader's mount, with all the trappings gone sideways with misery." (130–131)

At the very heart of the novel the twin *pissoir* passages condemn the upright. A woman curses her lover in the toilet: "May you die standing upright! May you be damned upward!" She curses her lover's genitals: "May this be damned, terrible and damned spot! May it wither into the grin of the dead, may this draw back, low riding mouth in an empty snarl of the groin" (95). The rest of this passage anticipates Robin on all fours at the end of the novel: For what do you know of me, man's meat? I'm an angel on all fours, with a child's feet behind me, *seeking my people that have never been made* [emphasis added], going down face foremost, drinking the waters of night at the water hole of the damned . . ." (95). The lesbian curse on the clitoris in the *pissoir* is terrifying. Why does Barnes set it next to the rollicking tales of happy homosexual cruising ("cottaging") and O'Connor's domestication of the Parisian *pissoir* as his cottage ("my only fireside is the outhouse" [91])? What is missing from the casual sex of the men is the possessiveness of "love." (Such passages obviously couldn't be written after AIDS.) Yet when Nora seeks solace in the arms of other women she misses Robin even more. Barnes seems to suggest that the dynamics of lesbian sexuality are different from homosexuality. Matthew longs to be someone's wife while Robin rejects Nora's wifely domestic ways and Nora's infantilization of her. In Latin *infans* means "speechless," and *Nightwood* creates the sex object as the silent subject.

Between them O'Connor and Nora try to analyze lesbianism, though she cannot give up her posture, derived from patriarchal conceptions of love, of the abandoned wife. The discussion centers on the figure of the doll as the lesbian's child, Robin's smashing the doll, Jenny Petherbridge's gift of another doll to Robin, and the figure of the prince. Robin says she chose a girl who resembles a boy as a lover from the figures of the prince and princess in romances. "We were impaled in our childhood upon them as they rode through our primers, the sweetest lie of all . . ." (137). When the love one has been told to expect never arrives, one chooses the androgynous figure of the prince.

Nora tells the doctor that the doll she shared with Robin was "their child," but she also says, "We give death to a child when we give it a doll—it's the effigy and the shroud" (142). O'Connor tells Nora that she really wanted Robin to *be* a doll, an "uninhabited angel," an object onto which she could project "sexless misgiving." But she does not really listen to him or respond to his analysis: "Do you think that Robin had no right to fight you with her only weapon? She saw in you the fearful eye that would make her a target forever. Have not girls done as much for the doll?" (148) He continues: "The last doll, given to age, is the girl who should have been a boy, and the boy who should have been a girl! The love of that last doll was foreshadowed in the love of the first. The doll and the immature have something right about them, the doll because it resembles but does not contain life, and the third sex because it contains life but resembles the doll." (148) So sleeping Robin is not really the princess but the prince.[18]

The moment when Robin raises the doll over her head as if to smash it, but doesn't, and the repeated moment when she smashes and kicks the doll—her "child" with Nora—have an element of the uncanny in them. We may compare the treatment of the doll figure in *Nightwood* to Freud's essay on "The Uncanny" (1919). When O'Connor tells Nora that she has "dressed the unknowable in the garments of the known," (136) he is giving a definition of the uncanny much like Freud's definition of a species of the horrifying that is also very familiar. Freud's essay is a peculiar example of the analyst as literary critic or, rather, father of patriarchal aesthetic theory. Like some contemporary theorists, he begins, "I have not made a very thorough examination of the bibliography."[19] He then claims that although he himself is not susceptible to the uncanny, he will nevertheless write the essay since most aesthetic theory deals only with "the sublime." Freud fills the gap with several pages from dictionaries (in various languages) defining *unheimlich*. *Heimlich* comes to mean not only *homely* in some cases, but its opposite, and magic is associated with it as well as the secret parts of the body. It never occurs to Freud that *heimisch* refers to the female world of the home with safety and comfort provided by woman. The transition of the word's meaning from holy to unholy, from the domestic to the horrific, clearly marks the historical change from male pleasure in the female to his fear of woman, her body and her space. Freud, albeit unwittingly, is one of the best examples of this ideological reversal. While Freud's definition is a workable one, there is a great discrepancy between his definition and his examples, most of which come from E.T.A. Hoffmann's *Tales*.

I maintain that Freud's notion of the uncanny (in examples) is gender biased, and that only certain men would experience the uncanny in the cases he cites—that women do not find these situations uncanny, and therefore they are not universal. It seems perfectly reasonable to suppose that male and female versions of the uncanny should be different from each other, and to examine the female versions of the uncanny offered by *Nightwood* in contrast to Freud's analysis. Since women have been the providers of *Heimlichkeit*, or domestic bliss, it is obvious that their experiences of the uncanny will be different. Freud, quoting Jentsch, starts his inquiry by finding the uncanny in our doubt as to whether something that appears animate is really alive or whether a lifeless object might really be alive (*U,* 132) as in waxwork figures or dolls.[20] Freud is at some pains to deny the importance of the figure of the doll, Olympia, in the uncanny effect of Hoffmann's "The Sand Man," the first act of Offenbach's opera, *Tales of Hoffmann*. (I wonder if one could read Manet's famous painting, *Olympia,* as another participant in the Freud-Hoffmann doll-making paradigm, the reduction of woman to the passive object of the male gaze. The painting seems to invoke an order of objecthood: white woman/doll, black woman/dog.)[21]

Hoffmann's fantastic realism and grotesquerie were a direct influence on Djuna Barnes. While Bakhtin regards Hoffmann as too alienated and morbid to participate in the Rabelaisian folk tradition of the grotesque, Djuna Barnes was influenced by and participates in both traditions. The Romantic concern with the sick self, the move of fairy-tale fantasy from pastoral forest to metropolitan café, the concern with night and dream and Anton Mesmer's experiments with hypnotism—"the science of the soul" as proof of the existence of the supernatural—these concerns, which come from Hoffmann to Barnes, are part of the intellectual origins of *Nightwood.* "The Sandman" was originally published in *Night Pieces,* and Hoffmann shared Barnes's love of Jacques Callot, the seventeenth-century engraver of grotesque creatures part beast and part human. Like Barnes, Hoffmann had an amazon grandmother, and he enjoyed disfiguring the margins of her Bible with figures of satyrs and hell. His portrait of Olympia seems to have come from his mother, described as rigid, cold, hysterical, and given to staring vacantly into space (*Tales,* 18, 19). Nathaniel's obsession with Olympia, the automaton, is based on her passivity: "Never before had he such a splendid listener. She neither embroidered nor knitted; she did not look out of the window nor feed a bird nor play with a lapdog or kitten . . . she sat for hours on end without moving, staring directly into his eyes, and her gaze grew ever more ardent and animated" (*Tales,* 162).

Through the spyglass he buys from Coppelius, Nathaniel sees his real lover, Clara, as a doll and tries to kill her. Eyes are the heart of the story, and Freud insists on reading through men's eyes a tale of fear of castration in the loss of eyes, and the hero's relation with his father and Coppelius as a good father/bad father drama.

I suggest that Freud's analysis represses his own interest in the collaboration of Professor Spalanzini with the mysterious charlatan Dr. Coppelius/Coppola ("eye-socket" in Italian) in which he may have seen his own collaboration with the eventually discredited Fliess, though the part of the body in question was the nose. The two doctors "create" a woman (the womb envy of the Freud-Fliess letters is obvious; Fliess believed that men had cycles like women, and Freud appeared to accept this idea).[22] What is at issue in the story is the male doctors' creation and destruction of the woman patient. Hoffmann's Olympia is a mechanical "La Somnambule." The intellectual history of "somnambulism," which meant hypnotism (not merely sleepwalking), is the direct forerunner of Freud's definition of the unconscious. In this history the line between science and charlatanism was very thin. For Fourier, Sue, Hugo, Mesmer, and Hoffmann somnambulism proved the existence of the human spirit, the collective unconscious, or God. This antienlightenment, antimaterialist doctrine of "illuminism" was also the mother of modern socialism; metempsychosis (Joyce's "met him pike hoses") and animal magnetism were some of its tenets as well as an androgynous god, a sexed universe, and a division of the world into animal, human, and angel.[23] Since so many of these ideas animate the world of *Nightwood,* I suspect that Djuna Barnes's intellectual origins are to be found here.[24]

When she labels Robin Vote "La Somnambule," Djuna Barnes is not aligning her with Lady Macbeth but with the innocent heroine of Bellini's opera *La Somnambula,* whose romantic story was written to prove the existence of the soul to atheists and rationalists. People are not simply "living statues," material automatons, it was argued, but animated by spirit. The count in the opera was a "scientist" who proved to the unbelieving folk that the heroine's unconscious spirit caused her to walk in her sleep, and that her rational self had no control over her actions. Unlike *Tales of Hoffmann, La Somnambula* no longer commands the immense popularity it had in the nineteenth century, largely because intellectual historians have not been willing to see the roots of modern thought, either socialism or psycho-analysis, in these romantic, irrational experiments. At a production of *La Somnambula* in Washington, D.C. (December 1984), the audience laughed through the scene in which the heroine sings of her love for her fiancé while sleepwalking to the count's bed. The unconscious power of her desire is the point of the opera, as it is the point of Robin's nightwalks into promiscuity in *Nightwood*—she retains her innocence, her association with the virgin Diana of Ephesus. This "virginity" of Robin's we interpret as control over her own sexuality. As a sleepwalker she is the collective unconscious of un-differentiated female desire. Felix says she has the "odour of memory"; her speech is "heavy and unclarified"; "there was in her every movement a slight drag, as if the past were a web about her" (118, 119).

Nightwood plays operatic allusions against circus allusions in a dialectic be-tween folk and highbrow art on the subject of desire. O'Connor introduces Robin to Jenny Petherbridge at the opera—the powerful *Rigoletto,* also based on a plot by Hugo, in which the father murders his daughter while trying to avenge her rape, refusing to accept the fact that she loves the count who raped her. O'Connor mocks the diva: "there's something wrong with any art that makes a woman all bust!" (103)

Though Felix asks for Wagner's music to be played in cafés, O'Connor turns Wagner's heroic chaste male ideal of brotherhood as well as the me-dieval patriarchal theme of the quest (which were used to great effect by the Nazis) into a joke (as well as a feminist critique of Wagner): "[o]ne woman went down through the ages for sitting through *Parsifal* up to the point where the swan got his death, whereupon she screamed out, "Godamercy, they have shot the Holy Grail!" (96) Barnes is taking potshots at the repres-sive ideal of celibacy for men, which displaces desire onto evil figures of se-ductive females, as articulated by Wagner. The operatic *motives* are also "answered" in the dialogue of the novel with lines from music hall and pop-ular songs. This pastiche of fragmented pieces from the past of Western cul-ture, which we now associate with the postmodern is also practised by Barnes in her painting and drawing, *faux* woodcuts, parodies of the Beard-sleyesque, copies of folk-art cartoons in which the faces are made into real-istic portraits while the rest of the drawing is derivative, oil paintings on cardboard.

The doctor tells the story of Don Anticolo, the tenor from Beirut, who—drinking with a dozen sailors—mourns his dead son, throwing up and down the box of his ashes, "no bigger than a doll's crate," recalling Robin smashing the doll. The whole of the chapter called "The Squatter" mimics the opera as well as a *commedia dell'arte* Punch-and-Judy show. When

Jenny dresses up in costume and takes Robin and her guests in old-fashioned carriages to the Bois, the grand masquerade scene is an abduction from the lesbian seraglio, the fighting and scratching of the lovers like a puppet show at a fair, where Punch and Judy are both women, and the child, Sylvia, who is caught in the quarrel, adds a melodramatic *frisson.* Djuna Barnes's father composed operas including the comic and melodramatic *Allan Castle,* whose heroine is stabbed as she poses inside a picture frame, anticipating the "framing" of Nora in *Nightwood,* in the window as she observes Robin with another woman, and in the doorway of the chapel in the last scene.[25]

To return to Freud, Hoffmann, and the uncanny, one may say that the (woman) reader (though woman is not a universal category) does not experience a chill when the mechanical doll is smashed and the eyes roll on the floor, whereas some women do have such a response to Robin's smashing the doll in *Nightwood.* The (woman) reader of "The Sandman" knows that Nathaniel will reject Clara precisely because she is not a doll, because she has a mind and uses it to analyze his obsessions as well as to criticize the poem in which he predicts that he will kill her. Hoffmann pictures the patriarchy in the persons of the two doctors, constructing "woman" as a passive, mindless doll and passing on this "ideal" to a young man who accepts the image, sees through the patriarchy's lens, its dark glass, and cannot relate to a real woman. "The Sandman" is, in fact, about the construction of the male gaze and the oedipal initiation of the son into the father's dominating I/Eye. Coppola's doll does not move the reader because she is so patently not of woman born, so clearly a creature of male science and male desire. When Robin smashes the doll the horror is caused by the erasure of the difference between sign and signified. Western culture has socialized girls by giving them dolls to develop their maternal instincts. A doll *is* a baby, they are told. It is precious and must not be broken. The uncanny moment is caused by Robin killing her and Nora's baby, the symbol of their union. The doll signifies as well the unnatural and illegitimate in their relationship.

The smashing of the doll is a recurrent scene in women's writing. The mathematician Sophie Kovalevsky tells in *A Russian Childhood* of her pathological fear of dolls; Jean Rhys in *Smile Please* almost defines her writing self as the doll breaker. Fear of objectification and abjection seem to be at work here as well as fear of motherhood. The classic story is Maggie working out her anger deliberately on a doll in George Eliot's *The Mill on the Floss.* Eliot calls the doll "a fetish which she punished for all her misfortunes." She has banged three nails into the doll's head in her fury, and the trunk is "defaced by a long career of vicarious suffering." What is interesting is that Maggie

never really destroys the doll, for in order to go through her ritual of comforting it after she has beaten it, she has to leave it some semblance of resemblance to herself. The doll as a toy or "baby" is a relatively recent
cultural phenomenon, but there is a long history of the doll as a magical ritual object. In the Russian version of Cinderella, it is the doll that brings Baba
Yaga to save the heroine.

While Freud claims that the doll Olympia is "nothing else but a personification of Nathaniel's feminine attitude toward his father in infancy"
and "a dissociated complex of Nathaniel's which confronts him as a person"
(U, 139). I suggest that she is Freud's patient, the female hysteric, who is
hypnotized and forced into "good" and wooden behaviour and eventually
destroyed by quarrelling male "doctors." Freud claims that one of his patients believed that her dolls would come to life if she looked at them with
enough concentration, but that "the idea of the living doll excites no fear at
all" (U, 140).[26] For a woman who is socialized to be looked at, who even
objectifies herself in the mirror, the uncanny is not figured in symbolic castration of the eyes, for she is the object being gazed at, but the fear of becoming a living doll or statue, of becoming *only* an object. When Robin and
Nora act as *kores* (in Greek *kore* means "pupil of the eye") or "living statues"
of the lesbian as eternal maiden while they look at a representation of such
abjection in the statue with the protruding blank eyes; as pupils (in the
other meaning of the word) of the eye, they deconstruct the process of
objectification/abjection of woman. Felix, with his monocle and false
portraits of ancestors as blank-eyed actors, returns the gaze of the Aryan at
the Jew.

Djuna Barnes's articulation of the female uncanny and its relation to writing in a complex of signs around images of dolls and eyeless statues participates in female modernism's larger interrogation of gender and the writing
self under the male gaze which also includes the problem of the struggle between the needle and the pen. (In "Il vole," set to music by Francis Poulenc
in "Fiançailles pour rire" [1939], French poet Louise de Vilmorin writes, "I
should like to sew but a magnet/Attracts all my needles.") Jean Rhys uncannily suggests in *Smile Please* the relation of the woman's eye to her "I":

Before I could read, almost a baby, I imagined that God, this strange thing
or person I had heard about, was a book. Sometimes it was a large book
standing upright and half open and I could see the print inside but it made
no sense to me. Other times the book was smaller and inside were sharp
flashing things. The smaller book was, I am sure now, my mother's needle
book, and the sharp flashing things were her needles with the sun on them.

Her nurse forbade her to read and told her a version of the Sandman story:

> "If all you [sic] read so much, you know what will happen to you? Your eyes
> will drop out and they will look at you from the page."
>   "If my eyes dropped out I wouldn't see," I argued.
>   She said, "They drop out except the little black points you see with."
>   I half believed her and imagined my pupils like heads of black pins
> and all the rest gone. But I went on reading.[27]

The relationship between the woman reader and the woman writer often reproduces the uncanny feeling of your own eyes looking up at you
from the page. God/father/book is indecipherable, but in reading a sympathetic writer and in writing for a sympathetic reader, the woman can look
at herself and be looked at without fear. The eye of God is the big book,
but in the little book the needles (pens) connect with the eyes of the mother
as the daughter's mirror. When the book is the mother's eye, the daughter
writing finds her "I."

Freud asks, "Who would be so bold as to call it an uncanny moment, for
instance, when Snow White opens her eyes once more?" (U, 154) Many
women would be so bold. Certainly we may read Nora's dream of her dead
grandmother in a glass coffin as her wish to be the prince who wakes Sleeping Beauty or Snow White. Her anxiety is caused by her wish to kill her father, who is already playing that role and standing in her way in the dream.
The dream, with its absent mother and hovering father, also enacts the
struggle to maintain female connection within the patriarchy, the desire to
remove the possessive father and incorporate the magic grandmother, to
erase the boundaries imposed by patriarchal culture. Robin, lying prone on
the bed, acting as a "picture" for others to look at in the "La Somnambule"
chapter, is the proverbial woman patient. Barnes brilliantly parodies the famous scene in which Jean-Martin Charcot and a group of upright doctors
hypnotize the horizontal female hysteric by exposing the erotics of the doc-
tor-patient relationship, its voyeurism and quackery. We see psychoanalysis
as circus in Matthew-I-am-my-own-charlatan-O'Connor, whose womb
envy is openly expressed: "[I]t was a high soprano I wanted and deep corn
curls to my bum, with a womb as big as the king's kettle . . . in my heart is
the wish for children and knitting. God, I never asked better than to boil
some good man's potatoes and toss up a child for him every nine months by
the calendar" (91).

O'Connor as transvestite-shaman knows by vicarious experience what
certain women want. His analysis of Nora and his advice, that "ritual con-

stitutes an instruction," amounts to a feminist critique of patriarchal psychoanalysis. "And do you need a doctor to tell you that it is a bad strange
hour for a woman? If all women could have it all at once, you could beat
them in flocks like a school of scorpions; but they come eternally, one after
the other." (101)

He recognizes female desire as different from men's, and it is difference
he urges on Nora. He claims to be "the last woman left in this world" (100)
though he is "the bearded lady." O'Connor's transvestism is a positive force
in *Nightwood*. The most powerful representation of the uncanny in the novel
is when Nora sees him in bed in his flannel nightgown and curly wig and
says, "God, children know something they can't tell; they like Red Riding
Hood and the wolf in bed" (79). In the typescript of the novel the following lines are crossed out: "with what cunning had his brain directed not
only the womanly, but the incestuous garment? For a flannel night dress is
our mother."[28] In fragments from the "Go Down, Matthew," chapter
Barnes wrote: "What sense is there in saying the girl went wrong at twenty,
that she wore a bowler hat by preference when but eight months old and
showed a liking for kissing her grandmother's ~~bottom~~ [crossed out in orig-
inal] left elbow; it's not that she did so that needs explanation, its what it
seemed like while she was about it."

Children liking Red Riding Hood and the wolf in bed is uncanny because
O'Connor is acting the role of Nora's grandmother in the other dream, the
version which is "well-dreamt" because Robin enters it "like a relative
found in another generation." Nora is looking down into the house "as if
from a scaffold" at her grandmother's high room, "bereft as the nest of a bird
which will not return" (Nora is mocked by O'Connor as "*Turdus musicus*,"
or European singing thrush) and Robin is lying below in fear with a disc of
light (obviously a spotlight) on her. Nora keeps calling her to come into the
"taboo" room but "the louder she cried out the farther away went the floor
below, as if Robin and she, in their extremity, were a pair of opera glasses
turned to the wrong end, diminishing in their painful love" (62).

The house is *unheimlich* because, though it contains all her grandmother's
things, it is the opposite of her real room and "is saturated with the lost presence of her grandmother, who seemed in the continual process of leaving
it." It is a house of incest, and if Robin enters it she joins the incestuous family. There are two grandmothers, a beautiful feminine one and one "dressed
as a man, wearing a billy cock and a corked moustache, ridiculous and
plump in tight trousers and a red waistcoat, her arms spread saying with a
leer of love 'My little sweetheart.'" Nora had wanted to put her hands on
something in this room, but in the past "the dream had never permitted her

to do so." I suggested that what she puts her hands on is "the plume and the inkwell" and the pictures of her ancestors mentioned in the beginning of the dream, to take up her grandmother's profession of writing.

The costume her grandmother wears is that of the master of ceremonies at the circus, precisely the role of the narrator of *Nightwood*. Robin is in fear because she is being written about. Nora experiences the dream as "something being done to Robin, Robin disfigured and eternalized by the hieroglyphics of sleep and pain" (63), that is, being made into "La Somnambule." Nora, as publicist for the circus, is dreaming herself into the male role of master of ceremonies, Djuna Barnes writing this novel as circus. Her grandmother is herself in drag. The grandmother is cross-dressed as herself, the writer. This role of narrator as master of ceremonies at the circus is spelled out in "La Somnambule" in the description of Robin's room as like a jungle trapped in a drawing room: "the set, the property of an unseen *dompteur,* half lord, half promoter, over which one expects to hear the strains of an orchestra of wood-winds render a serenade which will popularize the wilderness" (35).

The performative structure of *Nightwood* is like an eight-ring circus, brilliantly controlled by the grandmother-narrator-*dompteur* as each "act" is performed and the living statues speak their lines. As Paul Bouissac argues in *Circus and Culture,* circus acts progress in a dialectic of control and disturbance, culminating in a triumphant assertion of the performer's mastery. The reader is never allowed to play any participatory role, but is eternally cast as "audience" at the circus or cabaret.[29]

In her dream Nora sees her grandmother as a "wolf" in both senses, and recognizes the ill-fitting male costume she must don as granddaughter-writer; when she constructs the doctor as her grandmother, a fine feminist transference for a workable psychoanalysis begins. Like Felix watching O'Connor's tricks at Robin's bedside, the reader experiences "a double confusion" (35) as the narrator alternates between *dompteur* and "dumb-founder," providing a sideshow and "preparing the audience for a miracle" (35). Barnes' rhetorical tricks are like the magician's feints with back and elbows, "honesties," to distract the audience from his hoax. Is *Nightwood* a hoax or a profoundly humanistic and political novel? When the woman acts the beast and the beast turns human in the last scene, do we laugh or weep?

Bakhtin would argue that Barnes, like Rabelais,[30] does not reverse the world for carnival as political therapy, or release, in the steam-engine model of social behavior; but that Barnes's characters represent the revolutionary potential in folk culture.[31] That is, *Nightwood* reveals that gays and outcasts

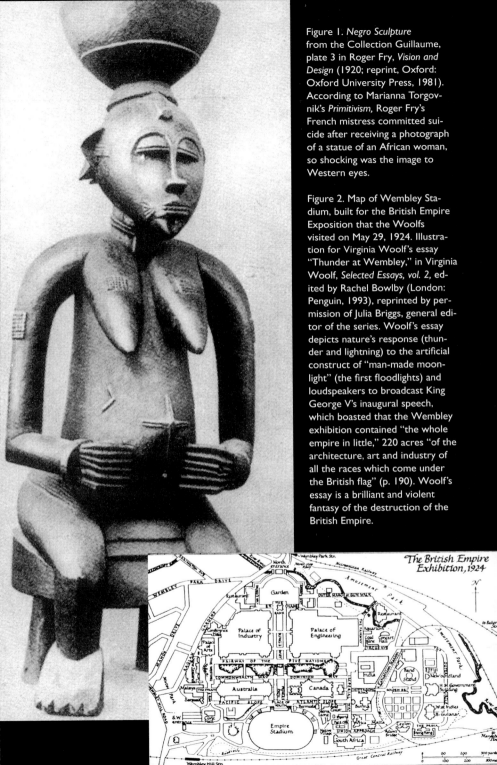

Figure 1. *Negro Sculpture* from the Collection Guillaume, plate 3 in Roger Fry, *Vision and Design* (1920; reprint, Oxford: Oxford University Press, 1981). According to Marianna Torgovnik's *Primitivism,* Roger Fry's French mistress committed suicide after receiving a photograph of a statue of an African woman, so shocking was the image to Western eyes.

Figure 2. Map of Wembley Stadium, built for the British Empire Exposition that the Woolfs visited on May 29, 1924. Illustration for Virginia Woolf's essay "Thunder at Wembley," in Virginia Woolf, *Selected Essays, vol. 2,* edited by Rachel Bowlby (London: Penguin, 1993), reprinted by permission of Julia Briggs, general editor of the series. Woolf's essay depicts nature's response (thunder and lightning) to the artificial construct of "man-made moonlight" (the first floodlights) and loudspeakers to broadcast King George V's inaugural speech, which boasted that the Wembley exhibition contained "the whole empire in little," 220 acres "of the architecture, art and industry of all the races which come under the British flag" (p. 190). Woolf's essay is a brilliant and violent fantasy of the destruction of the British Empire.

The British Empire Exhibition, 1924

Figure 3. *Mädchen aus Kowno* (1918) by Karl Schmidt-Rottluff, one of many German expressionist works influenced by African art, from *Graphik des Deutschen Expressionismus* (Stuttgart, 1986), p. 40. French artists are generally cited in this context, but African influences are evident in German modernism very early.

Figure 4. Elvedon Hall, the model for the Big House in *The Waves,* a Georgian building enlarged by John Norton 1863–1870 for Maharajah Duleep Singh "into an Oriental extravaganza unparalleled in England. The palace has "a central domed hall with glass lantern, with the walls, pillars and arches covered with the closest Indian ornamental detail, all made of white Carrara marble and carved *in situ* by Italian craftsmen." Nikolaus Pevsner, *The Buildings of England (Suffolk)* (London: Penguin, 1974), pp. 199, 63. Thanks to Julia Briggs for the source and the reference. Elvedon in *The Waves* clearly refers to this instance of the empire's collaboration with Indian princes, as well as to the whiteness that the novel attempts to investigate. See Sonya Rudckoff, *Ancestral House* (Palo Alto, CA: Society for the Promotion of Science and Scholarship, 1999).

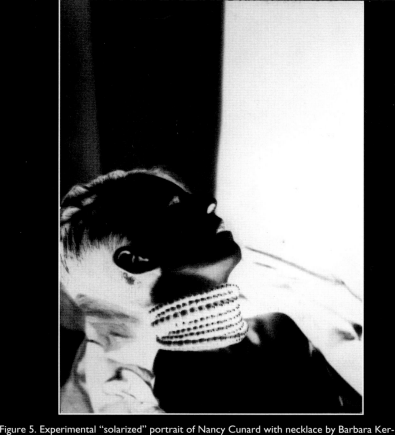

Figure 5. Experimental "solarized" portrait of Nancy Cunard with necklace by Barbara Ker-Seymer, Harry Ransome Humanities Research Center, University of Texas. Barbara Ker-Seymer (1905–1993) was an important modernist experimental photographer who began work as the assistant of Olivia Wyndham and was influenced by the German magazine *Der Querschnitt,* and, along with Man Ray, solarization and negative printing. She collaborated with other experimental modernists John Banting, Curtis Moffat, Brian Howard, and Humphrey Spender.

Figure 6. Nancy Cunard with bound head and veil against tiger skin. Harry Ransome Humanities Research Center, University of Texas. This portrait by Barbara Ker-Seymer was misidentified for many years as the work of Cecil Beaton. Ker-Seymer studied art at the Chelsea Polytechnic, the Royal College of Art and the Slade School. Her circle included the painter Edward Burra, the dancer William Chappell, and the choreographer Frederick Ashton.

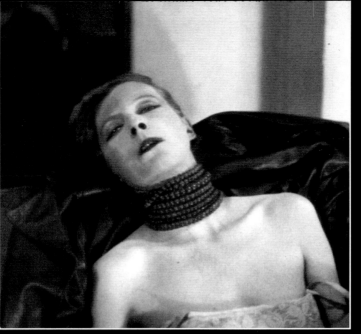

Figure 7. Nancy Cunard with beads, head thrown back, by Barbara Ker-Seymer, Harry Ransome Humanities Research Center, University of Texas. Ker-Seymer did fashion photography as well as work for Mass Observation. She took many daring photographs of her friends, including Jean Cocteau, in the archive given by her partner, Barbara Roett, to the Tate Gallery, London.

Figure 8. Nancy Cunard with leg warmers, by Barbara Ker-Seymer, Harry Ransome Humanities Research Center, University of Texas.

Figure 9. Nancy Cunard, hat and bracelets, by Barbara Ker-Seymer, Harry Ransome Humanities Research Center.

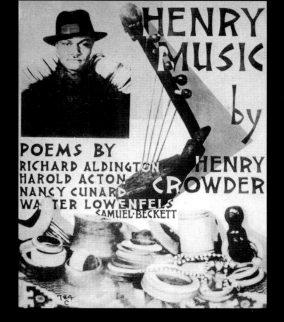

Figures 10 and 11. Jacket design (back and front) for *Henry-Music*, published by Nancy Cunard at her Hours Press in Paris, 1930. The collage of Cunard's bracelets and figures from her collection of African art was made by her friend, Man Ray, as a "cameraless photograph." Cunard's arms may be seen behind Henry Crowder, the jazz pianist whose music for poems by modernist poets was published in the rare volume. Schomburg Library, New York.

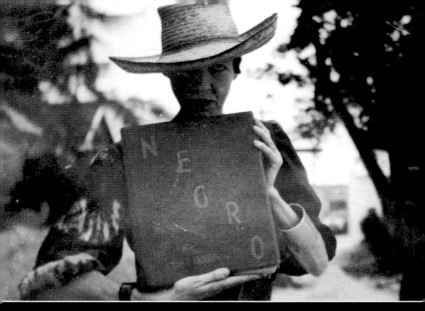

Figure 12. Nancy Cunard holding a copy of the *Negro* anthology at Le Puits Carré, her house in Normandy. Her own copy is in the Harry Ransome Humanities Research Center, University of Texas.

Figure 13. Greta Garbo in *A Woman of Affairs*, 1928, the silent film made from Michael Arlen's 1926 best-selling novel *The Green Hat*, with Lewis Stone. Douglas Fairbanks, Jr., gives a remarkably uncensored gay performance, despite the picture's rewrite of the suicidal husband's sin as embezzlement.

Figure 14. Greta Garbo as the Nancy Cunard character in *A Woman of Affairs*, with John Gilbert. Censorship spoiled the film, as did the fact that it was a belated silent film after talkies had begun to appear.

Figure 15. Katharine Cornell as Iris March in the 1926 Broadway hit production of *The Green Hat*, a role that established her career. The original green hat from this production was given to the Actor's Club. The two green hats Miss Cornell wore in each performance were then raffled off. Riboux designed the original, and two-hundred thousand copies were sold commercially in the United States. Tallulah Bankhead played Iris in the London stage production and wore the green hat in public as well as on stage.

Figure 16. Michael Arlen, author of *The Green Hat* and many other successful romances, and his glamorous wife, Atalanta. Nancy Cunard called him "the Baron."

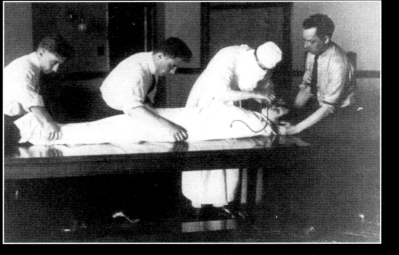

Figure 17. Djuna Barnes as a reporter in the United States, being force-fed as a publicity stunt to understand what the hunger-striking English suffragettes were enduring.

Figure 18. Indian writer Mulk Raj Anand.

have a culture, a linguistically and philosophically rich culture, encompassing high and low art, opera and circus, psychoanalysis and religion, and that this culture is a vital political force.

Inversion reveals the essence of the particular historical moment which we construct as the "rise of fascism" in the "upright" defining their differences from the abject, by race, gender or sexual practice. At this historical moment the outcasts constitute the essence of human culture. Fascism chooses to eliminate from "civilization" those very figures who are the "symbolic forms" of humanity in ancient traditions, circus folk, lesbians, homosexuals, transvestites, and the Jew who is the recorder of history and culture.

The "splendid and reeking falsification" of the world of carnival and circus in *Nightwood*'s reversals is redemptive. As in Rabelais the circus folk take royal titles: Princess Nadja, Baron von Tink, Principessa Stasera y Stasero, a King Buffo, and a Duchess of Broadback. In carnival, enthronement of the fool implies dethronement of hierarchy. They are "gaudy, cheap cuts from the beast life" (11) as the butcher is a stock figure in old European carnival (O'Connor compares penises to mortadellas. Carnival parades often featured enormous phallic salamis). Nadja's spine curves like a lion's, and Frau Mann's costume is like Nikka's tattoo:

> She seemed to have a skin that was the pattern of her costume: a bodice of lozenges, red and yellow. . . . [O]ne felt they ran through her as the design runs through hard holiday candies, and the bulge in the groin where she took the bar, one foot caught in the flex of the calf, was as solid, specialized and as polished as oak. The stuff of the tights was no longer a covering, it was herself; the span of the tightly-stitched crotch was so much her own flesh that she was as unsexed as a doll. The needle that had made one the property of the child made the other the property of no man. (13)

Here the novel's themes converge: Circus performer=doll=lesbian. In her 1935 *Fires* Marguerite Yourcenar creates Sappho as an aging lesbian trapeze artist, in a mode described by Susan Gubar as preserving "the utopian grandeur of the lesbian aesthetic project in the modernist period." [32] Memoirs of Paris in the twenties and thirties recall the circus, the elegant trapeze act of Barbette, the Texas Transvestite, the human gorilla. [33] In *Nightwood* the lovers meet at the circus and mix circus figurines with ecclesiastical hangings in their apartment, continuing carnival's tradition of mixing the sacred and the profane. Robin laughs in church and goes home to read de Sade on the day she gives birth, and—in one of the novel's most hilarious scenes—

O'Connor masturbates in church as the Transvestite of Notre Dame. Bouissac defines circus as a *language,* "a set of rules for cultural transformations, displayed in a ritualistic manner that tempers this transgressive aspect." It enacts freedom from culture and inverts the ordinary. He claims that "individuals who have not been fully integrated into a culture find it more acceptable to enjoy this type of performance, as do individuals with a marginal or unique status, such as poets and artists."[34] As Claude Lévi-Strauss says, we see the circus as supernatural, a place where human beings can still communicate with animals and with our own "higher powers." One of *Nightwood*'s most fascinating aspects is that it has more animal characters than people, from lions to mouse meat, cows, horses, fish, and an extraordinary number of birds, adding to its archetypal qualities.

Like the circus *Nightwood* is polycentric; it makes the reader uneasy with time and history for political purposes. Robin Vote, Nora Flood, and O'Connor (whose names intersect in their *o*s and *r*s and *n*s) are performers of archetypal roles. The hybrid form of the fiction reinforces the hybrid experience of the characters. O'Connor says, "take away a man's conformity and you take away his remedy," and tells of the paralyzed man in a velvet box at Coney Island; "suspended over him where he could never take his eyes off, a sky-blue mounted mirror, for he wanted to enjoy his own difference" (146). Robin is the androgynous ideal, the archetype of the savage virgin Diana, a feminist version of the noble savage; *Nightwood* is her "sacred grove." The name "Vote" signifies the suffragettes, often martyrs and victims of police and government brutality. As a young reporter, Barnes investigated the violent force-feeding of hunger-striking suffragettes by having herself force-fed and writing "If I, play-acting, felt my being burning with revolt at this brute usurpation of my own functions, how they who actually suffered the ordeal in its acutest horror must have flamed at the violation of the sanctuaries of their spirit?" (*New York World,* 1914, Barnes Collection). The photograph that accompanied the article of Barnes, the prone victim, being violated by a group of doctors, echoes the picture of the hysterical woman being hypnotized by Charcot and the French doctors. The image conflates the subordination of the politically independent woman with that of the medical model of the aberrant woman. Barnes experienced force-feeding as a kind of rape, as many of the brave movement women did. Christabel Pankhurst was figured as Joan of Arc on the front page of *The Suffragette.* Martyrdom, sainthood, and the androgynous militant figure of the woman in men's clothes were part of the mythology of this feminist modernism, and Barnes draws on its culture for Robin.

But *Nightwood*'s uniqueness lies in its language, its billingsgate and, to use a phrase Freud coined for the analysis of dreams in his letters to Fliess—a nice combination of Yiddish and Greek—its "dreckology," the continual use of animal and human excremental imagery, from "whale shit" to "dinosaur droppings" to bird turds. Djuna Barnes is the female Rabelais. Only ribaldry is powerful enough to carry *Nightwood*'s political vision. For she was writing, like Nora in the dream of her grandmother, at what Victor Hugo calls "noirceur sublime de l'écritoire," the sublime blackness of the inkstand.[35] Despite fascism or political repression, folk art survives among the marginal and in the circus: "Clowns in red, white and yellow, with the traditional smears on their faces, were rolling over the sawdust as if they were in the belly of a great mother where there was yet room to play." (54)

If I am right in reading *Nightwood* as a prophecy of the Holocaust—an attack on the doctors and politicians who defined deviance and set up a worldview of us and them, the normal and abnormal, in political, racial, and sexual terms, a world that was divided into the upright and the downcast— the horror that in fact took place is still very difficult for us to contemplate. Certainly *Nightwood* was not read at the time (1936) as a prophecy of the Holocaust. In Yvonne Mitchell's *Colette: A Taste for Life,* she describes Sarassini, the "great circus king," who invited the European press to performances in Berlin in the early thirties in order to get bookings in France for his troupe of five hundred animals. Djuna Barnes and Thelma Wood may well have been there with Colette and other journalists. Because the circus performers were Jews, Yugoslavs, and Negroes, and Sarassini chose expatriation over firing his crew, they were scapegoated by the Nazis. The night before he left Antwerp for South America, "the tent housing his twenty-two elephants caught fire, and most of them were burned to death."[36]

The abjection Barnes figured in *Nightwood* is mild compared to the murder and dehumanization (including medical experimentation) of the Nazi concentration camps. When American soldiers liberated the camps, the stench of excrement and death overpowered them. They could not identify with the tortured, starved prisoners as fellow human beings. One soldier wrote of them as a "horde of gnomes and trolls. . . . Some hop on crutches. Some hobble on stumps of feet. Some run with angular movements. Some glide like Oriental genies." Another described the emaciated victims as resembling "huge, lethargic spiders," and others described the "absent-minded apes" of Buchenwald, while many said the scenes resembled a bestial circus nightmare.[37] While the soldiers had difficulty identifying with the humanity of the Nazi's victims, civilians refused to believe the newsreel evidence of the massacres. Eventually the press began to focus on individual perverse Germans as perpetrators of the crimes, since people could not deal with the idea of sadism on such an immense scale as to involve the whole nation. Interestingly the press concentrated on two women, Irma Grese, "the Beast of Belsen," and Ilse Koch, "the Bitch of Buchenwald." It seems to me immensely significant, though it has not been noted before, that the press singled out individual women as symbols of Nazi sadism and cruelty, as objects of hate, when Nazism itself was such a patriarchal ideology, and the crimes were committed almost entirely by men. Ilse Koch is relevant for us, for she collected pieces of tattooed human skin from camp prisoners. Did she write on the skin as a direct challenge to Leviticus? Were Felix and Guido among her victims? Certainly Nikka's body as the black backside of Western culture and the mutilated body of Mademoiselle Basquette challenge us to remember the inexpressible horror of the Holocaust. *Nightwood* reminds us that the human condition is a sister- and brotherhood of difference, and that ideologies that seek to erase those differences and define only themselves as human are indescribably dangerous.

5

Bonding and Bondage

Nancy Cunard and The Making of The *Negro* Anthology

Longfellow Hall. Radcliffe College. Cambridge, Massachusetts, 1992. Do the members of the audience for a seminar called "The Semiotics of Exile" imagine that the speaker is herself an exile, returning at this very moment to the primal scene of resistance to assimilation into the ruling class? The scene of speaking at the English Institute in 1992 overlaps on the screen of memory with a scene from 1956 when I took my first college examinations in this room. Then, as now, Harvard as an institution had problems with Others—problems about gender and culture and class and race. I was a problem then. The discrimination against Catholics was a peculiar Boston thing. A peculiar institution. Now people find it hard to imagine. The dean said I was an "experiment." This room was to have been the scene of my assimilation, the place where, like other Others, I was expected to become one of Us instead of one of Them. Harvard's announced Catholic quota when I was here more than forty years ago was seven percent. The Jewish quota was forty percent. The class president was a Jamaican. My idea of honor came from the nuns at Mount Saint Joseph Academy in Brighton, Massachusetts. It turned out that their teaching and training was far superior to anything I was to receive at Harvard. But I didn't know that then. I was being trained to mock their devotion, to erase their imprint on my character, to reject my Irish working class family and culture.

Radcliffe's exams were then being proctored on the Honor System that Harvard had abandoned. I'm feeling very odd going to the ladies room in this building. The ladies room in Longfellow Hall was a place where I learned to face what my place was. What if the marble walls still echo with the laughter of those WASP girls when I interrupted their cheating? "She's going to report us," they giggled.

They were going to grow up into ladies. This and all the other rooms in the college were theirs. Why didn't I report them? Who knows? I stayed away from the students and the kindly dean who reminded me of my place. But this was the moment of recognition of the institution as the enemy. Other institutions less dangerous to the welfare of the planet have tolerated the disloyalty I pledged to them on this spot. I re-member it as clearly as my First Communion, this moment when I decided to refuse to be grateful to Harvard, to bite the hand that fed me. 'Suspicion is the best policy' is deeply engraved on the chip on my shoulder. Someone ought to tell all the women who try to deal with Harvard, "fair" Harvard,—all the Blacks, Jews, Asians—others—that WASPs cheat. Their institutions needed the rest of us to keep up "standards," the grade point average.

The second scene is at a long table in Widener Library. A Black student sits down across from my friend Sally from Louisville. She faints. This is what I remember about the place when after my talk Skip Gates stands in Harvard Square and throws out his arms to indicate "the Black Studies Empire" spanning the second floor of a whole block. He wasn't joking. The feminists here told me that the Women's Stud-ies Program was a joke. Can't have two Others at a time.

It's ridiculous for a grown woman, the mother of grown children, to hate Harvard. What's there to hate? I hate the way they get to decide between Women's Studies and Black Studies. I hate the way they can set white women and Black men against each other instead of bonding in alliances. The scapegoats are Black women, forced to choose one identity, not both, regarded with suspicion by both. After all these years I still hate the institution that wanted to steal all my ethnic Catholic-girl intellectual and moral energy and assimilate it for its own ends. That's how they operate, by can-nibalizing the brains and the work of quotas of smart and assimilable Others. The dean was right. Harvard was taking a risk.

What am I doing here? Well, I suppose I'm here to talk about Nancy Cunard, a flamboyant Englishwoman who spent her life in the cause of Black liberation. I like Nancy Cunard. She hated racists. She made public scenes. She was always making a spectacle of herself—for political reasons. In making a spectacle of her spectacle, re-cycling her radical vision, here at Harvard, I hope to claim a place for Nancy Cunard in the knowledge factory being built here, so that the Negro anthology will reach the readers for whom it was written.

This prologue was written for the essay below when it appeared in Mae Henderson's *Borders, Boundaries and Frames: Cultural Criticism and Cultural Studies (Essays From the English Institute).* The editor at Routledge cut this anxious autobiograph-ical caveat concerning the host institution for the English Institute. There were im-portant autobiographical essays in the volume but their authors didn't hate Harvard. The editor of the collection, who had commissioned the talk and the essay wrote a critique of Nancy Cunard's motives for devoting herself to the cause of black libera-tion, and mine, for reviving interest in her.

So I return to the scene with some curiosity. I have spent the intervening decade researching and writing about Nancy Cunard in a cultural studies project called

White Looks, Black Books. *But the issues raised in this first set of arguments re-main important. This first attempt to talk about Nancy Cunard touched a nerve and I want to place its arguments on the record in* Hearts of Darkness. *Unless and un-til black critics and readers find the exiled white radical "race woman" sympathetic, I believe, she will not find her place in history. My obsession with historical justice for Nancy Cunard, as Mae Henderson intuited at the time, is a way of chanelling my own critical concerns from gender to race. I have learned a great deal more about her since writing this essay. But I have not solved the dilemma that first confronted me when I saw the photographs taken by Barbara Ker-Seymer. The white negress atti-tude that Nancy Cunard adopted is still in force today, and still in fashion. It remains to be seen what today's dark hearts will make of her disturbing images.*

Radcliffe College has now completely disappeared into Harvard, leaving little trace and a few disgruntled feminist alumnae. At the point when Carol Gilligan left the institution, Jane Fonda funded a chair in the Harvard School of Education in the name of the pioneering feminist, since cancelled. But research was to be done on both girls and boys. Henry Louis Gates and his W.E.B. DuBois Institute have a visible public profile, an "empire" as he predicted. But all is not well. The institution and its Others are very much at odds and always in the headlines. One of the oddest things in the 1934 Negro anthology is a piece by that racist in exile Ezra Pound, insisting that no progress would be made until there was a chair of African Studies at Harvard. Clearly it will take more than that.

BONDING AND BONDAGE

It ought to be self-evident that Judaism in no way touches on the mass murder of Jews by Gentile Germans and their Gentile European helpers; nor is the Holocaust, though its victims were Jews, a product of Jewish history or civilization. Oppression belongs to the culture of the oppressors.

Cynthia Ozick—*Times Literary Supplement,* July 5, 1991

If it is true that oppression belongs to the culture of the oppressors, then it is also true that cultural historians need to remember that they are the ones who name and catalog histories. Blaming the victim has too often been the result of attributing oppression to those who were oppressed. For slavery continues to be studied as a problem in black history, when it is surely (first of all rather than also) a subject in the story of white cultures. Yet the iden-tity of the historians and producers of knowledge about subject peoples has recently been scrutinized mercilessly for purity of motive and mind-set. Anyone who might possibly belong to the family of "oppressors" has been eliminated as an authority. Or at least I'm assuming that it was Nancy Cu-

nard's gender, her color, her class, her politics, and her several sexualities as
a set of (shifting) identities that set all the red lights flashing on everybody's
indicators of "political correctness" well before the popularity of the phrase
but not the activity—to discredit Nancy Cunard as an intellectual historian
of black culture. If slavery is not just a problem in black history, then why
are a white European woman's extraordinary efforts to understand it and to
write and circulate its many complex and overlapping different histories
ignored or vilified by black intellectuals and activists as well as by white
historians?

My project is to ask why Nancy Cunard (1896–1965) has been eliminated or discredited as a producer of knowledge in all the fields to which
she contributed, why her voice has been silenced in the histories of the several modern(ist) discourses to which she contributed. Given her apparent
indifference to feminism, it would be ironic if the chief cause of the loss of
Nancy Cunard's presence as an radical intellectual was her gender. She was
not the kind of role model usually offered to aspiring young crusaders for
social justice. She'd be a failure as a heroine in a Lives of Great Women series, and feminists will not find a long-lost champion of women's rights
when her achievments are reviewed. Her life was not a happy one, nor was
it stable in any sense. Women are supposed to to live stability and provide
stability for others. Nancy Cunard was a revolutionary, dedicating her life
to political upheaval, committed to changing the world. But the standard
narratives of revolutionary lives provide no pattern—except perhaps the
lives of Russian upper class anarchists. Revolutionaries are supposed to come
from the working class. British intellectuals and historians of that class have
not rushed to claim her as their own and books continue to appear describing her as a mindless debutante. (The attitude is similar to the encourage-
ment of class suspicion of Virginia Woolf's socialism and feminism. They are
suspicious of her motives.) From the point of view of Cunard's birth, she
was a class traitor, and so she was seen by biographers, as well as by spies for
national and international intelligence agencies. Her other survival is as an
English eccentric, a stagey and flamboyant "character," like her fellow poet
Edith Sitwell. The place where she most deserves to be honored is the history of the struggle against racism in Britain, the United States, and the
Black Atlantic She was a major figure on the Left in the British black liberation movement in the thirties, forties, and fifties. When the stories of African anticolonial struggles are finally written, perhaps it is here that she will
find her place in history.

Half-educated by governesses, by her rich Irish American mother (neé
Maud Burke) and her father, Sir Bache Cunard, of the Cunard shipping

family, she renounced family and fortune and educated herself in the history of racial oppression and trained herself as a writer, publisher, journalist, and amateur anthropologist. As an English expatriate in France, a self-made expert on black culture and the history of slavery, she does not fit easily into the one antiracist discourse that does exist—that created by white Englishwomen who worked in the antislavery movement, documented and analyzed by feminist intellectual historian Moira Ferguson in *Subject to Others*—unless it proves to be the case that the missing feminism in her story is really there and has been suppressed.[1]

Her name did her more harm than good. As brilliantly as her mother, Lady Emerald Cunard, after she changed her name, had shone in her London literary and artistic salon with her (also married) lover, the conductor Sir Thomas Beecham, Nancy's Hours Press office at 15, rue Guénégaud in Paris gave off a different sort of aura, a modernist multicultural glow made of blue notes and red flags and ivory bracelets—a certain surrealist glamour composed of sex, primitivism, Left politics, and jazz. And there she staged a series of salons in the twenties and thirties around the intersections of surrealism, communism, avant-garde writing, African art and ivory artifacts, jazz, antifascism in Spain, a center where African intellectuals and political leaders and black artists and expatriates from all over the world were apt to meet Samuel Beckett or Janet Flanner, Louis Aragon or even the old guard writer George Moore.

But she was not a hostess or a lady with a salon, as a historian of women surrealists, who had never heard of her, assumed when she asked contemptuously, "Did she *do* anything?" Nancy Cunard was primarily what we used to call in the civil rights and anti–Vietnam War movements, a full-time political organizer. One of the things she did was to contribute a model for the form of future political protests by intellectuals throughout the twentieth century in organizing and publishing *Authors Take Sides on the Spanish Civil War* (1937). She was a living network, a one-woman permanent walking demonstration against racism and fascism, and a celebrant of black culture in all its forms. She had a voice in shaping many of the competing and conflicting discourses of modernism, but in their histories there is only the marginal trace of a husky whisper, a streak of kohl across those hooded piercing eyes, remembered in a malicious footnote, and a stunning visual history in photographs, portraits, and sculpture by major and minor modernist artists.

She was an autodidact, a self-made intellectual and political organizer. And she was very successful at her work. She produced an enormous amount of knowledge to combat racism and to invite Europe and the West to see Africa and its diasporic cultures as civilization. Her work and the work of those she organized to produce the monumental *Negro* anthology,[2] an international body of progressive intellectuals and artists of all races working together to produce and disseminate knowledge about black culture—was ridiculed, lost, dismissed, made fun of, ignored—and then it was done all over again. This is what gives me a chill. The case of the loss of the *Negro* anthology reveals what happens to the histories of all oppressed groups when they have no indigenous institutions—universities, libraries, museums, art galleries of their own—to protect and value, cherish and circulate them. (I always tell my students that my collection of books on feminism and by women writers was bought in book sales by university libraries. I was buying what the institutions of knowledge preservation were throwing away.)

ARMS AND THE WOMAN

Nancy Cunard is remembered as a bad bold body, the subject of some stunning photographs by Man Ray, Cecil Beaton, and their colleagues in the visual avant-gardes of London and Paris. The problem with this limited role on the margins of the numerous fields in which she worked, or, rather, with her image as an illustration of texts, trends, and ideas, is that her political generative activity is denied—as if Hemingway, for example, were remembered only in the louche snapshots of his friends and not for the shape and length of his sentences.

That body and its self-fetishizing is indeed one of my subjects. Nancy Cunard participated with her photographer friends in making images that epitomize modernism's heart of darkness.

I also want to open up the ethical question of what it means when a white woman of the mistress class stages herself as a slave, binds and shackles her body and her head in shameless and fashionable display of political solidarity with black oppression that—contrary to her intention—highlights both her difference and her whiteness. What happens when she revels physically in the primitivism she is articulating as modernism? How much irony is there in Cunard's costumes? Who shared it? And who shares it now? We can begin to think about some answers when we acknowledge that it is not uncommon for the arc of desire to intersect with the arc of intellectual activity, for art and work to focus on exchanges between the body of the self and the Other, especially in the encounter between surrealism and anthroplogy that shaped Cunard's imagination and generated so much of her cultural work. Hemingway's body might be studied in the same way, along with his fiction and reportage. The sex life of the ethnographer has become the focus of recent geneologies of modernist anthropology, and Michel Leiris has become a hero to his successors. But none of the writers cite Cunard. I believe her work was just as important as that of Leiris, who does, in fact, cite her political bravery and devotion to the cause of African art. But then, he had the institutional protection of the Musée de l'Homme to allow for the playfulness of surrealist autobiography to mask the fact that he served the state as curator of African and other forms of primitive art as they were collected, studied, and displayed. He truly had an empire.[3]

Cunard's ivory bracelets have come to symbolize the primitive in modernism's so-called Negrophilia. The photographs both mask, and divert attention from, the role of institutions, missionary churches, wealthy collectors, anthropologists, and ethnographers and their state-supported expeditions to the colonies. The image of Nancy Cunard has become a scapegoat for the white man's rape of Africa. And yet it was the white man's rape of Africa that she spent her life trying to document, expose, historicize, and record for posterity.

If geneology is history, then it is becoming clear that one of the ways hegemony is maintained is the writing of the biographies of the great men as a form of history of the field. For example, Lévi-Strauss made it clear that structuralism was founded by Jane Ellen Harrison. He continually acknowledged his debt to her pioneering work in inventing the modern discipline of anthroplogy as a materialistic rather than a linguistic enterprise—where fieldwork and the study of objects in context was to replace the study of ancient texts alone. But his followers eliminated her from history, creating Lévi-Srauss the founder, the origin, of their field. Their geneological persistence has effectively marginalized a central figure of modernist anthropology.

Is it that Nancy Cunard's desire to know and to reproduce and circulate what she found out by diligent research and a massive campaign of self-education offended or threatened everyone with a territorial interest in some aspect of the cultural history of modernism? Is it that, as Sabena Broeck argues, her desire and her politics were both centered on black men? Like Carl Van Vechten, Cunard was acknowledged as an important bridge figure between black and white cultures in Paris, London, and New York. Is it necessary to burn the bridges to write the history of that period? Or was it her "conflation of matriphobia and political radicalism," as Susan Friedman claims, that shocked her contemporaries most?

Was it that she raised "troubling questions about the mother-daughter bond within the psychodynamics of gender, race and class," by breaking the taboo of class loyalty and washing the Cunard family linen in public? She died a raving alcoholic in a public ward in Paris, still working on her epic poem on world peace. Why is there such a taboo about the lives of women alcoholics?

Her biographer creates her as a misguided nymphomaniac, assuming that sexuality determined her politics just as her ex-lovers, black and white, attributed her lack of the monogamous impulse to a fundamental moral and intellectual flaw, when such behavior by themselves or their male friends was glamorous and enhancing to the image of the expatriate heroic artist. A strange posthumous as-told-to "autobiography" by her jazz musician ex-lover Henry Crowder, circulates to discredit her role in the history of black liberation and in particular the amazing production of the *Negro* anthology—which he had inspired by his tales of life in the American South.[4]

Mocked and belittled in the histories of the Harlem Renaissance, Nancy Cunard was left out altogether from the story of the culture she did so much to shape, the story of the Communist Party in Harlem in the thirties; she is basically a missing person in Valentine Cunningham's history of British writing in the thirties, barely mentioned in the histories of the English expatriates and the Spanish Civil War, ignored as a journalist and war correspondent, marginalized as a modernist poet, erased from her role as organizer of the international protest movement on behalf of the Scottsboro Boys, her Hours Press listed on the fringe of small press and avant-garde publishing world (discovering Beckett, printing Pound's *Cantos*), reduced to a footnote in the biography of her lifelong friend Langston Hughes, or demonized or left out of the lives of her former lovers, such as Louis Aragon, so that, incidentally, her role in the Paris Left as well as in surrealism itself is summarily cut. Her role in collecting and showing African art in Paris early in the century and her pioneering of the revaluation of ethnic objects as art for museums and private collectors changed art history. Roger Fry is remembered, but even he is excluded from recent studies of primitivism.

Where is Nancy Cunard? Her work for the *Negro* anthology revitalized the field of anthropology and introduced fieldworkers and ethnographers to one another's work as well as to positive ideas about Africa as a place of historically civilized rather than savage cultures, and had a major influence on French ethnographic practice, as Michel Leiris says in his memoirs. But she exists neither in the history of art history's modernist turn to African image nor in the history of the new participatory and positive practice of ethnography. Leiris has become the hero of postmodern anthropology because he wrote his own autobiography instead of an ethnography of the Africans he was sent to study. While building a career in and through the institution of the Musée de l'Homme, Leiris managed to maintain a reputation as the opposite. He created a public persona as a radical surrealist intellectual with a harrowing inner life, while maintaining himself and working for the state as a bourgeois bureaucrat. He posed as a social outlaw while subjecting the "Africa" he plundered and brought home to the rules of private property and the state. Nancy Cunard left no public autobiography and buried what personal memoirs she wrote between the lines of her biographies of the minor men of letters George Moore and Norman Douglas in the 1950s. Presumably she had no inner life. Her biography is a blank space that can be filled by whatever theory one wants to apply. In her lifetime and ours her image survives as the princess of primitivism when primitivism is figured as a negative force. Nancy Cunard really was an outlaw. And she still makes us uncomfortable.

But it is also true that modernism in almost all its aspects could be explicated with a work of Nancy Cunard's, a poem, a broadside, a news item, a book, an African carving, a revolutionary pamphlet, an ivory bracelet, or photographed in a close-fitting leather costume or solarized with an elongated neck wound with beads, head flung back as if awaiting the kiss of a vampire. Her body is here very much part of the history of the period, draped in tiger skins, wrapped in leopard, or backed by metal as in a *Metropolis* landscape of thirties Berlin. Breastless, white, and phallic, stretched in pleasure (or perhaps it's pain), caught in soft cloth manacles, bound by silken scarves, held by ivory chains, she becomes a boy or an androgynous creature (a different kind of woman, the imaginary lesbian of sapphic modernism?) from the African fertility figures with their pointed breasts, which stand at the center of modernist primitivism.

Is this white woman's staging of herself as a prisoner or a slave the visual equivalent of feminism's use of the discourse of slavery to articulate its own demands for freedom discussed earlier? Does the cross-gendering and cross-sexualizing of these poses make racial divisions between reproductive and non-reproductive sex? Marking the African woman's body for motherhood (see the Ernst Neuschul painting on the cover.) Modernism leaves a space for that other kind of white woman's body that its photographers celebrate, in white top hat or cat's whiskers, in mask and cape and Spanish broad-brimmed hat, or coat and tie and Eton-cropped hair, a body that breaks the rules of gender, a body that suggests sex without motherhood, interracial sex, and intersexual race-ing. We know from our own lives that such fashionable cultural creations as our own bodies are perfectly compatible with intellectual careers and creative professional lives. Why do we deny this doubleness in women in history? Why can't we accept Nancy Cunard

as a producer of knowledge who inhabited a strikingly beautiful and provocative body?

Nancy Cunard's monumental work, the oversize 855-page *Negro* anthology
(with 385 illustrations), published in 1934 and paid for with the fifteen-
hundred-pound proceeds of lawsuits for interracial sex slanders against her
in the English newspapers, was one of the first works to attempt the production of knowledge about African cultures on a global scale. Two-thirds
of the 150 contributors were blacks, and the enormous volume (begun in
1930) covered every aspect of black people's art and civilization, from individual African countries to the United States, the West Indies, South America, Haiti, and Cuba. The object was to showcase the splendors of African
civilizations at the same time as Europeans were being subjected to Colonial Expositions and fairs that treated Africans as cannibals and headhunters,
savages who were subject to the military campaigns and the missionary in-
vasions of Europeans.

   She and her team of scholars study racism in the United States and the
comparative history of slavery; they write about jazz, blues, and gospel.
Zora Neale Hurston's important folklore essays, first published there, have
been reprinted without acknowledgment of their source in *Negro*. Many of
the articles are dated, but many are so fresh and comprehensive today that
it is shocking to think that the work done for these essays has been lost to
the field. Black Studies in the United States would have come to recognize
the African diaspora a lot sooner if readers had had the *Negro* anthology in
print and available to them. Questions raised and issues studied and documented here in the thirties were raised again in the seventies and debated as
if this knowledge had never been accumulated. Hugh Ford's abridged version used images of Cunard herself in place of the hundreds of pictures of
black people she had published in the original. The loss in time and effort
to progress in Black Studies is enormous. If such a gap existed in in physics
or mathematics, the scientific community would be justifiably outraged.
Was it the whiff of communism attached to the book that frightened readers off? Or was the press campaign to portray Cunard as an English heiress
slumming in search of sex with black men effective in discrediting the intellectual importance of the book? Cunard's letters to black intellectuals,
from Claude McKay to Langston Hughes, Arthur Schomburg to George
Padmore, make clear the importance of her role in the struggle.

*Henry Louis Gates was perhaps right to think of the Black Studies Department at
Harvard as an empire. He was right to demand money for books and professors,*

scholarships and grants, space to expand. This history must not be lost again. In the Negro anthology in 1934, no less a modernist intellectual than Ezra Pound demanded that Harvard should immediately fund such a chair of African Studies. The idea was also argued by Arthur Schomburg, whose own personal library was so important to the research done for the Negro anthology, and formed the basis for the library that bears his name in the New York Public Library. Empires, it appears, need armies. If Women's Studies demanded an equivalent empire in space and money and research institutes, would we get it?

Only an autodidact could have imagined such a grandiose intellectual scheme requiring immense amounts of research in primary documents in libraries all over the world as Nancy Cunard's *Negro*. Only a committed left-wing activist could have called on the worldwide ideals of cross-racial brother- and-sisterhood to bring such a project into being. Only a mad surrealist poet would have thought that its dynamite collections of artistic power and beauty would blow up in the face of bourgeoisies of all nations and colors, and that the scales of prejudice would fall from their eyes at once. Only an intrepid Englishwoman in exile would have believed that she could bring it off, commissioning, cajoling, editing, revising; dealing with bruised egos and suspicious intellectuals, underground leaders, separatists, photographers, professors, anthropologists, folklorists, and politicians; discovering new voices; letting controversial voices be heard; publishing manifestos, and always having the last word—presuming to edit the then conservative W.E.B. DuBois, and to criticize his newspaper, *The Crisis,* in which she had published a version of her surrealist antiracist manifesto, "Black Man and White Ladyship"—arguing with Marcus Garvey, proclaiming in her feckless fellow-traveling footnotes that the way and the only way to racial freedom was the Communist Party.

STRASBOURG PRIMITIVE: MISSIONARY KITSCH AND POSTCOLONIAL SHAME

Living in Strasbourg as a foreigner, I notice that primitive folk motifs decorate the village prints on tablecloths, aprons and casseroles for cooking regional dishes. These charming Alsatian designs in fabric and pottery are sold to the tourists, while the locals buy bright Turkish and Moroccan handicrafts and look to Paris for fashion. Peasant crafts denote purity, the natural, and the exotic, and in exile one is aware of the competing claims of various foreign and homely primitivisms. Anthropologists have shown us how Africans carved figures of the people who came to study them, and given evidence of tribal people who incorporate the debris of the modern world into

*contemporary art forms. But I have seen some products of the clash of cultures that
produce no smiles of assent or knowing nods.*

*All winter I have walked to market through the flea market, curious to see what's
being bought and sold. It is full of strange representations of Africa and Africans, of
misshapen palm trees and sawed-off jungles. They look as if they were made by children or mental patients, by people with something missing in a sense of the beautiful, or lacking perspective. These odd and ugly drawings and paintings of African
landscapes and people in clumsy, homemade wooden frames from the twenties and
thirties are a version of the primitive I cannot place. On the blankets and tables of the
local farmers they stand apart from the watercolors and oils of familiar rural scenes,
wine-making peasants, and snow on the Vosges. They are too childish to be kitsch,
too earnest and grimly limited to compare to the naïf/native productions from Haiti
or Greece that entrance tourists. Sitting next to pornographic postcards of French soldiers with African women, they lack wit or élan or anything I can conceive of as value
from my cultural perspective. They are unbelievably ugly.*

*I read that the French city of Nantes has produced an extraordinary exhibition,
documenting its own carefully hidden history of centuries of extensive and enormously
profitable slave trading. The cover-up is what interests me, the kind of cultural con-
sensus that locks generations of people into living historical lies. What, I wonder, is
the connection between Alsace and Africa?*

*Puzzled by these peculiar portraits of naked black women in exotic spaces, and
sensing their participation in some obscure discourse of professional pornography, a
kind of "domestic obscene," I learn from a bookseller in Colmar that the region is
rich in Africana, souvenirs of the Protestant missionaries who followed Albert
Schweitzer, the local hero, to Africa. What's left in the flea markets is what serious
collectors of Africana disdain.*

*They were not at all what I feared they might be, products of Christianized
Africans who had lost their talent on conversion. For I had assumed that these were
unwanted and uncollected artifacts of Christian colonialism. They have none of the
vigor and vibrancy of the folksy saints and sinners painted by Alsatian farmers on
their walls and windows, but were made by white people in exile in Africa—missionaries who returned home with their homemade fetishes. This is the way some Al-
satians saw Africa and Africans.*

*The ugliness of the paintings is exceeded by the ugliness of the carvings. The
crudely hacked wooden objects appear to come from the Stone Age when compared
with the elegant sleek polished figures from Africa that fill the ethnographic museums
of the West. The woodcarvers of this region make primitive figures of bears. But these
bare-breasted African female figures look as if they were hacked out of firewood by
butcher knives. The Brothers Grimm might recognize them as versions of bears, beasts
perhaps from the jungle of northern European nightmares. They do nothing to de-*

light the eye. But it is not just a Schweitzer Protestant fertility figure I am seeing. For the Péres Blancs have their headquarters here too: Catholic missionaires Africains. *And they too return from exile.*

When Roger Fry claimed in Vision and Design *(1920) that African carvings were the purest forms since those of the Greeks in the history of art, he echoed the modernist painters who had already begun to steal from the Musée de l'Homme to energize their moribund cultures. What he could not visualize, situated among the high modernists rushing to fill their paintings with the forms and colors of the Far East, Africa, and Hawaii, was what would happen when low white European cultures appropriated the arts of their colonial subjects. Picasso and Matisse they were not. The poverty of their own culture shows through their appropriation of the Other in ways that allow for none of the justifications made by Western art historians and curators for the wholesale use of the primitive by modernist artists because it produces what is called great art.*

Inhabiting some as-yet-unmentioned site in the semiethnographic, the flea market fetishes that obsess me often have labels that mask their purpose as works of respectable scientific observation rather than objects of masturbatory fantasies for peeping priests. This dismal and lugubrious provincial primitivism disguises the erotoreligious rapacity of the missionary gaze. The awkwardness of the unskilled hackwork of the woodcarvers and painters produces an embarrassment in this viewer—but I nonetheless return—that I will call it postcolonial shame.

Neither the exquisite purity of form that Roger Fry found in African sculpture, nor the ruthless genius of the appropriating modernist Picassos can be found in this messy detritus of cultural adventurism. For here at the level of popular culture or what we may call pop primitivism, there is a kind of Missionary Kitsch that deserves to be set alongside Tarzan and Tintin comics as a herald of the postmodern. The question is whether the invocation of fake anthropology on the part of these self-deceiving Christians was less socially damaging than real academic and institutionalized anthropology, disguising its service to empire and commerce?

Determined to buy one of these strange carvings before leaving, I go back to the flea market once more. But it's spring. The tourists are here, and the missionary Africana has gone back to the attic.

HATING HARVARD?

Ages ago at Harvard I studied and worked in a hidden and secret space where no one bothered me—the library at the Agassiz Museum, at a table between glass cases of ethnographical displays. My father had given me Van Loon's Geography *as a teenager and I fantasized a life of exploration in exotic places. Working in a Board and*

Room job as a scholarship girl, I was maid to a wealthy family in a rich suburb of Boston. It was hard to make friends or fit into Radcliffe social life. So I spent four years studying alone in the Agassiz, dreaming of becoming an anthropologist. The same dean who said I was a Catholic "experiment" insisted I study Physical Anthropology first. I barely passed. So I majored in English. Almost all the information taught as scientic fact in that course is now discredited. Writing now about Nancy Cunard, the most unorthodox "anthropologist" imaginable, I enter the field at last.

Something in Nancy Cunard's rejection of white culture and English imperialism was enacted in an exile more threatening than scholarly research into the history of slavery. By writing and publishing *Black Man, White Ladyship* (1931) she repudiated England as mother country and denounced her American-born mother as a racist, mingling matriphobia with the idea of the struggle for black power. The sexualized black male body becomes the site of her political (and personal) rebellion, as she publicly gives up her inheritance, both culturally and literally, in a gesture that frightens everyone concerned, even her black lover. The version of this pamphlet currently in circulation in *The Gender of Modernism* is a reprint of the edited pamphlet from Hugh Ford's *Nancy Cunard: Brave Poet, Indomitable Rebel,* and it omits her discussion of English homophobia and her relating of American lynchings to male fetishization of womanhood. *Black Man* will repay study as a surrealist political manifesto rather than the product of personal spite. In her role of undutiful daughter, however, Nancy Cunard gives us an alternative story of modern female development, a radical refusal of the reproduction of motherhood, a rejection of the mother in class and race terms as the representation of imperialism, and a declaration of the daughter's independence from the sacred bonds of mother-daughter love. This heartbreakingly severe move may have enabled Cunard's break with her mother country and secured her future as a race activist. But its harsh terms also disabled her emotionally, and she carried with her in her revolutionary work an unbearable burden of unresolved anger and existential loneliness.

If Nancy Cunard were here today, doubtless she'd be dressed in some witty version of what French designers call the bondage dress—a series of crisscrossed bands similar to the chained/unchained images she performed for the avant-garde camera in the thirties. When the bondage of the moment is a form of foot binding, Cunard's leg warmers will be in style again. Nancy Cunard's reenactment of black slave bondage in the self-staging of her white body as a site for political protest against racism has not been read inside *her* semiotics, but instead as a perverse pornography, both political and sexual. But she really meant the performance of bondage to signify her political bonding with black culture. She meant it as literally as she meant to break the biological bond with her mother by publishing *Black Man, White Ladyship.*

The semiotics of exile that Nancy Cunard staged on her skeletal body signal a motherlessness and lack of nurturing that we are used to constructing as anorexia. Did she feel she was bonding with her black sisters when she was photographed as a white slave, her neck encircled by beads, her arms by bracelets? Even her leg warmers—this is the early thirties—are a form of chic shackles. She also almost always kept her head bound—in hats and scarves, veils and close bands or ribbons. Her twenties permanents and marcel led waves bring her straight hair closer to the bounce and spring of black hair. Today she'd have beaded cornrows in an elaborate headdress. What does a bound head signify to a free woman? (Think of how suspicious political commentators were of Hillary Clinton's headbands.) A double message is being sent by these photographs and by the left-wing diva's dress in the costume of the androgynous twenties boy-girl for the rest of her life.

While many of the most famous photographs of Nancy Cunard were taken by Man Ray and Cecil Beaton, some of the most interesting ones were taken by Curtis Moffat and Barbara Ker-Seymer, a London photographer whose work was often misattributed to the more famous men, rediscovered by Val Williams in *The Other Observers.*[5] She used bold images from German cinema, leather, silver, and corrugated iron to photograph glamorous gay London in the thirties, and Nancy Cunard's photos join those of Brian Howard, Raymond Mortimer, and Eddie Sackville-West in her portrait gallery. After the scandal of *Black Man, White Ladyship,* Ker-Seymer suggested that she make solarizations—negative prints that would make the white subject appear black, a technique also used by Man Ray and Curtis Moffat. Figures 5–9, of Barbara Ker-Seymer's photographs, have never been published before. They were circulated privately, and there is some evidence that they were partly staged by another talented artist-photographer, John Banting. Banting, a lifelong friend of Cunard's, later went to Harlem with her to research *Negro,* and published a piece in the book. He gave his talents to designing political banners for London demonstrations on behalf of the unjustly imprisoned Scottsboro Boys, and he joined her in Spain during the Civil War.

Ker-Seymer's solarizations of Nancy Cunard are an interesting visual parable of her desire for a black body of her own. They also "expose" her neck and torso, stretched with ropes of beads into an elaborate mimicry of lynching, emphasizing in the thrown-back head, the red lips, dark nostrils, and kohl-blackened eyes of both the vampire's victim and the vampire herself. These images still have the power to confuse and disturb us. On the one hand it is outrageous that the white woman presents us with her tribalized body, appropriating African images of the elongated neck from ethnographic photographs of the exotic, as in the semi-pornography in the pages of *National Geographic,* for fashion's pleasures. But the photos send other messages as well—messages about pain, sadistic torture, perhaps drugs. Her body looks drained. The straps of her dress are pulled down. Is she about to be raped or abused? Has she just had an orgasm and is that the open-mouthed edge of abandonment? Or does she just want to be fed?

Since Nancy Cunard, the crusading reporter and left-wing poet, wrote so passionately against lynching and lynch mobs in America, protesting the violence against black men, the pictures are all the more disturbing. They suggest an absent violator of that exposed white female body, the same image called up by Southern lynchers of black men. Her bound and exposed neck, along with the heavy makeup, make her appear to be in thrall to an evil power. They are sadomasochistic and melodramatic. The brilliant Ker-Seymer photos of Nancy Cunard as the white woman appropriating the suffering of the lynched black man, the Southern racial and political martyr in the struggle for freedom, capture the ideological issues of the era as little else in art has been able to do—the white male construction of black manhood as exclusively a violent threat to white womanhood, a threat that justifies lynching and implicates white women in terrible crimes.[6] What does it mean when Nancy Cunard switches roles and performs the role of white woman being lynched when in reality black men were being lynched in the name of revenge for white woman's lost purity? Can the figure of the white woman hanged, bound, manacled, enslaved—ever disrupt in private performance the racial fears of sexual mixing that she wants to explode? Or is she unaware of the act she is putting on? Having seen some examples of studio photos taken as late as the fifties, of black men with tribal spears, feathers, and drums, from her own collection, I find it hard to think that she was unaware of the power of the performance of pain in these photographs. It is clear that there was some private connection between Cunard's enactment of the erotics of the white slave in photographs made for her own pleasure, and her unshakable commitment to the politics of protest against racism. Are there kinds of "drag" that are not ethically permissible? I recall the fury of reviewers and audiences at Lina Wertmüller's representation of a German woman concentration camp commandant forcing a starving Italian prisoner to have sex with her. When a white woman makes a visual claim to the victim status of the lynched black man, can we read the performance of cross-racial and cross-sexual "lynching drag" as an attack on white males? Nancy

Cunard's sexuality remains a challenge to our categories. But the racial dimensions of that sexuality constitute no reason to doubt her utter political devotion to the cause of racial justice.

As I have argued in regard to Djuna Barnes's having herself photographed while being "forcibly fed," in order to experience the ordeal of the English suffragettes on hunger strike in prisons, there is a strange mixture of the political and the sexual in Cunard's exhibition of pain.[7] Her bound head and limbs bring her body into play in a very complex crossing of sexual fetishism and commodity fetishism. Djuna Barnes's photographs of herself being force-fed show that the prison doctors were in fact "raping" and violating the bodies of the hunger-striking suffragette political prisoners. But by choosing to be violated (and photographed in the act, with all the paraphernalia of tubes and clamps invading the sheet-bound body) in order to "feel what they felt," to experience for themselves in a public staging the suffering of the suffrage martyrs in Holloway Gaol, Djuna Barnes, also a crusading reporter, calls into play in 1917 a certain modernist high masochism that we are more used to seeing in the works of male surrealists. It would be interesting to compare these Barbara Ker-Seymer images with those of Man Ray, which have become classics. Both Barnes and Cunard put their bodies on the line, exposed *themselves* in order to expose political evils. Photographs were weapons in the struggle against sexism and racism for the women activist-reporters, but they were also opportunities for erotic performance. The erotic performance of pain of the victimization of blacks, women, slaves, and sex objects may have allowed certain white women modernists empowerment through fetishism.

One stunning Ker-Seymer photograph shows Cunard lying uncomfortably on a corrugated steel "bed," as if flung into the corner of a factory floor, fully dressed, gazing with fear (and anticipation?) at an absent attacker, head bound, throat encircled with scarves, heavy ivory bracelets on both wrists. A particular kind of urban terror is being invoked here, especially signaled by her large black glove, the melodramatic signifier of the murderer in the movies—she is both criminal and victim—caught in the act of stealing, perhaps, by an outraged employer, but just as easily an innocent victim grabbed on the street and thrown into a back corner of the metropolis for who knows what purpose? Contradictory as the black leather glove is, the homeliness of the knitted leg warmers above the elegant strapped and buckled pumps sends the viewer into further confusion. They, like the straps and bracelets and scarves, are about bondage. But what are these schoolgirl's skating socks doing with the figure's designer suit? They suggest that she is cold, has been there a long time, locked up. It is as if she is in prison in a modernist opera's set, a Lulu or Carmen in dancing shoes, exhausted after a steamy performance. Has a sympathetic warden smuggled in the homemade leg warmers? Or do the stripes and straps and high-heeled shoes merely make her legs into a phallic fetish? Or, is she, like the heroine of *The Red Shoes,* the woman artist in thrall to a puppet master? The leg warmers are incongruously *heimisch* and domestic, trading places with the corrugated steel bed on which she lies. The bed by rights should be soft and woolly, like the leg warmers, but shackles are supposed to be made of metal.

As a series of substitutions, Ker-Seymer's picture places the white career woman in the city at the scene of the crime. But she refuses to tell us whether she is the victim or the perpetrator. Uncannily, the figures stage a certain gendered and classed homelessness. In another substitution, the leg warmers recall the puttees worn by soldiers in the muddy trenches of World War I. Cunard's voice as a poet was shaped inexorably by the horrors of that war. Like many women of her generation, she never lost the guilt felt about the senseless killing of millions of young men. The figure of the woman alone and abandoned in the city may call on some of these emotions as well. She may be dressed for her own battles.

Nancy Cunard certainly influenced museums and collectors to buy and display African art, to pay attention to primitivism. She was a walking advertisement for Pan-Africanism. She was a white signifier of Black Is Beautiful. The ivory bracelets that became her signature, worn from wrist to shoulder as a badge of exotic identification with African sexuality and power as well as of imprisonment, as reminders of the shackles of slaves and of the harem, were signs of the sincerity of her White Negress act, however suspiciously the origins of the ivories and their cross-cultural meanings would now be regarded, however politically incorrect her seeming appropriations may appear. Visually her imprisoned arms retain their erotic charge.

Though slaves died by the hundreds, and so did elephants, to satisfy the taste for ivory, both inside Africa and in Europe, Asia and America, to Nancy Cunard her bracelets bound her like shackles to the history of slavery and the struggle for freedom. The ivory itself was a signature of her willing enslavement to the cause that she championed in her *Negro* anthology. It was—like her—off-white. How can one say that anyone's motives are pure? Or deny the agency Cunard earned by performing the bondage of blacks in dress, art, and sexual style as an aid to political bonding in the struggle against racism?

Her braceleted arms embrace the figure of Henry Crowder in Man Ray's brilliant collage for the cover of her 1930 Hours Press volume, *Henry-Music.* Her face does not appear. She stands behind her man in a form of simultaneous effacement and exhibitionism—saying, "He is mine, but I'm not there." This was her role in editing and organizing the *Negro* anthology, with poems and essays by hundreds of contributors and the express command that all of the hundreds of photographs in the book be of black people. Part of her capture of Crowder, the jazz musician, consisted of insisting that he learn composition to write down his music, and she enlisted her friends Harold Acton, Richard Aldington, Walter Lowenfels and Samuel Beckett to produce poems to be set to his music. The essence of the style of Crowder's band, Eddie South and His Alabamians, was, of course, improvisation: One of the things that made it jazz was the difficulty of pinning it down. But she desperately wanted to capture all the energy of this dynamic music to pass it down historically. So, in a way, *Henry-Music,* her last publication at the Hours Press, is a rehearsal for the *Negro* anthology. Her own poem in the book, very much a part of thirties protest discourse, like her "Equatorial Way," her "Appeal for the Scottsboro Boys," seems to derive from the dramatic monologues of black poets. She writes in the voice of the redneck white sheriff, and one can sense her involvement with and adoption of techniques of black American folk and poetic forms. Like much angry black protest poetry of the period, "Equatorial Way" also seems to anticipate certain forms of contemporary black music. The anger in black culture that produces rap and hiphop music also produced Nancy Cunard's "Last advice to the crackers:/Bake *your own* white meat—/Last advice to the lynchers:/Hang *your brother* by the feet."

EQUATORIAL WAY
For Henry

Not yet satisfied
But I'll be satisfied
With the days I slaved for hopes,
Now I'm cutting all the ropes—
Gettin in my due of dough
From ofays that'll miss me so—
Goi-ng . . . Go-ing . . .
Where the arrow points due South.

I dont mean your redneck-farms,
I dont mean your Jim-Crow trains,
I mean Gaboon—
I dont mean your cotton lands,
Ole-stuff coons in Dixie bands,
I've said Gaboon—

This aint no white man's nigger
Nor was—but I've grown bigger
The further away from you
Further, longer away from you
My cracker moon.

Doin my own stuff now,
Equator, Pole and Pole—
Fixin to board the prow
And let the Ocean roll and roll
And roll me over, even,
To where the Congo waters roll.

Wont take from the old lands
But twelve bottles of gin—
Wont leave on the old lands
But my cheque cashed in—
Then make clear to the Black Folks
They can't but win.

Goin to drink to the last damnation
Of the son o' bitch U.S.A.—
Goin to send for a conflagration
From down equatorial way—
Feelin kind just at this moment,
(Kinda callin in my debts for pay.)

Last advice to the crackers:
Bake *your own* white meat—
Last advice to the lynchers:
Hang *your brother* by the feet.
One sittin-pretty Black Man
Is a million-strong on heat.

Goin to beat up Fear on the octaves,
Tear the crackers limb from limb—
Goin to take on each-every vengeance,
Drum one blood-blasting hymn—
And laugh laugh LAUGH in the shadows
Louder'n Death—I'll be watching him.

[Nancy Cunard, *Henry-Music*, 1930]
The glossary that follows is Cunard's.

1. Ofay; white people
2. Redneck; appellation given southern-states farmers, necks scored by sun—petty tyrants.
3. Jim-Crow trains;

Published by Wishart in London, the *Negro* anthology's printing was paid for by Nancy Cunard herself, mostly from fifteen hundred pounds earned as a result of English newspapers' publication of slanderous stories from the American press connecting her with Paul Robeson while she was on her second research trip to Harlem in 1932.[8] It remains to be seen what role the United States and British governments had in these attacks. It is clear from her FBI file that spies in London reported to the United States on the preparation and publication of the *Negro* anthology. The local censors intervened, insisting that Rene Crevel's "The Negress in the Brothel," translated by Samuel Beckett, be removed from *Negro*. Undaunted, Cunard had the three pages set secretly by the radical Utopia Press and tipped them in while binding the volumes herself. The essay, though not listed in the table of contents, is actually in the printed book—a reminder of her radical resourcefulness. She boasts of her conquest to Arthur Schomburg, but Hugh Ford apparently didn't notice this when he revised and reprinted parts of the anthology.[9] This subversive set of pages—significantly on Black women's sexuality—there in the text but unmarked, surviving the censor in unnumbered pages, may serve as a sign of the suppressed referent of the *Negro* anthology itself, of Nancy Cunard's career as a white activist for the cause of black freedom, and this attempt to restore her to history as a producer of knowledge. It increases the material value of the volume to bibliophiles. Refusing to accept censorship, Cunard recaptures her book from press, publisher, and censor. (Renata Morresi points out that a set of pages on Jesse Owens's Olympic triumph is in the copy of *Negro* in the Schomburg Library.)

"Gone Negro": The Files

Two of the U.S. State Department files on Nancy Cunard have now been declassified, 800.00B Nancy Cunard, and 811.4016 Scottsboro. Secret Memorandum No. 1384 dated London, April 22, 1932, reports that Nancy Cunard has sailed to New York on the SS *Albert Ballin* and is now acting as intermediary between Ben Amis and a Negro committee in New York and A. Ward of the Negro Welfare Association in London. Ben Amis was "one of the colored representatives" associated with Earl Browder and William Z.

Foster (leaders of the American Communist Party) on the National Executive Committee of the League of Struggle for Negro Rights: "This young woman has 'gone negro' in her sympathies and proclivities. She has been living at 18, rue Guenégaud, Paris, which she has made a sort of depot for negro 'art' and 'culture'. She has taken up both these and has been compiling a book about them. Politically she is now ultra-leftminded, and has been in touch with and furthering the interests of the League Against Imperialism."

Memo number 1388 says that "this young lady gave orders to sell the books and furniture in her negro shop in the rue Guenégaud and it is now closed. It is understood that her colored friend, Henry Crowder, preceded her to the United States." Other memos contain copies of her Scottsboro appeals, along with copies of letters demanding that the passport of Ada Wright, (mother of one of the Scottsboro Boys), who had been on a speaking tour in Europe, be revoked for "disloyalty," and inquiring why Nancy Cunard, "British subject living among negroes" was allowed into the United States.

Number 1539, London, March 8, 1933, describes Cunard as widely known as a supporter of Negro "emancipation" and "concerned in the endeavor to set up a negro center in London."

The author of the memo has opinions:

> There is now reason to believe that this young lady, owing to the stress of the times, no longer enjoys her former financial prosperity. She still proposes to bring out at her own expense and at the cost of some £600, the volume entitled *NEGRO,* on which she has been working, with colored collaboration, for some time, but it is thought that this is pretty well the last shot in her financial locker, at any rate for the present. Despite her financial situation, Miss Cunard appears to continue improvident and impenitent. She seems to be quite capable of sharing her last £10 with any organisation connected with the I.L.D.

The International Labor Defense Committee supported the Scottsboro Boys, and was a communist organization. In other files she is listed as "Nancy Cunard, Communist," and there are copies of letters to her from William Patterson of the International Labor Defence, regarding organizing in Britain, and especially colonial work. On April 4, 1933, she gave "the negro Amis" one hundred dollars for the Scottsboro case, from "collections made at dances, meetings, etc., in England."

Even though this essay threatens to become one long aside or digression, may I suggest here that the vilification by the press, like the lies and fabri-

cations about a white woman who stayed in Harlem in the Grampion Hotel, deserves further study. The hate mail generated by the press outcry also
should be looked at as a literary genre. The letters are predictable in their
pornographic wishes for Nancy; their death threats and bad sexual puns on
her name often come from those who sign themselves members of the Ku
Klux Klan. Obviously presidents, movie stars, and public figures of all kinds
must receive a great deal of hate mail, but to my knowledge it has not been
studied as a literary genre.[10] One of the most disturbing of these letters in
the Humanities Research Center collection at the University of Texas,
comes from someone who styles himself "Master of one of the fine steel
monsters of the deep," a Cunard Line ship. He says he would sink the ship
if she were on it, how could she sink so low, and so on? Nancy Cunard kept
a batch of these letters and sometimes read them aloud to friends in later
years, trying to figure out the psychology of the letter writers.

The book weighed eight pounds and included 250 articles, as well as
hundreds of photographs and illustrations. The oversize volume, printed in
Caslon Old Face type, on fine paper, the pages measuring twelve by ten
inches, is itself a semiotic signifier of both the dignity and gravity of the subject of international black culture(s). Hugh Ford's 1970 reprint (out of print
and also considered a rare volume) reproduces parts of a text that had 315
pages on Africa, an enormous section on the United States, the West Indies,
the Caribbean, and Latin America and a sixty-page section on Europe. (In
2002 this volume brings several thousand dollars at Sotheby's or in the book
trade, *if* one can find a copy.) The sections on African art in particular, and
the long and detailed histories of slavery in various countries, as well as the
naming, quoting, and publishing of the works of black writers, political
leaders, philosophers, and rebels, are an astonishing accomplishment, an act
of cultural work in its seriousness and international scope, all of it a tribute
to Cunard's organizational and editing skills and the immense power of her
own writing and research, as well as her ability to build international networks of scholars, historians, anthropologists, photographers, and poets to
present this collective effort to the world.

Was it precisely because it *was* a collective effort that it has been lost to
history? (Nancy Cunard's genius for collective efforts for the causes she believed in later extended to her Speak Outs of intellectuals' opinions and
chapbooks of poems on the Spanish Civil War and collections of poems for
France in World War II.) We now often associate such monumental international cultural projects with feminism, as in the Arkin and Shollar *Long-
man's Anthology of Women Writers of the World,* which took ten years to
prepare, or the massive Feminist Press volumes of the work of Indian

women writers, but the *Negro* anthology is outstanding because it refuses to remain in the domain of art and ventures bravely into politics, anthropology, and history. People are suspicious of the motives of the organizers of such collective cultural efforts. But Nancy Cunard has not been accused of megalomania, merely of using the making of the anthology to work out her own exile from white Western culture.

Cunard did in fact enlist many people to help her, and Raymond Michelet is acknowledged for his assistance. Samuel Beckett, whom she discovered when she published his *Whoroscope* at the Hours Press, did many translations for the volume (and there is a faintly obscene echo of her name in *Waiting for Godot*). In sifting through what is left of her files and correspondence for the making of the volume (what is left survived the fate of all her files used in the latrine and on the floor of her French village house when Nazi soldiers were billetted there), one is impressed by the very existence of her black literary and political networks all over the world. Holding these handmade scrapbooks, the reader notes Cunard's penciled reminders that the mud on these pages came from Nazi boots, that much else was used as toilet paper or for target practice, and that her famous collection of ivory bracelets was scattered in the nearby fields.

CULTURAL CAPITAL

It is my opinion that Nancy Cunard was very much aware of the form of the anthology as cultural capital, and that she produced a weighty and dignified tome with cultural market value in mind to participate in other economies driven by money and power, as well as in the discourses and debates about race sparked by her fury at what she considered the neglect and denial of African art in the Colonial Exhibition in Paris in 1931. As a British subject (despite her exile in Paris) she was aware of the use of poetry anthologies, especially Palgrave's *Golden Treasury,* as an instrument for the dissemination of ideology in the colonies, to insist on the superiority of English culture to indigenous forms, often constructed as the savage traces of all that was *not* culture or civilization. What we now can see, sadly, is that the utopian production of such a cross-national tribute to black culture— which we would call multiculturalism—was practically meaningless if she could not also secure the anthology's dissemination to her intended readers. Because *Negro* was banned in many African countries and in the West Indes, it could not reach the readers it was meant for. Anthologies of English poetry were required reading in colonial schools all over Africa and India, cheaply printed and circulated widely, and people like us read and taught these works in the schools and colleges of the former colonies. Unless she could get the *Negro* anthology into those schools or into the hands of the readers who needed it, it would be practically impossible to convince any but a handful of intellectuals (including some West Indian radicals, who kept the banned book hidden under their beds during World War II), and those who had access to particular libraries, that black culture was indeed culture and could, in fact, be compared to Wordsworth on its own terms. Censorship, banning, and its "communist" connection contributed to its disappearance.

The *Negro* anthology also got caught in the crossfire of local battles for cultural hegemony in Harlem, and Cunard herself seems to have been constructed either as a white woman who stole black men or as a frigid nymphomaniac with whom respectable black folks would not want to associate. The role of the FBI in savaging her reputation has yet to be determined, and the influence of agents or blackmail on friends is not to be underestimated.

Friends of Langston Hughes have suggested to me that it was the combination of "Communism" and unorthodox sexual practices they shared that damaged the reputation of the book and its editor. (Her witch status parallels that of Zora Neale Hurston, whose splendid essays inform the volume.)

Or was *Negro* lost to history, basically ignored despite being reprinted, because, although she published his essay, Cunard criticized W.E.B. DuBois? Because she wrote scornfully of the accomodationist NAACP, and proclaimed for all to hear that the future of blacks everywhere was tied to the Communist Party? I suspect that the Communist connection may be the real problem here, for, although she published the works of all sides in her Harlem section, she marked the volume with the semiotic stamp of her Left convictions, opening with "I, too, sing America," a Whitmanesque poem by the leftist Langston Hughes, like herself not an actual member of, but very close to, the Communist Party, and Howard Lester's photograph of a black worker in a cap titled *An American Beast of Burden.* She used her editorial privilege to mark her democratic inclusiveness by publishing articles she disagreed with and then disfiguring them with footnotes marking her differences with the author.

I suspect that Nancy Cunard's brilliant anthology (first called *Color*) was conceived as a work of propaganda for black liberation. She dedicated it to her lover Henry Crowder, an Afro-American jazz pianist she met in Venice in the late twenties, claiming that by drawing her attention to the plight of blacks in the United States he gave her life a purpose and shape. It is quite conceivable that this is true. Where the problem lies is in people's troubled and often hostile responses to her choice of cause and crusade. It is not possible for a white feminist in my position to claim the inaugural place for Nancy Cunard's *Negro* anthology that Alain Locke's *The New Negro,* a small, strictly artistic anthology of 1925, was given in Houston Baker's *Modernism and the Harlem Renaissance* and is now canonical. Though I may quote Alain Locke's letter to Cunard, my voice still does not have the authority of Houston Baker's. (For the *Negro* anthology to take its place in cultural history, black readers must read it.) Alain Locke's letter, dated April 14, 1934, begins:

> I congratulate you,—almost enviously, on the finest anthology in every sense of the word ever compiled on the Negro. When I saw the announcements, I feared a scrapbook, but by a miracle of arrangement, you have built up a unity of effect and a subtle accumulative force of enlightenment that is beyond all contradiction and evasion. . . . The serious analysises of Jazz by Antheil and Goffin are path-breaking. You will have endless vindications in the years to come. Thanks for your discrimination in presenting my talented young friend, Zora Hurston.

A woman exile is an uncanny figure, I have argued elsewhere, for her very body means home and hearth; it signifies the womb/home of humankind. If a woman chooses homelessness, becomes a voluntary and even sometimes exultant exile, like Nancy Cunard, she frightens people. She certainly was a threat to "family values." She not only publicly repudiated her mother, her class and her country, Nancy Cunard never settled down, never made a home. Exile was her element, and she exulted in it. For her home was where her press was, her instrument for her reaching the world with pleas for her political causes. Even before it was destroyed by the Nazis, her cottage in a Norman village near Paris was, to her friends, another example of her uncanny, unfeminine homelessness, a parody of the idea of home as a sanctuary for privacy. She had designed it while living with Louis Aragon, and it was a bizarre tribute to surrealism's radical attacks on home and family. One had to go through everyone's bedrooms to get to the kitchen or common rooms, wrote Henry Crowder about Nancy's seduction of Michelet, the young French student who had run away from school and helped in the research for the anthology—under the very nose, as it were, of her present lover. Women are supposed to be homemakers, and Nancy's restless wanderings, the very publicity of her life in the limelight or the café in the square—made her seem unnatural. Her tragic death in Paris, drunk and raving lines from her last long poem pleading for world peace, was an exile's death. Sometimes—in fact one might say that all the time—she felt like a motherless child.

Working with modernism has taught me to wrestle with categories of periodization and geography as well as sexual identity and literary value. Accustomed as I was to challenging the hegemony of literary estates and biographers of writers from Virginia Woolf to Rebecca West, Djuna Barnes to Sylvia Townsend Warner, it was a shock to find that a healthy suspicion and a basic skepticism about received wisdom are as necessary in reading (and believing) the biographers, autobiographers, and literary historians of what is called The Harlem Renaissance. It seems obvious to me that by concentrating on the twenties as a renaissance, historians have constructed the thirties and political activism as somehow anti-art. How can I reconstruct a modernist time line that will highlight the publication of the *Negro* anthology in 1934? Working outside my field, I find myself possessed by the mad desire to collate David Levering Lewis's *When Harlem Was in Vogue* with Mark Naison's *Communists in Harlem During the Depression.* I am confused by the marginalization of Nancy Cunard in odd footnotes and peculiar sideways citations in the lives of people like Langston Hughes and Claude McKay, who seem so central to her life in the period. As I work in the Cunard papers, I do not make copies of Langston Hughes's poems, expecting that they can be found in his *Collected Poems* in the library. [Now there is, but it is not entirely reliable.] But what am I to make of the fact that there is no volume of Langston Hughes's *Collected Poems* in the library? There are two separate but not equal volumes; one is "selected" and the other is marked "revolutionary." I read the biography. Langston Hughes, who figures in Cunard's life as a brother radical, a Communist Party fellow traveler like herself, a lifelong close friend and comrade whom she met in Paris, in the Soviet Union, in Harlem, and above all in Spain in the struggle against fascism, the Langston Hughes who was also the friend of her Latin American radical writer friends, the Langston Hughes who shows up smiling, with his arms around the comrades, in her photo albums, the Langston Hughes I had assumed from his letters to her (and her attitude) to be homosexual, like most of the men in her circles—this dynamic modernist figure is written out of history. By himself? By his literary estate? By the biographer who calls this lively, lusty figure asexual? In whose interest is Langston Hughes being desexed and whitewashed?[11]

Not only did I assume that homosexuality was part of the Hughes persona, but that he and Claude McKay were linked to European modernisms through some of the people in Cunard's gay radical circles. I also thought it would be an interesting problem in gay history to open that folder on writers and the Spanish civil war in Cunard's papers at the Humanities Research Center, to think about the relation betwen radicalism, race, and homosexuality in the context of the Spanish Civil War. I am struck here by the tremendous gap between "modernism" as I was taught it and the modernism I teach. In that folder is W. H. Auden's handwritten copy of "Spain," along with Nancy Cunard's typescript for her volume, a typescript full of mistakes because she had trouble reading his handwriting. This is the poem Auden later repudiated when he named the thirties that "low dishonest decade." It appears that he sent the poem only at the insistence of his and Nancy's common friend Brian Howard. Are we to believe that Langston Hughes's heart was not in his poems for Spain either?

I am learning is that it is necessary to chart these cultural journeys in both directions, to figure out whether or not we can get from here to there or from there to here. My questions began blithely enough with Nancy Cunard's exile from England. What would happen if one tried to take the Cunard Line to Harlem, I asked. Does the A Train still travel express to Paris? The historical problems are centered on recuperations of the aesthetics and politics of the thirties, not at the century's temporal extreme but always placed at the cultural extreme in a dualist dynamic that insists on setting up art and politics as natural enemies. Nancy Cunard's work as poet, avant-garde publisher of the Hours Press (where she discovered Samuel Beckett and published Pound's *Cantos* and many other major modernists), as the editor of *Negro,* which I am claiming is the monumental internationalist forerunner of all our current work in Cultural Studies, as the organizer of several volumes of artists speaking out on the Spanish Civil War, as author of the *Scottsboro Appeal* and *Black Man and White Ladyship* and of a major contribution as a journalist for the Associated Negro Press reporting not only the war in Spain but the Geneva meetings on Ethiopia, race issues in World War II and African questions through the 1950's—has fallen through the cracks of several different maps of modernism in which one would expect to find her foregrounded. What are the reasons for this?

As one maps out any subject for inquiry, a center and a periphery develop. If I examine my own process, will I be able to explain the cultural and historical processes that have denied Nancy Cunard recognition as a major intellectual and political figure of the twentieth century? Why is Nancy Cunard an embarrassment in black modernism, or never mentioned at all when one could claim *Negro* as the inaugurating effort in claiming an

Afro-American culture? The answers are not simple. But if I compare, for example, what feminists name and work against as the dominant texts, either as works of art or criticism, with those Houston Baker challenges in *Modernism and the Harlem Renaissance* or James de Jongh names in *Vicious Modernism: Black Harlem and the Literary Imagination,* there appears to be little agreement on what is hegemonic. One can say that white male modernisms, from "the Pound Era" to "the Auden Generation," include one white woman artist as monster—Woolf or Stein or Amy Lowell. When feminists have rewritten these narratives, as in Shari Benstock's *Women of the Left Bank* or Bonnie Kime Scott's *The Gender of Modernism,* new categories and paradigms emerge, as in the subject of the sex war, "sapphic modernism," or expatriate women writers. Race has remained peripheral to many of these new modernisms as well (despite good intentions), and one of the critical or historical solutions for scholars has been to study what has been left out separately—engendering ethnic modernism in the United States, for instance, or looking at race as part of the passion for primitivism in European modernisms. But nothing seems to change in the way elite institutions teach an elite culture of high modernist texts and writers. Women or blacks or gays or chicanos may form alternative canons but never enter into (or mess up) the existing order of now "classic" texts and writers. They're "it": Everyone else is read and judged around or in relation to these texts. They may be allowed to form a separate order in themselves or in relation to one another.

Coming to Harlem via the Cunard Line in the thirties, I have different expectations and different cultural baggage than if I were coming to avant-garde Paris on the A Train. But I already know that I would be allowed to write certain narratives about Nancy Cunard. Nancy Cunard was constructed as a nymphomaniac in order to explain her affairs with black men. This effectively made impossible any simultaneous claims that Cunard was an important radical intellectual and cultural historian. The biographer uses the category "nymphomaniac" to signify heterosexuality, though it is clear that she had lesbian affairs, slept with younger men, older men, homosexuals, sailors, and boxers, and claimed to be the third in some lesbian relationships. In Shari Benstock's *Women of the Left Bank,* Nancy Cunard is recuperated for a vision of radical modernism that stresses the vision of the Hours Press, and her brave and committed journalism for Republican Spain. Benstock points out Richard Aldington's disgust at Cunard's publication of *Black Man and White Ladyship,* and his creation of her repudiation of her class as a dangerous form of bohemian eccentricity, in a caricature short story called "Now She Lies There": "Its 'hysterical relish' [Benstock writes] constitutes a stronger, more virulent form of an underlying assumption that women of a certain social class and economic background discovered in the expatriate experience a means of open rebellion against their families and a method of killing time" (*WLB,* 393).

Among Benstock's avant-garde expatriate women publishers, patrons, poets, journalists, and editors on the Left Bank in the twenties and thirties, Cunard's left-wing politics, her commitment to the cause of blacks and the Spanish Civil War differentiate her from the surrealist fellow travelers she enlisted as allies in terms of her very seriousness. But what is it that kept them (and us?) from a recognition of her seriousness, her intense hard work as a researcher and reporter and writer? Is it that her cause was not the enfranchisement of her own sex, but rather the recognition of the claims of a whole downtrodden race across national lines and boundaries?

Lady Cunard's salon, un-bohemian as it seems now, was a novelty in its day, and her unconventionality was protected by a cover marriage. In some ways Nancy's outrageous artistic circles were extensions of her mother's social practices. She published with Edith Sitwell a series of poetry anthologies called *Wheels,* and Virginia Woolf published her brilliant poem *Parallax* at the Hogarth Press in 1925; her 1921 volume was called *Outlaw,* and at the Hours Press she published surrealists, homosexuals, and radicals from Louis Aragon to Laura Riding, Havelock Ellis to Brian Howard. But, as Claude McKay wrote to her from Tangier after his house and belongings had been destroyed by what he thought was the British secret service or international police, it was one thing to stick to championing black arts and artists. Once she advocated political action for racial justice as in her international *Appeal for the Scottsboro Boys* and publicly associated herself and the Black cause with the Communist Party, she was bound to be hounded by the yellow press and bombarded by tons of sexually explicit hate mail (or "hate-MALE," as one of her American radical friends called it, when he wrote from Max Eastman's Dutchess County farm that he had burned a bushel of it).

McKay was worried about how the adverse publicity would affect the reception of *Negro,* and yet the outside pressures on him succeeded in alienating him from Nancy and making the claim in his memoirs that he did not contribute because she refused to pay him—when no one was paid for their collective work.

A great deal of work remains to be done on the history of the making of the *Negro* anthology, and for all of Nancy Cunard's writing on race to be recuperated. Nancy Cunard's route out of the hypocrisy and racism of her class is not easily dismissed. One cannot, one *must* not, despise a white woman who devoted herself to the cause of black liberation. Sex and race are dangerous subjects and very complex, especially when tangled in a woman's political life, as she and her friends lived, and as we read their lives.

Where does my partisanship come from? I ask myself, realizing with a shock that black culture, politics, and music were my own route out of the stifling Irish working-class Catholic school world of my youth. Since Nancy Cunard claimed that when she was six years old she dreamed of blacks dancing, and of herself joining the dance and somehow knowing the steps, earning the eternal suspicion of biographers and critics who are perhaps not so naive as to expose the dark hearts of their dreams, *I* have to risk saying it:

From Father O'Connor's (he was known as the "Jazz Priest") Sunday afternoon-Teenage Jazz Club sessions, at Storyville in Boston, to surreptitious trips to clubs in Roxbury, hiding my school uniform under my trenchcoat, I came to the politics of race through music. Later, during the struggle for civil rights, I worked with my future husband teaching in Freedom Schools in Roxbury. We named our son for Malcolm X. This narrative has been very much suppressed in our family legends. The main story has been "How I became a feminist," not how we struggled for racial freedom along with our black comrades. Now it seems so obvious that I, like others of my generation, developed the sense of agency for a white feminist identity through black culture and the struggle for civil rights. This narrative, that the struggle for racial justice empowered many white feminists and their work, is, as I try to place myself in cultural history, the most important story of all.

6

Laying Down the White Woman's Burden

Michael Arlen's *The Green Hat* and Mulk Raj Anand's *Coolie*

Iris Storm (the Nancy Cunard figure in *The Green Hat*) is "unreproductive," to use Angela Ingram's term; her sexuality is not related to motherhood, nor her behavior to traditional maternal self-sacrifice.[1] She is agent (and sign) of the end of European civilization. Primitivism, the wholesale European modernist appropriation of Africa in the arts, is only partly explanatory of the white artist's identification with African culture. Her unreproductive (androgynous) image relies on the power of the cultural projection of erotic exotic motherhood onto to the African woman. Joseph Conrad's image of Africa as Europe's "heart of darkness" works so well and has worked for so long to express the West's ambivalence because, I believe, the word *heart* is a euphemism for breast. (And, in the psychodynamics of fetishism, the breast is a substitute for the genitalia. Writers like Rider Haggard in *King Solomon's Mines,* of course, more often mapped female genitalia onto their African fictions, and "racial scientists," as Sander Gilman points out in the case of "The Hottentot Venus," sought to differentiate the genitalia of African women from those of Europeans.) The phrase "heart of darkness" figures Africa as pro- and pregenerative, the creator and nurturer of the human species, the universal "mother country," now infantalized by usurping European colonials who demand allegiance to themselves as "mother countries," in the pernicious loyalty-demanding family metaphor devised by James Stephen as first head of the Colonial Office in England, and later by anthropologists digging for the oldest bones, the origins of human life, and ethnologists anxious to preserve and collect the "primitive."[2] Current debates about the African origins of human life have a long history.

It is not so much Africa as Oriental womb or even Africa as primal female sexuality that haunts all the texts of modernism, not just Conrad and

Forster, but also the fictions and essays of Virginia Woolf, Dorothy Richardson, D. H. Lawrence; expressionist and cubist painting; the sculpture of Brancusi, Lipchitz, and Giacometti; classical music's confrontations with jazz, gospel, and the blues; the dance from Diaghilev to Josephine Baker, as well as the mystical-political fiction of W.E.B. Du Bois, the poetry of Langston Hughes, and the work of Claude McKay—and the ethnographies, colonial expositions, museum shows, the new consumer culture of exploration and travel from advertising posters to the collecting of exotic objects and hunting trophies. It is the African woman's breast as it appeared in the sculpture and carving and anthropological photographs newly being looked at by European eyes. The black woman's breast abstracted into a powerful protruding phallic form by African sculpture is a visual shock to Europe. Their own artistic traditions had valorized a pink-and-white breast as the model of female beauty. Round and soft, the European breast suggested maternal comfort.[3] The breast in African sculpture says in no uncertain terms that woman is creature of the outside as well as the inside. She is a public figure whose body enters into the world. The hard phallic breast terrified and fascinated the Europeans. [Note Claude McKay's description of the white woman's response to the African Statue in *Banana Bottom,* as well as Woolf's claim that she would have to be a very different person to put such a statue on her mantelpiece.] The entrance of the African statue onto the cultural scene at the same time that European women demanded their political rights, and the "New Woman" was choosing to look flat chested and to avoid childbirth, without renouncing sex—reminded men of female power. The breast in African sculpture is an emblem of power, and there is no mistaking it. Woman in African culture, the statues' message was, occupies outer as well as inner space; she is active politically and publicly, a presence rather than an absence in the world. If the carving occupied space with such aggressive three-dimensionality, the African woman must be a power in her own culture. The thrust of black breast into the cultural space of modernism was a challenge to the white phallus.

Modernism cannot be understood without reconstructing its primal scene: The European artist looks at the African fertility figures and masks in the studio of Appollinaire or Derain and imagines a new way to liberate spatial energy, taking from African sculpture a three-dimensional language of volume that Picasso (and other painters and sculptors in Paris) use to transform Western art. Virginia Woolf's trope of the white Western gaze transfixed by the sight of a "very fine Negress" and struggling with the problem of "passing" the figure without possessing it, is central to understanding the way gender informs the politics of representation, identification, and difference in modernism and discourses about modernism.

"Passing" a "very fine Negress," a version of the ubiquitous female African fertility figure that I believe is at the center of all modernist discourses, as the narrator does in the classic feminist text *A Room of One's Own,* the woman writer wants to boast that she does not participate in the male colonizing gaze because she has no wish to make an "Englishwoman" of the "negress." But the astonishing sentence reveals that she cannot conceive of such a fellow creature as a black Englishwoman. As she passes she doesn't see a sister, a citizen, a version of herself, but someone outside, alien, other, not, as she says of her white self, "woman," in relation to the British patriarchy.[4]

Nancy Cunard, a contemporary of Virginia Woolf, also concerned with transgressing gender and class boundaries, was also unable to pass an example of a "very fine Negro" or a "very fine" object of African art without insisting on the difference between her "look" at the other and the male colonizer's need to make the African into a British subject. The gender difference is important here. In fact the "passing gaze" objectifies the other in a different way from the colonizing gaze, which wants to make the other a political subject of the empire. The "passing gaze," as it is employed in Woolf and in the writing and politics of other white women who identify with working-class outsiders or people of color as victims of white patriarchy, is still capable of reducing the other to an aesthetic object, as in the vision of a "fine" negress or the "beautiful" body of a worker, just as the "passing gaze" may make the Other into an object of sexual desire. Cunard's gaze participates in the primitivism of Picasso, Derain, Appollinaire, Brancusi, Giacometti, Ernst, Man Ray, and other modernists, who do, in fact, wish to own the African objects as well as to incorporate their magical spatial genius into their own artistic production. Nancy Cunard's relationship to these cult objects and fetishes is complicated by her own experience of being looked at as just such an icon, and her obsessive practice of self-fetishizing.

Perhaps I can try to express it this way. Virginia Woolf's narrator says she can pass a "very fine negress" without wanting to make an Englishwoman of her, proclaiming her innocence in the face of the other's oppression by white Englishmen. What could make the Negress into an Englishwoman, in the sense of citizenship? At the time (1928), in fact, only marriage to an Englishman. There were not a lot of black "Englishmen," and the law was not sympathetic to the claims of the colonized to citizenship in the mother country; and white ones were not likely to "marry" a black woman in the legal way. Perhaps Woolf is haunted by desire here, her own desire to "marry" or have sexual relations with the black woman? Is she saying, then, "I can't pass her without desiring her body?"

The relation of the passer to the passed in the phrase is very complex. If we stress "making" in "making an Englishwoman of her," what is being suggested is mental colonization, the "forcing the soul" demanded by the Goddess of Conversion in *Mrs. Dalloway.* The narrator wants to dissociate herself from missionaries who deprive Africans of their belief systems. She could also be saying that she doesn't wish the Negress to suffer the kind of political indignity she suffers as an Englishwoman without rights, when in Africa, it is clear from the statues, woman has power and status.

Again, we may ask, what if the negress were not, in some Western aesthetic sense, "fine" at all? Suppose she were old and crippled? Would the narrator still care about being seen as innocent of her oppression? Why doesn't she see that there are "English" negresses or black women living in her country, and some for generations, some since before slavery in the eighteenth century? Making an Englishwoman of her means, among other things in the context in which Woolf was writing, appropriating the labor power of her body, or, in terms of some forms of slavery, the reproductive power of her body to produce more slaves.[5] Woolf must have been aware that (certain) Englishwomen could vote for the first time in the year in which she was writing. The problem of race had to be faced regarding her Jewish husband in terms of sexuality, nationality, and gender identity. But she did not face it.

One could certainly argue that she created herself as a "woman" writer and an English writer against the alien Jewishness of her husband, as Nancy Cunard created herself as a radical journalist against the history of the treatment of blacks as it manifested itself in the life of Henry Crowder. The troubling language of Woolf's letters and her disturbing use of the word "Jew," is another form of modernist primitivism, akin to Cunard's discourse along with other race radicals of the day, of "racist anti-racism" regarding "pureblooded" Africans. The widespread anti-Semitism of the modernists was derived from a racial crisis among white Europeans, an identity crisis that coincided with the cults of African art and music and the fad for reading ethnographies of the sex life of "savages" and case studies of "aberrant" sexual behavior among fellow Europeans. When they write "pure black," of course, they are denying the white blood infused by slavery and rape into generations of blacks. The language of science, eugenics, and evolution encouraged thinking of Others as "races apart" or atavistic throwbacks to the apes. It is the serious use of these discourses that dates Huxley's novels dreadfully, while Michael Arlen's frivolous romance still provide reading pleasure.

If one rewrites Virginia Woolf's disturbing passage in terms of Nancy Cunard's stance, or imagines it as another kind of European "passing gaze," where the white woman is the one who looks and the black person or image stands still and [this is crucial] *does not look back,* then one may also imagine her saying, "I cannot pass any example of a 'very fine Negro,' real African man or African artwork, without wanting to possess him/her/it." She wants to take on its *mana,* or magic being, to make her black like them or to wear as armor in her role in the struggle against white European cultural supremacy. Despite the fact that Arlen's and Huxley's fictions and the popular image of Nancy Cunard was based on exploitation of her sexuality and her ambivalent gender identity, and that, in addition, the primal identity that Virginia Woolf and other modernist women explored in their work was gender, for Nancy Cunard, her racial identity as "white" was far more important psychically than her identity as a woman.

Virginia Woolf could not look at her "very fine negress" for long, one imagines. Nor could she hold her gaze at the sight of a black man outside of a colonial exposition. This is a fine line to draw between (certain progressive) white women and white men in relation to colonialism, perhaps too fine a line for us to read now. But at the time, the impetus to separate the anticolonial white self as a fellow victim of British patriarchs, and to identify with and champion the African struggle for freedom, to bond with black men, seemed a possible political position for Nancy Cunard to occupy.

However, the blind spot in Nancy Cunard's position was that, however much she created her body to be looked at by colonizing or possessive or "passing" gazes, in solidarity with blacks as ethnographic objects or not, she was never (because her white body never could escape the mark of its class, and, I would argue, was always also a type of the English national "body" when seen abroad) in a position in which she could not turn the tables on the viewer and boldly look back, directly into the eyes of the camera or the beholder or the artist or sculptor making an image of her. Even if she were acting as a stable sex object, or subject of vulnerability, it was clear that she could easily occupy the objectifier's position. Her acting out of abjection was not an instance of "real" abjection or the utter abjection of "social death" experienced by blacks.

Black men could be, and were, lynched in the United States for less than that kind of knowing looking, that bold return of eye contact that was her signature. When she encouraged her black lovers to cast their eyes upon her, she did not, perhaps, understand the psychic rage and violence that could be released by her transgression, though later it appears to have been a response she courted. One would have to call Nancy Cunard's *white looks* at the figure of the Negro in modernism neither innocent nor wholly complicitous in the empire's regime of scopic domination. Her white looks at the black figure are meant not so much as a controlling mode of being in relation to blackness as they are the sign of a crisis of self-consciousness in the culture of whiteness. Of course, the fragility and instability of this posture (and the moral and ethical problem of the exploitation of the Other) must be pointed out and deconstructed. We see how she saw herself in relation to African men, and, to some extent, we may imagine the way some Africans and black men in the diaspora saw her: as a comrade in the struggle against the same enemy as well as an exploiter of their sexuality. I would argue, however, that not all examples of the "very fine Negro" were immobilized or emasculated by her look. Some, like George Padmore, Langston Hughes, Claude McKay, or Eugene Gordon, were inspired by the *Negro* anthology or her pamphlet "Black Man and White Ladyship" to join her in imagining a rebellion against the power of the colonizing "mother country"; many Africans testify to being empowered by her writing and organizing. The personal bravery of her act of rejecting class and country as well as the shocking break with her mother, a surrealist blow at the universally acknowledged connection to the woman who brought her into the world— should not be underestimated as a powerful incentive to political solidarity.

But the history of the relations between white women and black men is so controversial, so fraught with tension, that it may be useful to move the discussion to another terrain.[6] While it would be natural to discuss Cunard's moves in relation to primitivism in English novels of the period, or even the use of blackface minstrelsy in the writing of her friends the American expatriate poets T. S. Eliot and Ezra Pound, and later, William Carlos Williams, her communist commitment to African struggles for freedom places her in a different position from their purely aesthetic explorations of transgressive or cross-race voices. What is interesting to us now is Cunard's participation in so many different discourses of modernist primitivism, from French surrealist theater, dance, and film and other visual arts, appropriating and reviving itself under African influence, to the anthropological discourses of Europe, the Americas, and the Caribbean, "respectfully" collecting and analyzing artifacts and transforming them into "art," to the spirit of anthologizing the poetry and oral traditions of African peoples that was so much a part of European intellectual life in this period, whatever its ideological intent.

THE GREEN HAT

The Green Hat (1924), Michael Arlen's chic popular novel of the twenties, its wicked and worldly heroine, that "shameless and shameful lady," Iris

March (Storm), based on Nancy Cunard (with later stage and screen performances by Tallulah Bankhead, Katharine Cornell, and Greta Garbo enhancing the image)—created the classic twenties figure of the perverse, independent boy-girl, consumed by desire for forbidden love. Presumably, woman having been repressed for so long, her desire is as insatiable as its objects are unsuitable. She is the English postwar "nymphomaniac," a figure from the contemporary medical discourse of sexology, cold-hearted and hot-tempered, a version of the "vampire lesbian from Sodom." Drink and drugs, part of another twenties discourse about the decadence of the newly emancipated woman, are suggested, and, in Huxley's novels in particular, the figure of this female is an evolutionary throwback to the primitive. That peculiar word *nymphomaniac,* which has haunted the reputation of Nancy Cunard, is actually used about Iris in *The Green Hat,* as it is about Myra Viveash in Aldous Huxley's *Antic Hay* (1923), and the even more outrageous Lucy Tantamount in his *Point Counterpoint* (1928)—and it moved easily from Huxley's best-selling, but now unreadable, highbrow fiction to the life. Arlen's romantic doomed heroine is as genetically unfit to live as Huxley's vamps, but it's her blue blood that damns her, not the atavistic sadism that revels in bloody and brutal lovemaking, linking the Huxley heroines to a savage biological past in which the twenties vamp is really a vampire (Viveash = the living dead?) or as forerunners of Robin Vote.

An abortion is hinted at (the rejection of motherhood is the key to the myth) and sexually transmitted diseases suggested—in the opening chapters, a contagion supposedly gotten from dark men in the new cosmopolitan world where rulers and slaves of empire and exotic sexuality mix with money and power, and Iris lies in a convent hospital in degenerate Paris, patronized by "cosmopolitan divorcées" to take care of the results of their "common harlotries."

Clean white men, the sex-mad girl's peers and childhood friends, and rich, club-going English gentlemen are the heroes of the genre of romance fiction to which *The Green Hat* belongs. It popularized, glamorized, fetishized, and then condemned the nymphomaniacal Nancy Cunard figure. Michael Arlen, an Armenian himself, known as "the Baron," presents such Englishmen as victims of Jews, "Dagoes," "niggers," "Semites," Latin American and Levantine millionaires, all of whom are now attractive to the newly bold English girls of the twenties. The novel reeks with fear of pollution—a fear embodied in romance fiction by the figure of "the eternal masculine." Their own institutions of empire and trade have brought to Europe the very pollution that attracts white women like Iris to cross class

and racial boundaries as sexual predators. *The Green Hat* fears the foreign—
Michael Arlen and his characters are horrified by French food and French
nuns. The fictional Iris defends the Jews from her friends' disgust with a
slightly more enlightened racism—she loves a certain "Jewish" materialism,
a cosmopolitan love of luxury and pleasure that is characteristic of herself
and her friends, a response in keeping with the often jarringly "racist anti-
racism" of Nancy Cunard and her activist colleagues in their celebration of
the "pure" black cultures of Africa, later in the thirties. [7]

Iris Storm might well be quoting Nancy Cunard when she calls herself
"the slave of freedom," or mocks the narrator:

> Wait till you're so free that you just daren't do what you like. Wait till you're
> so free that you can be here one minute and there another. Wait till you're
> so free that you can see the four walls of your freedom and the iron-barred
> door that will let you out into the open air of slavery, if only there were
> someone to open it. Ah, yes, freedom. . . ." (131)

Thin and pretentious and faux-Wildean as *The Green Hat* is, it plumps
the reader down in one of the English clubs where Nancy Cunard's reputation was made and her character dissected. It allows us to see a world in
which one woman's desire can be equated with the loss of England's place
in the world order. What did her affairs have to do with affairs of state? we
ask now. What, indeed? She let down the side, deliberately dropped "the
white woman's burden" (155), not a mission to the unwashed pagans, but
wearing her own chastity as a sign of England's image of itself as a racially
pure superior nation. The novels give us the discourse of national purity, arguably the same discourse that later produced Hitler, in an undiluted form.
The flouting of the "laws" of sexual purity and racial purity is a threat to
the state. For, if a blue-blooded English lady sleeps with a dark foreigner,
no one will respect England.

White Women and Black Men

The complexities of the situation may emerge more clearly if we move the
discussion away from its obvious context, to think about it with a contem-
poraneous novel by an Indian writer, where the issue of a white woman's
power under colonialism is brilliantly related to the casting of men in the
colonies in the role of house servants to European women.[8] The discourses
of sexual desire and political freedom intersect with and contradict each

other as the educated woman of the cosmopolis, eager for citizenship and aware of her body, collides with the voice of the dispossessed and disenfranchised colonized male. The psychological and political plight of masculinity under colonialism, as described by Frantz Fanon or Ashis Nandy is, to my mind, brilliantly articulated in Mulk Raj Anand's novel *Coolie* (1936).

I want to use the Indo-Anglian writer's "coolie" figure as a way of understanding the situation of men of color like the Afro-American jazz pianist Henry Crowder; to the Spanish peasants, waiters, boxers, and African students in Europe; and even, to some extent, the white homosexual men who were Nancy Cunard's sexual partners, political comrades, traveling companions, and fellow artists, researchers, and translators of her collaborative projects. Anand's "coolie" figure is the Third World male uprooted from his traditional culture and thrown into contact with the First World female who is alienated from patriarchal culture and in search of sexual and intellectual emancipation. (*Coolie* is more than this, of course. Unlike the colonial fiction Homi Bhabha describes as mimicking European forms, Anand's novel subverts both the Anglo-Indian novel and the English popular romance.)

In *The Green Hat,* Iris March's glamorous clothing, made of exquisite fabrics tailored by Paris couturiers, is described in fetishist detail by the fussy and fixated narrator. He raves over her hats and stockings, and faints over her green and silver shoes. If the narrator of *Coolie* confides in the reader like a native male servant who "knows more than the all-knowing" about his white mistress, the narrator of *The Green Hat* seems to gossip in a cafe as the discreet homosexual dancing partner of the lady in question, the voice of her "cover" boyfriend, involved in her queenliness and creating her as a tragic diva. *The Green Hat* survives not because, as its narrator says of himself, it is too much "of its time," but because racist remarks punctuate Michael Arlen's fashionable gush—largely, one thinks, not in his own personal racist tone, but pitched to sound like the kind of Englishmen he writes about, in mimicry of upper-class manners, and because writing itself is a "dingy" kind of work for him. The word *dingy* recurs in *The Green Hat's* discourse of English national purity—"there is an immense, unalterable dinginess in being human," he confesses. (15) Deep in "self-dinginess" before the "purity" of Iris and her alcoholic twin brother, Gerald, the narrator abases himself before their images in an excess of nostalgia for English aristocracy:

> For I was what Gerald was not, what she obviously was not. I could somehow "cope with" my time and generation, while they were of the breed

destined to failure. I was of the race that is surviving the England of Hora-
tio Bottomley, the England of lies, vulgarity, and unclean savagery; while
they of the imperious nerves had failed, they had died the slow white death
which is reserved for privilege in defeat. (15)

A SMALL WHITE FACE

Iris Storm's "small white face" obsesses her creator. When Michael Arlen
fictionalized Nancy Cunard, he was also writing nostalgia for the loss of the
English national body. She is a figure from a glossy magazine of the twenties, a woman in white, wrapped in an ermine cape, which sets off her intense blue eyes ("like two spoonfuls of the Mediterranean in the early
morning of a brilliant day") and her emerald ring (a sign of Lady Cunard,
Nancy's socialite mother), as she drives off in her enormous sleek yellow car.
Michael Arlen sighs, "She was fair. As they would say it in the England of
long ago — she was fair. And she was grave, so grave. . . . And white she was,
very white, and her painted mouth was purple in the dim light." (10, 11)
Arlen describes Iris Storm's Hispano-Suiza as lovingly as he does her
clothes — it was a "gallant and suave" "battle chariot," "open as a yacht,"
"like a huge yellow insect that had dropped to earth from a butterfly civilization." (Huxley's fetish was cars, despite his novel's claim that he was, by
heredity, "under-acquisitive," and the fact that he couldn't see to drive. His
wife drove, and a special seat was built to measure for his outstretched legs
in the scarlet Bugatti racing car with dove-gray leather upholstery that they
bought with the proceeds from *Point Counterpoint*.)[9]

Iris's bridegroom commits suicide for "purity," she tells people, on their
wedding night, ruining her reputation and making a hero of the martyred
"Boy"; then her twin brother, cited in the newspapers for "bothering
women" in the park, "blows his brains out." These are the causes, presumably, of her shame, to become the object of gossip and pity of her former
friends. They are the romance novel's way of turning the immense social
cost of the death of a whole generation of men in the war into a figure of
sexual suicide. It is worth thinking about the cultural work done by the romance novel in making the lost generation of young men agents of their
own destruction to displace realistic accounts of the carnage of mutilated
bodies on the World War I battlefields. This narrative assuages social guilt
about World War I and deflects responsibility for these devastating losses
away from the government. It also provides an "explanation" for young
women's search for sexual partners among the forbidden Others, because the
golden boys of their own class are all dead.

The *déclassé* Iris is surprised at being called "a renegade from her class," someone who "had betrayed her caste to perfection": "Rushing about Europe like that, . . . you let England down. You've no idea, Iris, how these young foreign blighters hold England cheap," (51) says her friend. Here Michael Arlen captures some of what Nancy Cunard had to live with as she tried to make herself into a serious Left political writer. Her "small white face" meant England and chastity to too many people, people who counted her move to the Continent and then the world as a kind of personal betrayal, people who saw her love affairs with Africans and African Americans as a national scandal. Britannia had succumbed to the waves, drowned in disarray in foreign waters. (The Huxley formula of talking heads, endless scenes of men talking, punctuated by murder, rape, suicide, and the death of children, projected the war's violence onto civil society.)

THE GREEN HAT

It is as dated as Mrs. Mainwaring's reading of it. [Her name is pronounced Mannering] *The Green Hat's* precious narrator tries to amuse us by telling us directly what he is doing as a writer ("This chapter can't reasonably be expected to bear the weight of that night," he writes, archly), and the text is tiresome as a result. Scandalous in its time, it now seems embarrassingly banal and strained [and just Mrs. Mainwaring's cup of breakfast tea]. And it does, I think, give one a sense of what Nancy Cunard's life was like before she began to take herself seriously as a writer and a political activist, as in glimpses of what illness, despair, and drink had done to her that show up in the surviving diaries. Michael Arlen also captures Cunard's self-made Outlaw persona and a sense of the incredible bravery—and foolhardiness— shown by a woman of her class and era in rejecting her home, family, country, and culture:

> [Y]ou could not . . . "place" Mrs. Storm. You had a conviction, a rather de-
> spairing one, that she didn't fit in anywhere, to any class, nay, to any na-
> tionality. She wasn't that ghastly thing called Bohemian; she wasn't any of
> the ghastly things called society, county, upper, middle and lower class. She
> was, you can see, some invention, ghastly or not, of her own. . . . You felt
> she had outlawed herself from somewhere, but where was that somewhere?
> You felt she was tremendously indifferent as to whether she was outlawed or
> not. In her eyes you saw the landscape of England, spacious and brave; but
> you felt unreasonably certain that she was as devoid of patriotism as Mary
> Stuart. She gave you a sense of the conventions; but she gave you—unaware

always, impersonal always, and those cool sensible eyes!—a much deeper sense that she was somehow outside the comic, squalid, sometimes almost fine laws by which we judge what is and what is not conventional. (20)

Michael Arlen's heroine is intelligent. She is gallant and honorable, like a man, like an English gentleman, in fact. She is as strong as Munoo in the Indian novel is weak. The feminization of the native male and the masculinization of the white upper-class female are seen clearly as responses to the conjunction of colonialism and World War I in the marginal fiction I am reading here.

The narrator first sees Iris standing "carelessly," looking "like a tulip with a green head," in a dashing green felt hat and a close-fitting light brown leather jacket *pour le sport,* a kind of jacket Nancy Cunard wore for many years as a kind of signature. She has a wide, clean forehead, like a boy's: "Above her neck her hair died a very manly death," he writes, "a more manly death than 'bobbed' hair was ever known to die, and so it comes about that Iris Storm was the first Englishwoman I ever saw with shingled hair." (42) The narrator speaks in the voice of the English upper-class homosocial order in admiration of her style and her courage. We might take this narrative voice as a clue to the deep and lasting friendships Nancy Cunard formed with homosexual men. They were comrades in a particular culture of between-the-wars outlawry. "She was untouched, unsoiled, impregnable to the grubby hand of *lex femina.* . . . The outlaw was above the law of afterwards, impervious and imperious. She was beautiful, grave, proud. . . . She was the male of the species that is more fearless than mankind." (45)

Listening to the rhythm of the blues, he is reminded "of a small, white face suddenly thrown back against your arm with a smile that disturbed the dance. It reminded you of the desire that pleasantly turns to dust when you are desired. It reminded you of things you had never done with women you had never met." (109) Something about a rebellious woman like the fictional Iris Storm and the real Nancy Cunard encouraged the devotion of a certain kind of man and the fear and contempt of other sections of society. White woman, black music. She reminds him of the jungle.

Femme Camp: Stars and Divas

This is the image that has survived. Her "small white face" set against a black arm, her thin white body dancing to black music. The national body of

England lost in the jungle of the Congo. The image survived because Nancy wanted it to. As the conscious icon of her age she performed crumbling imperial whiteness in crisis as Marilyn Monroe performed a certain necessary whiteness for the American fifties and Madonna performed whiteness for the multicultural eighties. There is a form of *femme camp* in Nancy Cunard's style, for womanliness was always a masquerade she had learned from her mother as a child. White skin concealed her black heart, playing to the political and social need for cults of whiteness, challenging but also participating in an iconography of national purity, all the more necessary after Europe's orgy of wholesale slaughter of their Aryan young men in the war, and the threat of the racial dissolution of empire. I think what we find in this iconography of unsatisfied desire in the romantic novels, as well as the famous photographs that make a fetish of Nancy Cunard, is a perverse glorification of the childless woman—at a time when the nation needed women to produce cannon fodder for the next war.

After Cunard was dead, Hugh Ford collected a volume of reminiscences from her friends. Many of the sketches could be slid into the texts of the novels about her without disturbing the flow. The romance genres fed on one another. In their memoirs all of Nancy Cunard's friends romanticize her in in one way or another as a glistening Rhine maiden, a girl of the golden West, a tragic alcoholic Aryan, whiteness incarnate. Allanah Harper, Mary Hutchinson, Raymond Mortimer, and Kenneth MacPherson donned Michael Arlen's romance novelist's hat when they recalled her "astonishing" and "turbulent" presence: "Nancy, impeccably outrageously extravagantly courageous, generous, violent, self-destructive, fanatically wrong-headed, waywardly elegant, incarnately alluring: [10]

"Nancy Cunard was a fiery and furious angel, like the angel in Mathias Grunewald's triptique or the angel in Rainer Maria Rilke's *Elegies*—a terrible messenger descending with a fiery sword upon bourgeois hypocrisy and those ignorant persons who discriminate between race or color of skin."

"Miss Nancy Cunard is wonderful, made of alabaster and gold and scarlet, with a face like Donatello's Saint George . . ."

"There she is with her extraordinary eyes, arctic blue, tiger's eyes, triangular eyes shaped like arrowheads, with their 'regard (there is no English word meaning not only the eyes but the way in which they confront the visible world).'"

. . . tigress-dragonfly. No: cheetah. . . . Then, seated, one *heard* her . . .
Nancy's voice was a miracle. And so was the way she walked . . . she flowed
swiftly forward . . . like a cheetah, and also like a slim and splendid fish.

"The mixture of delicacy and steel in her build, hips, legs, ankles all of
the slenderest, weighed with massive ivory bracelets . . . that they seemed
too fragile to support . . . the head held high with its short fair hair, and one
foot placed exactly in front of the other, not with mannequin languor, but
spontaneously, briskly, boldly, skimming the pavement."

The icon of the emancipated woman, the desirous boy-girl, the active intellectual, the dangerous avant-garde artist—was not too fragile to support
the weight of its message. Women, in fiction and in life, wanted their freedom in sex and in politics.

The circulation of impersonations of Cunard's small white face and emaciated bold body in "the age of mechanical reproduction," in photographs
and fashion magazines, novels, sculpture, and painting, participates in a
modernist economy of the end of empire, and a crisis of white identity, co-
inciding with a postwar homosocial displacement of mourning for loss of all
the young men in the cult of Cunard as a daring diva. Race and gender categories, disturbed by the war, gave the new theaters of social life the "white
Negress" and the "boy-girl," as well as "the roaring queen" and the black
boxer, as familiar characters.

But Nancy Cunard was capable of manipulating the image for her own
ends. Her signature look was the bound head, and it had another kind of
message to relay, a sexual one about sado-masochism, as well as the political
message that the white European nations were having an identity crisis.
Smudged kohl-black eyes in a dead-white face sent a message about pain,
pain in the small white body and the body politic.

THE DEATH OF AN ENGLISH GENTLEMAN

In the last chapter of *The Green Hat,* Iris Storm, wearing a new version of
the green hat *pour le sport,* drives to the countryside of her childhood, rescues her rival from drowning, confronts her enemies in the library of the
Big House, wins the married white Englishman, and then retreats from the
battlefield in disgust at his lack of "honor," when he can't resist telling
everyone that she wasn't really impure, but just protecting Boy's reputation.
The plot unravels very fast, and in the dialogue of a drawing room "comedy" by Noël Coward. The plot tells us that Englishmen have lost their

honor—or, perhaps, that women have inherited what's left of male honor after the war. John Banting says that Nancy always laughed about Arlen's portrait of her in *The Green Hat*. They met him once after a late night in Cannes. "Never mind. The Baron (Arlen) made some money from it," she said. (BPIR, 180)

It turns out that Iris Storm's convent abortion was the stillborn child of her childhood lover, who had made love to her on the eve of his marriage, on meeting her after ten years' exile (his father had refused to let the childhood sweethearts marry because her family had lost its money) and the revelation that Boy's suicide "for purity" had been motivated by his discovery that he had given her syphilis. His need to tell this story, to bring her back into the fold of English honor, as it were, she finds unpardonable of him, robbing her of her one good deed, and she drives off to crash the yellow Hispano-Suiza into the tree that was the scene of their youthful pledges. The curtain falls on this melodrama as the narrator and Sir Maurice agree to say it was an accident. Pollution is driven out; the woman who fights for her right to desire is dead. English society is safe and, again as in a Noël Coward play, revealed to be based on a system of lies and cover-ups. Iris Storm is now our hero. The narrator has obsessed over her small white face and the slow white death of her class. He leaves us with a picture of the yellow car smashed into the ancient tree, the green hat lying on the ground. Robin Hood is dead.

There are, of course, strong cultural reasons for fictional creations of women of courage and honor at this point in English history. After all, most of the men in Europe were killed in World War I, whether or not they were courageous. Gallantry was now largely the province of women, and many women were delighted with the empowering role. But many women, faced with life without their men, committed suicide, convinced by society that they were "superfluous," the crash of a glorious car being a favorite way to remove the gallant heroine from the scene, in novels and in life. When *The Green Hat* constructs the men of the period as drunken, syphilitic suicides instead of heroic soldiers, it rewrites the reasons for women's behavior in the face of their overwhelming private and social losses in the war. Iris's suicide is made to appear as romantic and frivolous an upper-class act as those of her brother and husband. The romance novel does the cultural work here of glamorizing, or perhaps disguising, the rash of suicides by women in England after the war.[11]

Nancy Cunard's response to the fictional figures of dashing adventuresses was to model herself closely on them, constructing a self from a figure that was already a fictionalized version of herself. In the late fifties W. K. Rose met her in Europe as a living version of all the Lady Bretts, Catherines, Daisys, and Nicoles, "the lovely martyrs to beauty and truth in a world hell-bent on pleasure." (317). He was astonished at the contradictions in the "notoriously immoral" icon of the twenties. "Why not be a passionate romantic, pursuing high principles and low pleasures, and at the same time a fiend for accuracy, worse than a librarian?" He saw her as one of the period's "classy thoroughbreds," whose integrity came "shining through her own licentiousness," the real thing who had posed for the figures in Hemingway and Fitzgerald: "Nancy, looking like a greyhound, telling the truth as if there were no choice, yet making a wreck of her personal life and always ready to fling obscenity and insult at offenders." (317) Her bold extraordinary looks, her bravery, and her anger are the things people remembered about Nancy Cunard. They are not the virtues encouraged in women.

Charles Burkhart recalls an interesting scene in the fifties when he brought Nancy to a performance of Sandy Wilson's *The Boyfriend,* in which his friend Hugh Paddick was appearing as an actor. To these young people she was "Lady" Cunard; how could the legend of the twenties still be alive? Princess Margaret was sitting in front of them, but it was the royal Nancy who stole the show by telling the author and the cast, "Oh, no darlings, the Twenties weren't like that!" In her memoir of Norman Douglas she asked "Why this apocryphal smarming over . . . 'the wonderful twenties?' . . . Those 'twenties,' in retrospect, seem not in the least amazing to me; nor can I think of any one word for them. 'Normal,' perhaps?"

But then, I seldom went to England and saw it already with a half foreign eye. My home was France, Paris, in fact. And in Paris where *Surrealisme* had come into being, was a permanent state of *avant-gardisme* whose activities and creativeness were for ever stimulating.[12]

However well *The Green Hat* may fit Nancy Cunard's head, she didn't die; she lived and breathed and became another person. She continued, and, one might say, continues still, to remind people of "things you have never done with women you have never met. . . ." The green hat was worn by some great actresses who each contributed to the aura around images of Nancy Cunard, as her look did to theirs—Katharine Cornell in New York in her first starring role, Tallulah Bankhead in London, and Greta Garbo in the 1928 film version of *The Green Hat,* called *A Woman of Affairs.*

Arlen was indeed briefly Nancy's lover, around the time she had a series of operations that left her unable to conceive, and she was less than kind in describing Huxley's inadequacies as a lover in their (*very* brief) affair. She still wore a leather jacket (it was very a dashing costume for her press

conference on the steps of the Grampion Hotel in Harlem in 1932), sometimes she sported Iris Storm's silver turban, and she spoke in a husky voice.
But Nancy Cunard grew out of the twenties, even if the twenties continues
to claim her walk, her talk, her bad-girl persona as an icon of the age. Nancy
Cunard's *look* combined Noël Coward's sleek, upper-class gay maleness with
Josephine Baker's saucy swagger. Her walk was the walk of a French mannequin. Today we would call it vogue-ing. It is a version of *femme camp*
and the "white Negress" combined, along with the highly artificial style of
the runway model, white top to Josephine Baker's "black bottom." Here is
W. K. Rose's enraptured description:

> Her gestures were inimitable. One involved holding her elbow against her
> side, the arm going straight out in front, and, at the end, the hand raised,
> palm outward, fingers slightly curved—like some Massenet heroine hold-
> ing off the worst. Or standing, she would move her knee out at some un-
> likely angle, her foot slightly raised and turned to complete the line from
> thin hip to long toe. At the same time an elbow would be crooked, so that
> the forearm made a right angle with her side. I know Nancy was aware of
> her "look," for she always arranged herself in one of these stances when I
> started to take a snapshot of her. But there was nothing of the poseur in this.
> Rather, it partook of the gay intelligence and unique style that enchanted
> so many of us. (319)

COOLIE

The Green Hat (1928), Michael Arlen's minor English novel of manners, inspired more than films and plays about femmes fatales. Mulk Raj Anand's
odd and fascinating character in *Coolie* (1936), the impure Mrs. Mainwaring (from a name dropped in *The Green Hat)* and picked up by the Indian
writer in exile), is a Eurasian reader of romances who adores the wicked and
"misunderstood" Cunard figure, Iris Storm. *Coolie* is, to me, a major work
of English and Indo-Anglian fiction; also, it was misread by Indian critics as
unsympathetic with Mrs. Mainwaring, when in fact her desire for an intellectual life is taken very seriously. Anand's novel shows that imperialism is
part of white patriarchy; it turns rebellious white women and orphaned Indian men into whores and thieves. Like African American fictions of the
"tragic *mulatta*" (or mulatto) from the same period, for example, Nella
Larsen's *Passing* (1929), the novel struggles bravely with the relations of race,
gender, and sexuality.[13]

This struggle succeeds, in the odd last chapter of *Coolie,* taking the text politically well beyond the hopeless mimicry and "self-violation" V. S. Naipaul decries in Indian novels "about poor rickshaw drivers" that "fatigue" him with their claims that "poverty is sad" [214–215]. Naipaul bewails the "aimlessness" of Indian fiction, its static negativity suitable to "devotional literature" or the sentimentality of escape literature—he is shocked that romance novels are read even by "male university students" in India, and he quotes Camus to support his claim that the novel is related to a nation's spirit of rebellion, arguing that India's art is formed of fairy tales and fables because there is no ambition but a fatal philosophy of acceptance in the culture (214–216).

Naipaul's annoyance with Indian students who read romantic fiction is doubtless a form of embarrassment as the "British" intellectual searches for his Indian roots. But romance fiction is giving the students something they cannot find in "high culture," just as it serves the needs of white colonials in Anand's Simla. *Coolie* is certainly not a prayer or a meditation, the forms Naipaul finds natural to Indian culture. (One may argue that Virginia Woolf wrote the Static Indian novel in *The Waves*.) Neither is it a fatalistic fable. *Coolie* is a novel in Camus's sense, in that it articulates very clearly the spirit of rebellion in the story of colonialism's attempt to rob Munoo of his masculinity and his caste identity—and its failure. The rickshaw carriers carry the weight of the novel's spirit of national rebellion. Dehumanizing labor has not robbed them of selfhood.

A revolutionary thirties novel, as well as a national fiction in Camus's terms, *Coolie* follows the struggles of the fourteen-year-old orphan Munoo as he is forced out of his Indian hill village to work as a servant in the town, then to the city to work in a pickle factory, then, hitchhiking with the circus to Bombay to work twelve hours a day in an English-owned cotton factory. His feminization as he is taken from his land and made into a servant shows imperialism at work on the bodies of colonized men. A nationalist leader tells the workers to be patient when they are put on "short time." But a Communist Party orator rouses them out of their torpor to go on strike. The anger of the aroused workers is turned into murderous internecine riots by the spread of rumors that Muslims have kidnapped Hindu children. Munoo escapes the violence into the Malabar Hills, where he is run over by Mrs. Mainwaring's car, in a scene so melodramatic (and playing on the scene of the overturned bullock cart in *Kim,* and the scene in the cave of *A Passage to India*) that it startles the reader. Afraid that she will be stoned by the mob for having killed him, the memsahib brings Munoo to the hill station in Simla as a servant.

But Anand's awful Mrs. Mainwaring connects the world of Munoo's "Oriental" passive suffering with the world of "Occidental" ambition, the ambition of the mixed-race woman to assert a self, in this case a sexual self, when what she wanted was a "culture" that was beyond her grasp. The Indo-Anglian writer attempts a critique of the English world that produced the empire that exploits his hero. Anand sees that there is a direct relationship between the aspirations of the emancipated "white" woman and the degradation of the poor orphaned Indian boy. Imperialism offers the white woman power over her servants in exchange for giving up intellectual and moral claims to the struggle for equality and education for herself and her sex. Reading *Coolie* with *The Green Hat,* one acknowledges a certain mutual intertextuality at the heart of these texts. The portraits of "shameful and shameless" women, whose achievement of sexual freedom, even in such comic and tragic fictional forms, makes it possible to understand a stage of Nancy Cunard's life before she took up her political version of "the white woman's burden," and to feel as well what it may have been like to a sensitive Third World boy to have been taken up by such a woman in her later years.

The fact that Mulk Raj Anand does not despise an English popular romance like *The Green Hat* shows him struggling with the notion of what woman's freedom can mean, not an easy question in either English or Indian cultures, still less in the "Black Atlantic" world of the African diaspora that the real Nancy Cunard sought to straddle—and complicated by caste and class. Iris Storm, the cigarette advertisement fantasy, is a heroine to Mrs. Mainwaring, descendant of an old Anglo-Indian family of mercenary soldiers, for she is consumed by the desire to be pure white and English, to erase the Muslim washerwoman grandmother from her family tree, to be "pukka." Like Iris, May is ashamed of her desires, and her perverse pleasures are guilty pleasures in Mulk Raj Anand's brilliant novel. She drives a Chevrolet, or, rather, her driver does, except when in Simla, when four coolies carry her and her guests in a rickshaw, the Anglo-Indian version of Iris's Hispano-Suiza. Is woman's freedom to be realized only in sexual terms? Of course Anand is giving us not only a slovenly Anglo-Indian version of the snow princess, Iris Storm (who is the epitome of honor in an English gentleman, after the gentlemen have disappeared), he is also rewriting Kipling's Mrs. Hauksbee in *Plain Tales,* or chronicling the exploits of her successor in Simla at the end of empire. At this point the culture of the Raj has become a mockery of itself; the rickshaw drivers see through the charade. And Anand sees only too well what happens when a woman gives up the struggle for her own freedom in exchange for power over others. Both woman and boy are pawns of their English masters.

In *Coolie* Mrs. Mainwaring reads *The Green Hat* in bed, sipping tea in the Anglo-Indian hill station of Simla, dressed in "a dirty black skirt over her pajamas and a red polo jumper over her nightcoat." This intimate view of the Englishwoman in her colonial bedroom, written by an Indian novelist, is itself transgressive. Readers will be reminded of the disturbing scene with the collar button in *A Passage to India* where a homosexual racial tension is invoked in the bedroom. The "unbuttoned" condition of the Indian in relation to the Englishman in Forster's novel is as suggestive as Mrs. Mainwaring's layers of clothing, suggesting intimate layers of selves that servants see and are supposed to forget. The emancipated white woman's dance with the eyes of African masks in *Banana Bottom* in the middle of the night is also invoked.

THREE WEEKS: HOW TO BECOME AN ADVENTURESS

As the fictional Mrs. Mainwaring reads *The Green Hat* in bed, identifying with Iris Storm's sexual adventures, the young Nancy Cunard, not quite twelve years old, in the hothouse atmosphere of her mother's country houseparties at Nevill Holt—where the rich met the aristocratic for luxury and sex while her father was away shooting in Scotland—smuggled into her room the scandalous novel of the time, Elinor Glyn's *Three Weeks*. She was in heaven. She had found her type, a woman she could aspire to becoming, the audacious "temptress . . . the green-eyed lady with red hair who spent so much time on a tiger-skin." (*GM*, 56) The child who became the icon of outrageousness signifying the sinfulness of "The Twenties" and the model for the heroines of all kinds of fictions of the period from Huxley's *Point Counter Point* to Wyndham Lewis's *The Roaring Queen*,[14] had found an "authentic" style in a silly novel of an earlier decade: "My week with *Three Weeks* in bed in the clandestine hours of the dawn was a very great enjoyment. So that was an adventuress—beautiful, perfidious, dashing, and exactly what I wanted to know about! She blazed awhile across the repressions of my childhood. It also chanced that *Three Weeks* was the very first novel I read." (*GM*, 56) The outrage caused by the idea of an innocent girl reading a book so closely related to what was going on around her at Nevill Holt was enormous. Her governess reported her and punished her in scenes fictionalized by Wyndham Lewis in *The Roaring Queen*. Her mother raged. George Moore defended her. At the same age he had read Miss Braddon's scandalous *Lady Audley's Secret* just as "eagerly, passionately, vehemently," and he was in disgrace with the grown-ups for coming to the rescue of the little girl, who was "crimson with defiance," and he was forever, despite subsequent failures to be anywhere near politically correct by her standards, remembered as an ally against authority. The two Nancys meet nicely in this reminiscence, the dashing creature of society fiction (as both reader and written-about), and the Angry Young Woman of the thirties. Lady Cunard flaunts her lovers in her husband's house and instructs the governess to beat her daughter for reading about a woman like her mother. What does the daughter of such a conservative adventuress do? She becomes a radical adventuress.

COLONIAL MASCULINITY

Mulk Raj Anand's portrait of Mrs. Mainwaring is as devastating as his creation of the drunken, brutal foreman of the Sir George White cotton factory, Jimmie Thomas. Like the heroine of *The Green Hat,* she is "frigid," in

> her curious coldness of mind. . . . Her warmth, her ardor, her immense capacity for desire, must have been due to the blood of the pagan Indian grandmother in her. . . . She indulged in a strange, furtive, surreptitious promiscuity. . . . If her mind had not been reacting against the deep-rooted sin of sex, she might have had an integrity of character which would have saved her . . . vacillating between a belief she felt to be wrong and a desire which was continually insistent, she became a bitch to all the dogs that prowled round her bungalow" [252].

She marries a German to whom she is the exotic other, divorces him for Aga Raza Ali Shah, a Persian captain in the Nawab's army, and a poet who, in the words of the narrator, "really loved her and would have made her happy, since he was a better lover than any she had met" [I rather like this touch of sexual chauvinism], but she blackmails Guy Mainwaring into marriage, in "her ambition to regain her English nationality" [250]. Back in Bombay, her older children deposited in English schools, Mrs. Mainwaring avoids her husband as much as possible, cultivates her health with food reform fads and doctors, and goes to Simla—for her the hill country means luxury and entertainment.

The narrative of Munoo's life throughout the novel has presented Indian women as long-suffering and self-sacrificing, though their tempers vary from good to bad. His mother dies from overwork, and poverty makes his aunt curse him and send him away. His mistresses when he works as a servant are either loving and kind or overworked scolds. They nurse him in illness and comfort him, and so does the wife of his friend. He visits a prostitute with another friend, a wrestler, but goes away in tears, as earlier he had been aroused by the sight of young Sheila, the daughter of his master, in her wet, clinging garments in the bath. (Taken from the fields into the house, he is supposed to suppress his masculinity, but no one teaches him his new role.) The Englishwoman's lust confuses him:

> He was to her a young boy with a lithe, supple body, with a small, delicate face, and with a pair of sensitive poet's eyes. "What is your age, boy?" she asked him. "Fifteen, Memsahib," he had answered. And she had looked into his dark eyes for a moment with her own dark brown ones, pinched him on the arm with a playful flourish of her long, thin hands, patted him on the forehead, drawing her olive-ivory, Modigliani face backwards till it compressed her thin lips to a voluptuous pout, smiled at him and giggled. For a boy of fifteen was just what she wanted. (250)

The picture Anand creates of the white woman grooming her servant boy's hands is a devastating commentary on the mutual dependency and degradation of mistress and servant in the empire. His hands have been taken from work in the fields and hers from useful work in England to idleness in India. Munoo responds to her advances as she gives him a manicure, "carelessly undraping her right leg before him, . . . in an orgy of tears and kisses" [259]. Angrily she sends him away, and punishes him by ordering only three professional "boys" to carry her rickshaw, Munoo, her servant, to be the fourth. It is carrying the rickshaw that kills him. He begins to spit blood and soon dies of consumption at fifteen, with his friend Mohan at his deathbed assuring him that he is a brave lad. Friendship is what sustains the orphan boy through all his trials, and, despite his small and slender body, he thinks of himself as one of the warrior race of Hindus because of his caste. His "brother" returns him to Indian identity and masculinity as he is dying, wiping away the exhausted, humiliated feminized creature the empire has made of him.

The English "have a caste system more rigid than ours," the rickshaw coolies say among themselves. "Any angrezi woman whose husband earns twelve hundred rupees a month will not leave cards at the house of a woman whose husband earns five hundred. And the woman whose husband earns five hundred looks down on the woman whose husband earns three hundred" [278]. Mohan tells the rapt coolies, looking on at the dance in the Viceregal Lodge, the underside of the story, the servant's tale: "The women perspire in their tight frocks and their underclothes get wet. And the men are uncomfortable in their trousers as they flirt with other people's

wives" [278]. Mulk Raj Anand tells the reader about the Reverend J.
Fordyce, who invented the rickshaw in Simla, and not, as Westerners suppose, some decadent Indian maharajah—"it was not difficult to train the
coolies to run like horses," he writes, and "the genius of Western man for
technical achievement" improved vastly on the original model. "The usual
length of the Simla rickshaw is nine feet, including the shaft, and the breadth
is four feet. The weight is normally 260 to 360 lb, exclusive of the weight
of the ladies and gentlemen who ride in them" [262]. This passage, with its
cameo portrait of the reverend and its factual guidebook tone, mocks (rev-
erently) the tourist bits in Anglo-Indian novels, describing the savage customs of the natives, sati, or women's lives in the harem.

Like E. M. Forster, Anand shows India as "a veritable paradise for the
white woman. . . . For India was the one place in the world where servants
were still servants. . . . One could hire a rickshaw for fourpence an hour. . . .
Why, here were all the luxuries and amenities of the West at the knockdown
prices of the East, so that even Golders Green and Ealing lived like Mayfair
and Picadilly" [262]. The white woman's sexual exploitation of the man
of color is a part of her privilege, and Anand uses Mrs. Mainwaring's
identification with the metropolitan Iris Storm from *The Green Hat* in his
tale of an adolescent Indian boy's degradation into a rickshaw coolie at the
hands of a (confused, pleasure-seeking) memsahib. The English romance
novel provides her with the vicarious justification for her seduction of
Munoo—that all the noble white men are dead—as well as a way to imagine whiteness and promiscuity as synonymous with a theatricalized tragic
upper-class identity:

> And yet she felt she was like Michael Arlen's Iris Storm, a much-
> misunderstood woman. "Why didn't the world understand," she said, "how
> a woman gives herself in love, in pity, in tenderness, in playfulness and in a
> hundred different moods? What right had people to judge one? Why can't
> I give myself to this boy?" she asked. The regular curves of his young body,
> its quick sudden flashes of movement, stirred the chords of her being in a
> strangely disturbing manner. But she, more than Iris Storm, had a pagan
> body and a Chislehurst mind. And she blamed the air of Simla which so
> conduced to thoughts of pleasure. (258)

Reading these passages, as well as others in which the emancipated
woman attaches herself to young poets in Bohemian London and Bombay,
one begins to imagine from their point of view what Nancy Cunard's later
life was like with her black lovers and her young Spanish poets, her class,

caste, and money making such relationships possible. The "Chislehurst mind" passage is a quote from *The Green Hat*. But it is not clear what either the Armenian immigrant writer meant by this or what the exiled Indian writer meant by quoting it. Are we to imagine woman's desire only in terms of sin and guilt? But neither Iris nor Mrs. Mainwaring are shown really wringing their hands. Anand attributes Mrs. Mainwaring's sexuality to her Indian grandmother's genes. Arlen quotes Conrad—"[S]he was of all time. . . . She was, when the first woman crawled out of the mud of the primeval world. She would be, when the last woman walks toward the unmentionable end." (21) This evolutionary discourse clearly, connects Iris (and Nancy Cunard), though perhaps unconsciously, to the African woman in the "heart of darkness."

Certainly the penniless men who lived with Cunard often must have experienced her "pity" and "tenderness" toward them in the way Munoo does his English colonial Memsahib's advances, kind and loving one minute and cruel the next, in confusing the roles of mistress and servant or patroness and artist with the role of lovers. Anand's fictional critique of such women is more sexually explicit than E.M. Forster's in *A Passage to India,* but Forster leaves the reader with the feeling that the horrors of imperialism are entirely the fault of white women, while Anand makes clear the connection between inter-racial sex or the white woman's impurity and the colonialist exploitation of labor and appropriation of land. The Indian novelist, as opposed to the Englishman, gives the white woman a history, and the reader is told of her thwarted desires—for a university education and then to become an artist. She "blackmails" a rich man into marrying her, but she is herself "blackmailed" into trading her desire to work in London for a life of exotic leisure in the colonies. It is a drama one thinks was very often enacted in the empire's relationship with aspiring women. *Coolie* dramatizes the relationship between the native servant and the semiemancipated European woman, the sadomasochistic rituals and role-playing demanded of them by empire, a deadly carnival dance of the downtrodden with the unfree.

THE EMPIRE WRITES BACK

The last chapter of *Coolie* builds a platform for the victims of empire to talk back to Europe. The last chapter lifts the novel from the level of the sad and sentimental Indian-Dickensian tale of oppression that bores Naipaul. It connects the island with the Subcontinent by trying to enter the mind of the Other—in this case, Mrs. Mainwaring, at the other end of the social scale from Munoo, as Virginia Woolf's Septimus Smith is the opposite and double of Mrs. Dalloway. May Mainwaring is given a history; her food re-form faddism and her "furtive" promiscuity are imagined as products of her uprootedness as a "white" victim of the politics of colonialism, just as Munoo's decline is symbolic of the destruction of Indian village life.

Imagine a version of *Mrs. Dalloway* called *Tommy*—with its focus on the decline of the English common soldier, Septimus Smith, with the story of Mrs. Dalloway as a subplot. *Coolie* is *Mrs. Dalloway* turned upside down, with its main text recording the destruction of the body and soul of a "sub-altern subject." Narratively speaking, in *Coolie* Munoo is given the deep inner life that belongs to Mrs. Dalloway in Woolf's novel [which distracts readers into thinking she's the heroine] as Mrs. Mainwaring is pictured mired in materialism, assumed by the reader to be the cause of Munoo's death and not a fellow victim. But *Coolie* is much more subtle than its critics. The excess of the last chapter bursts out of the well-tempered (and -edited) prose and neat structure of the body of the book to link the mixed-race woman and the casual laborer as human beings—"dingy" human be-ings, Michael Arlen would say—destroyed by colonialism, as Septimus and his generation are destroyed by a war of imperial rivalry.

Mrs. Mainwaring is actually a native of the Subcontinent, the daughter of generations of white adventurers in the paid service of various Indian armies, but she desperately wants an English national identity. The romance novelist is only too happy to oblige. Munoo's identity is with his Kshatriya caste of Hindu warriors, despite his utter poverty and homelessness and his physical fragility. Both woman and boy are, in a sense, romantically cast by their author as high-caste outcasts of empire. If she had been provided with an inner life as rich as Kim's, Mrs. Mainwaring's adventures in sex might have made a stirring tale. Alas, she reads *The Green Hat*.

But Mrs. Mainwaring is not merely the object of the Indian writer's sat-ire. She is not as ridiculous or as unsympathetically portrayed as Forster's mendacious memsahibs or the bungling or brutal Burtons and Turtons in *A Passage to India*. Anand is eager to explore the results of the empire's social upheavals as well as to enter the discourse of racial hybridity. As a Eurasian with "dusky" skin, Mrs. Mainwaring attracts another hybrid figure, Major Marchant, the health officer of Simla, an Indian Christian, a cobbler's son who changes his name from the low-caste "Mochi" in England, where he learns to speak and regard himself as a perfect English gentleman. Anand associates Marchant's stinginess and incompetence with his mixed back-ground. Mrs. Mainwaring longs for an English education, but her literary aspirations are wasted in the search for "pukkahood" among the alienated Anglo-Indians rotting in Bayswater: "She recognized the need to integrate herself with real culture, for these Anglo-Indians lived completely in a void, having won the whole world and lost their souls in the bargain [254]."

But she is seduced by the luxury of India for a white woman and power over servants corrupts her. Her mixed racial background is overplayed as the origin of her immorality as well as her social insecurities. She is the ideal reader of *The Green Hat,* identifying with the "honor" of its romantically doomed outcast English lady. But Anand's Mrs. Mainwaring should be read with Kipling's Mrs. Hauksbee, and more importantly, with Forster's Aziz, as characters created by empire and crossed by it. In the next generation, one imagines, Anand's Mrs. Mainwaring would write novels herself, about star-crossed lovers under the Raj, or even (I'm projecting here) *The Green Sari,* a filmscript for *Masterpiece Theatre.*

It is surprising to see that Saros Cowasjee agrees with critics who find the last chapter of *Coolie* "very near disaster" as a digression into "unjust" chastisement of the Anglo-Indian community. While the critic believes it is fitting that Munoo should end his days in the hill country from which he was driven, he is disturbed by the "pillorying" of Mrs. Mainwaring and her "shady" past and present, which distracts the reader from Munoo's tragic end. But this reading misses the way the compromised "rise" of the "white" woman is linked to the "fall" of Indian masculinity, to show that both are manipulated by "Englishmen." *Coolie* is not only a simple tale of a Hindu peasant boy who dies of overwork and tuberculosis, a caste tragedy. Nor is it only a powerful realist propaganda novel of the thirties, a working-class tragedy, though it is that, too. With its controversial last chapter, so critical of Anglo-Indians in London and Simla, of the sexual habits of the sahibs, their unsuitable and ugly clothing, their invention and improvement of the rickshaw, that backward vehicle thought of as typically Indian, and of English society itself—the novel becomes a cosmopolitan contribution to world literature. Mrs. Mainwaring is a minor character in the way that Peter Walsh is a minor character in *Mrs. Dalloway.* They would make a good pair, actually. Failed artists, obsessed with sex, dancing together at a viceregal dance in Simla, or some other hill station, at the end of empire, almost comic figures in the twilight of what I call in the chapter on the Waves, the post-colonial carnivalesque.[15]

THE WRITER AS THIEF

In a brilliant move, Mulk Raj Anand digresses in this final chapter, as in his disquisition on the rickshaw, into an ethnography of the English and their customs, as if he were writing for a literate Indian readership for the

Indo-Anglian novel (which he knows is not quite there yet, though he anticipates that audience as well as the global audience of postcolonial readers, among whom I count myself) to get his jokes about the "savage" customs of the English colonialists. The last chapter is a great comic turn in its making the English and their strange habits (like dancing, an ancient, classical and highly polished art in Indian cultures: "What is the meaning of pushing a woman about here and there so stiffly?" asks one of the coolies (279).—making the English and their manners and mores the object of sociological commentary. "Look! they are walking about in couples in the garden," says one of the rickshaw carriers. All of Anand's characters, mixed race, Indian or white, are concerned about color and color's relation to caste and status. The description of the viceregal dance from the point of view of the rickshaw coolies is brilliant, and it is one of the things that make it possible to read this novel now.

I imagine Anand writing with some of the "weird light" he describes in the eyes of Mrs. Mainwaring's Muslim servant, Ala Dad, when he sets the Hindu boy to carrying the rickshaw. Ala Dad is a thief, and he is annoyed by how much his mistress knows about India: "This memsahib knew too much. She was a *kali* [black] Mem, *natu* [native]. The real Sahibs did not know the prices in the market. [260]" If he'd known she was a "black mem," he wouldn't have taken the job. "He was going to endure it as long as possible, and see how much she knew, because even the all-knowing did not know all that he knew." The author of *Coolie* is like Ala Dad. His betrayal of "what he knows" about the English in his fiction is not likely to be appreciated. Anand creates the figure of servant under empire as a thief. This is a paradigm of the plight of the native intellectual—the author, like Anand himself—as well as a paradigm of the plight of masculinity under empire. The native intellectual is stranded between two cultures as a translator, in the position of stealing knowledge, the secrets of his own culture, and making them available to the conqueror. His theft from the white woman for whom he works, is a way of retaining his identity, returning something to his people. Mrs. Mainwaring, the *"kali mem,"* is like Ala Dad, the educated Muslim in India. Both are created by empire, turned into thieves and whores by the unbearable stress put on them by the actions of colonialism, and bound together inextricably in hatred, fear, and desire, deflecting the rage of two oppressed groups from their common enemy and exploiter. Native men have their masculinity stolen by being made subservient to white women. White women are depraved by the move from total powerlessness to the seductions of power over men of color. It is time to revive *Coolie* as a subtle and important commentary on colonialism, a great Indian novel, a great Indo-Anglian novel, a great English novel.

The last chapter, like significant passages in other chapters, indulges in such ethnographic descriptions of the Other as punctuate the novels of Kipling or Orwell about India. Except here the Other is white. In *Coolie's* powerful last chapter, the Hindu hero is brought into contact with the impure, with the hybrid woman (clearly a kind of Kali figure) who will preside over his death on an "unreal white night." "We belong to suffering!" is what his friend Hari's wife croons to him when he is in despair, not—I must disagree again with the critics—a passive position approved of by the text, but the cry of the culturally displaced Indian woman. Again, a comparison with *Mrs. Dalloway* is in order.

Munoo is as much of a scapegoat for the prepartition Indian social order as Septimus Smith is for the English. Septimus dies for Mrs. Dalloway's sins, inasmuch as she represents the Home Front in Woolf's novel, for which so many boys and young men sacrificed their lives in World War I. Munoo dies for the sins of the Anglo-English in Simla. He dies from being far too frail to carry a rickshaw up the steep hill, past the military barracks, ascending the Mall to "the straight, prim beauty of the English shops," where empire and commerce meet in the person of the *kali* memsahib. Anand shows how colonialism transforms Munoo's quiet agricultural hill-country home into a playground for Europeans, like Simla—an imitation Brighton where they consume pleasure without having to work for it, or pay European prices. One of the pleasures is reading a novel like *The Green Hat*.

What all the revivals of the plays and the dresses and the dances of the age do not, and perhaps cannot, convey is either the deep despair of the real Nancy Cunard's diaries—like other women of the age she was bereft forever of the men of her generation—or her desperate and intent search for a life's work. It might seem out of place to think of Cunard's life as a kind of *Testament of Youth* to be read with "classics" like Vera Brittain's. But is interesting to consider that Vera Brittain's response to the loss of the men of her time in war was a lifetime's work for feminism and pacifism. The result of Nancy Cunard's experience of the loss of her male friends and comrades was to devote herself to the cause of the emancipation of black peoples.

Samuel Beckett's "shining whore" had a mind of her own, and soon she found a revolutionary politics that appealed to her immense intelligence, and it was that politics that gave her the courage to go on beyond the limitations of that small white English body and face. Left politics took her into the thirties as a blazing radical. Reading Mulk Raj Anand's Mrs. Mainwaring reading Michael Arlen's *The Green Hat* as she identifies with the Nancy Cunard figure, Iris March Storm, I have been reading a crisis of whiteness in England and its empire as the cultural context of the iconization of Nancy

Cunard in the twenties. The white woman "reader of romance" has traded the struggle for emancipation and education in Europe (her political freedom) for sexual freedom and power over servants in the colonies. The male colonial subject has been alienated from his labor in the fields and moved from one menial service job to another as the empire's market dictates, his masculinity and identity at stake as he is placed at the service of white women. The relationship between the two figures, Anand's "coolie" and Arlen's adventuress, is a version of a powerful social dynamic at work between colonized and ex-colonized men and white European women at the end of the twenties and the beginning of the thirties, in particular for this narrative the African students and Spanish peasants who served as Nancy Cunard's lovers. In the interest of defusing the issues, it also allows me not only to place Nancy Cunard in her period but to approach the cultural meaning of her long life as vamp/vampire in modernist primitivism: it enables me to look at the image from a new and different perspective, and, by moving the scene from idealized primitive "Africa" to fictional "India" to reduce some of the anxiety, polarization and partisanship which still surfaces around the problem of the figure Cunard created with her "Black Man and White Ladyship."

Coda

How to Recognize a Public Intellectual

When I say that in about April 1934, human character changed, I am revising Virginia Woolf's declaration of a revolution in (bourgeois European) seeing, engendered by the 1910 Cézanne show in London. Nancy Cunard's huge collaborative book, *Negro,*—an anthology of writing, photographs, music, drawings, ethnographies, and poems from Africa and its diasporas—signifies another change in the way certain white people might have seen the world at the time of its publication by Wishart in London in 1934. As a major thirties documentary, *Negro* gathered hundreds of writers to explode the myth of the racial inferiority of blacks. Cunard's work and the cultural work of the book are part of a lost legacy of active public intellectuals, Africans, West Indians and South Asians who worked with London leftists as a new breed of public intellectuals with an international perspective. One could argue that the three-dimensionality of cubism that Woolf and Roger Fry found so exciting in 1910 had been discovered by Western artists in Paris in their encounter with African art. That same three-dimensionality was evident in the hundreds of drawings and photographs in *Negro*. But now the reader had no choice but to see that the artists were black.

When Nancy Cunard finished her book and left the printing press to walk out of London to meet the hunger marchers from Jarrow, she had managed to produce a major paradigm shift in western culture. There was no longer any excuse for empire now that Africans could be seen in *Negro* as the authors of such sophisticated art. This very impressive book was evidence that black people were not racially inferior. Africans and their descendants, and by extension, other peoples of color, must now be accepted as sharing that quality Woolf called "human character." In addition Nancy Cunard, George Padmore, and the other black intellectuals who made the *Negro* anthology must be recognized as public intellectuals and no longer dismissed as outside agitators. Seven decades have passed, and it is time to reclaim this heritage.

To Nancy Cunard in the thirties Africans and the starving working classes of England were linked by their common humanity. But to others both groups remained as inhuman as Woolf's Victorian leviathan cook, "formidable, silent, obscure, inscrutable." What was it that broke the racial taboo in one white woman writer and not the other?

Both Cunard and Woolf knew Mulk Raj Anand. And Cunard was very close to the African and West Indian intellectuals in London at the time, in particular, Padmore. To Cunard they were all members of an international Left. Virginia Woolf and her husband were also members of the Left intelligentsia. But their personal lives and their political lives did not mix in the ways Cunard's did. They may have passed Claude McKay at the 1917 Club or at the exhibition of Negro Art, but they never met. The cultural life of Bloomsbury in the thirties has been written as if there were no blacks or Indians in it, and as if the women in Bloomsbury, and even then her social and critical ideas are not taken seriously. Nancy Cunard is not on the map of English intellectual life in this period at all. In spring 2002 she was present in two major London exhibits, the Spanish Civil War Exhibit at the Imperial War Museum, and the Paris, Capital of the Arts, Exhibit at the Royal Academy. The seldom-seen sleek bronze version of Brancusi's elegant abstract sculpture called *Nancy Cunard* was captioned by a dismissive reference to her as an heiress and a socialite. The Spanish Civil War exhibit made few concessions to women, except for the fact that La Passionaria's very small black dress hung from the ceiling. Showing, courtesy of Hugh Ford, Cunard's own copy of *Authors Take Sides on the Spanish Civil War,* the exhibit's caption mentions Cunard as merely one of the organizers of the classic protest pamphlet, when she did all the work herself, and says nothing of her tremendous contribution, in poetry and journalism, to the struggle against Franco and fascism.

Authors Take Sides is the center of most discussions of the literature of the thirties. Critics (and libraries) not only fail to acknowledge Cunard's authorship, they discuss only the signatories who were famous writers. One of Cunard's brilliant coups in this pamphlet was that she included statements by black intellectuals C.L.R. James, George Padmore, and Marcus Garvey, a fact never discussed by historians of the period, but a fact that seems revolutionary to us now. She also included a statement by the Indian writer Mulk Anand.

If Cunard, the poet and activist, is dismissed as an heiress, Mulk Raj Anand is not described at all. And yet he was at the center of Bloomsbury cultural life in the thirties and forties. It is my opinion that the study of the period would be greatly enriched by wresting it from the hands of those who leave out the women and the people of color who were active in the struggle for social change in Britain. It is important for students to know that leftists in the thirties were not all leviathans on the questions of race, gender, and class. Not all their hearts were dark.

Re-placing Anand's *Coolie, Untouchable,* and his World War I novel, *Across the Black Waters,* along with Cunard's anthology *Negro* onto our reading lists, along with the work of Eliot, Lawrence, Forster, both Woolfs and Orwell, would take us a long way toward seeing that there was a brief period of racial progress in Britain in the thirties. It would also make clear that the critics before us deliberately left us in the dark about the presence of black and South Asian intellectuals on the cultural scene. Now we want to know the name of the "fine Negress" and we want to read what she wrote. Many black women writers may be found in *Negro.* Ironically, Mulk Raj Anand was published only when Forster provided an introduction—and that introduction still prefaces the reader's approach to *Untouchable.*

In *Conversations in Bloomsbury* (reprint 1981) Anand remembers a London cultural scene in which Nancy Cunard was a respected activist intellectual and T. S. Eliot and the Woolfs surprised him with their love of empire and Kipling. He wrote and read proofs for *The Criterion* and for the Hogarth Press. Cunard railed at him about Untouchables: "To think a truly great people could fall so low as to throw millions into dustbins," she said (38). He was sweating "from the confusion of having to accept the blame, even though I was not responsible for the discrimination," and decided then that what she was doing for the Negroes should be done for the Untouchables. It is perhaps hard for the cynical reader of today to imagine this conversation in a Bloomsbury that has been represented as apolitical. When Anand told Cunard the story of Ghandi's being turned out of a first class compartment on a South African train, she replied, "Nothing like a personal insult to make you into a rebel." Anand agreed, remembering "how seven stripes of the cane in Amritsar in 1919 had made me hate British rule."

It is unsettling to see Leonard Woolf through the eyes of one to whom he talked about the big breasts of women in the Kandyan Hills in Sri Lanka. Though E. M. Forster helped him personally, when he gave a lecture at the Indian Students Union, Forster coughed and choked but didn't answer the Indian leader Krishna Menon's question about whether there was a political cause behind *Passage to India*. Mulk Raj Anand wrote to me in 1997:

My novel *Coolie* was written from a wordy quarrel with T. S. Eliot. I used to do short notes for *Criterion* magazine. One day, at teatime, Eliot said that "Kipling's novel *Kim* [was] the first fiction on India he had read." I had read the novel before going to London in 1925. I was immature and naive, but I had felt that Kipling's orphan boy hero was a fantasy of himself when he was growing up in Lahore [India] where his father had been principal of the School of Art. . . . I was so stunned by Eliot's admiration for this pseudo-hero orphan that I went to my room and started writing about the real orphan boy whom I had known in Kangra Valley of the Punjab Himalayas and later in Amritsar. . . . I had already published *Untouchable* when this incident about Eliot's praise of *Kim* happened. This novel is written from passionate protest about the millions of children growing up in hovels in big cities of India, rolling tobacco bidis, or working as house servants or offering to polish shoes."

Anand wrote that some critics thought the novel was "communist propaganda" because he showed

the coolies in Shimla [*sic*] under the shadow of the lofty Viceregal Lodge. . . . But, from inside me, I felt that, unless I was able to relate the plight of the coolies to the Viceroy's summer capital, my symbolic reactions to imperial rule would not be reflective of the real situation of pervasive imperial might and the whole crushed humanity spread out on the vast land.

I would like to read students' papers comparing *Coolie* with *Kim* and *Untouchable* with *Sons and Lovers*. *Across the Black Waters* relieves us from the repetitions of most World War I novels. In the classroom the *Negro* anthology gives us back the words and images of a whole generation of public intellectuals and starts us off to recover one of the most important Pan-African diasporic discourses of the thirties. It was the moment when Bloomsbury met the young radicals of the colonies, when some white hearts struggled out of darkness, when women and people of color became public intellectuals without the anxiety that hounds the self-appointed guru Bernard, of *The Waves*. The listener, collared by Bernard on a ship out to Africa, has returned to England. He speaks. Then she speaks.

Notes

I. THE EMPIRE IS WRITTEN

1. The Non-Jewish Jew is a figure described by Isaac Deutscher in his eponymous book.
2. Leonard Woolf, *Empire and Commerce in Africa: A Study in Economic Imperialism* (London: Labour Research Department and George Allen & Unwin, 1920).
3. Phyllis Lassner, *Colonial Strangers: Women Writing the End of the Empire* (New Brunswick, N.J.: Rutgers University Press, forthcoming).
4. After this was written I was invited to write an entry on Cunard for the *DNB* through the kind offices of anthroplogist Helen Calloway.
5. Michael Arlen, *The Green Hat* (New York: Doran, 1924).
6. Mulk Raj Anand, *Untouchable* (1933; reprint, Penguin, 1986).
7. C.L.R. James, *Minty Alley* (1936; reprint, Jackson: University Press of Mississippi, 1997).
8. See the recent work of my students, Gay Wachman, *Lesbian Empire: Radical Crosswriting in the Twenties* (New Brunswick, N.J.: Rutgers University Press, 2001), and Robin Hackett, *Sapphic Primitivism: Productions of Race, Class, and Sexuality in Key Works of Modern Fiction* (New Brunswick, N.J.: Rutgers University Press, 2003), where these theories are brilliantly argued. Their prizewinning CUNY dissertations (1999, 2000) were the result of a very stimulating intellectual collective, our own form of crosswriting with one another over the last several years, as we gave papers at conferences and tried out our ideas. Their influence on me is certainly as strong as mine on them and theirs on each other.
9. Sinkwan Cheng, "Decolonizing the Body From the Law of Private Property: The Mohammedan Women Hunger Strikers in Forster's *A Passage to India,*" in Sinkwan Cheng, *Law, Justice and Power: Between Reason and Will* (Palo Alto: Stanford University Press, forthcoming).
10. Mary Louise Pratt, *Imperial Eyes: Travel Writing and Transculturation* (London and New York: Routledge, 1992), 7.
11. Jane Marcus, "Britannia Rules *The Waves,*" *Decolonizing Tradition: New Views of 20th Century British Canons* (Champaign, IL.: University of Illinois Press, 1992).
12. Jane Goldman, *Critical Guide to Virginia Woolf* (New York: Columbia University Press, 1998).

13. Robin Hackett, "Supplanting Shakespeare's Rising Sons: A Perverse Reading Through Woolf's *The Waves.*" Tulsa Studies in Women's Literature. 18(2):263–80. 1999 Fall.

14. Leonard Woolf, *Empire and Commerce in Africa* (London: Labour Research Department and George Allen & Unwin, 1920).

15. Nancy Cunard, "Black Man and White Ladyship," and *Negro.* (London:Wishart, 1934).

16. Shari Benstock, *Women of the Left Bank.* (Austin: University of Texas Press, 1987).

2. "A VERY FINE NEGRESS"

The research and writing of this chapter were done with the generous support of a Guggenheim Fellowship and a Visiting Fellowship at Clare Hall, Cambridge University. My thanks to librarians in the Rare Book Room, Cambridge, U.K. for help with the James Stephen antislavery pamphlets, Lionel Carter at the South Asian Studies library for some Leonard Woolf materials and especially Bet Inglis at Sussex for courteous and generous help in the Monks House Papers on Leonard Woolf and Ceylon, and Trekkie Parsons for permission to quote. I am grateful as well to those who responded with spirit to its arguments as they were shaped in lectures at the Universities of Bergen, Oslo, Uppsala, Anglia Polytechnic (in two different versions), Birmingham, Greenwich, Cambridge, Jerusalem, and Frankfurt, as well as Bard College. Discussions with Lisa Marcus, Mary Hamer, and Claire Tylee have been helpful to this project, which was been reconceived in dialogue with the recent work of Catherine Hall, *White, Male and Middle Class: Explorations in Feminism and History* (London: Routledge, 1992), Vron Ware, *Beyond the Pale: White Women, Racism and History* (Verso, 1992), and Paul Gilroy, *The Black Atlantic: Modernity and Double Consciousness* (Cambridge, Mass.: Harvard University Press, 1993), and Beverley Bryan, Stella Dadzie, and Suzanne Scafe, *Heart of the Race: Black Women's Lives in Britain* (London: Virago, 1986).

1. *A Room of One's Own* (1929; reprint, New York: Harcourt Brace, 1957, p. 52). Virginia Woolf's work came out of copyright briefly in the UK in 1993, and there are now several new editions of the text, notably an Oxford publication edited by Morag Shiach with *Three Guineas,* 1993, and a Penguin, same date, edited by Michele Barrett, also including *Three Guineas.* The collected feminist introductions to the Penguin reprints are available in the United States in a volume edited by Julia Briggs, general editor of the series (London: Virago, 1994). See also *Women and Fiction: The Manuscript Versions of A Room of One's Own,* edited by S. P. Rosenbaum (Oxford, England, and Cambridge, Mass.: (Blackwell Shakespeare Head, 1992).

2. For a discussion of Virginia Woolf as *flâneuse* in relation to Walter Benjamin, Kafka, and Baudelaire, see "Thinking Back Through Our Mothers" in my *New Feminist Essays on Virginia Woolf* (London: Macmillan, 1981).

3. See my *Virginia Woolf and the Languages of Patriarchy* (Bloomington: Indiana Uni-

versity Press, 1987), for a full discussion of *A Room*'s concern with the tropes of interruption as they relate to the campaign for woman suffrage in England.

4. Moira Ferguson, *Subject to Others: British Women Writers and Colonial Slavery, 1670–1834* (New York: Routledge, 1992).

5. Paper presented at the conference "Modernity, Culture and the Jew," University of London, May 1994. The conference was notable for the absence of reference to the work of feminist theory, Gender Studies, or Black Studies. Much of the discussion was about the film *Schindler's List,* but no mention was made of the glaring fact that the viewer is offered scenes of sadistic sexual torture of women instead of the expected torture of Jews, a more socially acceptable pornographic pleasure, as a reward for viewing a difficult historical subject, displacing racial terror for the audience.

6. John Stuart Mill, *On the Subjection of Women* (1869, reprint, London: Virago, 1983), p. 145.

7. See Ferguson, *Subject to Others,* and Ware, *Beyond the Pale.*

8. William Thompson, *An Appeal . . .* (1825, reprint, London: Virago, 1983), pp. 67, 84.

9. Mary Wollstonecraft, *A Vindication of the Rights of Women* (1792, reprint, London: Penguin, 1985), p. 286.

10. Mill, *On the Subjection of Women,* p. 147.

11. Ware, *Beyond the Pale,* p. 109.

12. James Stephen, *The Slavery of the British West India Colonies Delineated as it Exists in Both Law and Practice* (London: Butterworth, 1824–1830. This and the following quotations from p. 364. See also Stephen's *Reasons for Establishing a Registry of Slaves in the British Colonies,* London, 1815.

13. For a discussion of the Stephen family's role in English history and the context of the making of *A Room of One's Own,* see "Liberty, Sorority, Misogyny," in my *Virginia Woolf and the Languages of Patriarchy.*

14. Lady Henry Somerset (1851–1921), organizer of the British Women's Temperance Association and friend of Frances Willard of the American WCTU, appears in Vron Ware's *Beyond the Pale* in her excellent cross-cultural study "'To Make the Facts Known': Racial Terror and the Construction of White Femininity." Ware analyzes the two powerful white temperance leaders' opposition to the Anti-Lynching Campaign of the black American journalist Ida B. Wells (1862–1931). In the end Wells pointed out that while the WCTU blamed the Negro for the defeat of Prohibition in the South, not a single colored woman was admitted to the organization. Lady Henry Somerset, of the beautiful Pattle sisters, was related to Virginia Woolf's mother, and her names Adeline and Virginia come from that side of the family. Their origins were in India among the French and "Anglo-Indian" colonial hierarchies. Lady Henry's campaign against alcohol began only after she had been socially ostracized by her own mother and her social circle for leaving her homosexual husband after being abused. For this crime she was

never allowed to see her son, who was taken by her exiled husband's family. This story is not told as an excuse for her defense of Frances Willard's attack on Ida B. Wells, but as another instance of the "monopoly on oppression" problem in the complex histories of white and black women. Lady Henry's intense, loving friendship with the U.S. temperance crusader may have influenced her judgment.

15. Quentin Bell, *Virginia Woolf,* vol. 1, (London: Grafton, 1987), p. 3. James Stephen's second wife was Wilberforce's sister, and he remained dedicated to the antislavery cause, resigning from Parliament when the government would not act on the question. At his death in 1832, Quentin Bell says, his son, Virginia's grandfather, took up the cause: "the protection of the Negro was the grand business of his administration." The white rulers of the colonies attempted to delay and thwart his efforts, according to Bell, but he succeeded in outwitting them and arguing them down. Virginia Woolf, p. 5.) See Peter Freyer, *Staying Power: The History of Black People in Britain* (London: Pluto, 1984), in particular "The Somerset Case," p. 120 ff; and "The Grace Jones Case," p. 130 ff, for a detailed look at the legal questions about slavery in Britain and the debates on whether or not English law applied in the colonies, and if slaves could be considered free English citizens when in England. The Stephens, *père et fils,* were deeply involved in these debates.

16. Freyer, *Staying Power,* pp. 177–178.

17. Leonard Woolf, *Empire and Commerce in Africa: A Study in Economic Imperialism.* (1920; reprint, New York: Howard Fertig, 1968).

18. Paul Gilroy, *The Black Atlantic: Modernity and Double Consciousness* (Cambridge, Mass.: Harvard University Press, 1993), p. 85. Actually Gilroy writes "gender is the modality in which race is lived," reworking Stuart Hall's remark that race is the modality in which class is lived.

19. Freyer, *Staying Power.*

20. Jane Gallop's infamous revelation of her anxious dream about the black U.S. feminist Deborah MacDowell to white critics Marianne Hirsch and Nancy K. Miller, in which she says that MacDowell replaces Lacan in her dreams, erases Deborah MacDowell's power as a rival (sisterhood does not appear to be an option) by hastily pointing out that it's the category of black feminist that haunts her: "for Deborah MacDowell read black feminist critic." (Marianne Hirsch et al., *Conflicts in Feminism.* New York: Routledge, 1988). In their published conversation, she manipulates her listeners into confessing their collective guilt in a gesture that naturalizes white feminist racism and makes it global, thus denying her own ethical responsibility, as well as the historical reality of the fact that there were (and are) many white feminists who were consciously working against racism. The real damage that is done is the denial of the historical reality that black and white feminists had been working together for many years. Gallop's prominence then gives circulation to the false notion that all U.S. white feminists were racist, and her personal anxiety is repeated as history. We can only ask whose interest is served

by Gallop's guilt-sharing gesture? Certainly it is not in the interest of forging future cross racial alliances or the joint production of knowledge. By taking Gallop's dream as its keynote, Elizabeth Abel's massive review essay "Black Writing, White Reading: Race and the Politics of Feminist Interpretation," *Critical Inquiry,* Spring 1993 on black feminist criticism repeats the gesture of globalizing her own misreading of racial categories in a story by Toni Morrison into a shared U.S. white feminist guilt that does not acknowledge any previous alliances between white and black intellectuals and activists in the United States, as in the Civil Rights Movement or the Anti-War movement. The confession of her problem as a reader (the difference in the story is based on class, not race) does not impair her sense of her capacity as a critical bibliographer to determine the worth of all recent work on black women writers. Deborah MacDowell puts in a telling phantom appearance as Jane Gallop's "very fine Negress" and feared rival, or as the ghost of slavery in America. But Abel actually decides to do "Deborah Mac-Dowell's" work as a black feminist critic. It is important that these territorial gestures be noticed and discussed.

21. Those of us who came to feminism from the Civil Rights movement in the United States, and the multi-racial antiwar movement, are surprised by descriptions of feminism as a white middle-class movement hostile to blacks, Asians and chicanas. Jane Gallop's ahistorical fantasy (*Around 1981,* New York: Routledge, 1990), an anxious and innacurate attack on the collective and mutiracial aspects of American feminist criticism, has lately been taken as fact by Europeans and by students. Aside from the fact that it was written from arbitrarily chosen texts rather than studying groups, organizations, meetings, position papers, demonstrations, and the like, this book never indicates what the real issues were in feminist criticism, based as it is on a denial that feminism was first a political practice. It is essential to point out that the book, like the piece in *Conflicts in Feminism,* appears to be a personal alibi for her own absence from the struggle for women's rights and an attempt to discredit the real collective alliances forged in the struggle. It does not take into account the fierce struggles to keep Left feminists out of the university by arguing that feminism was easily assimilated into the academy. What seems most to enrage her is the claim of marginality from blacks, women or leftists. The then jobless Lillian Robinson is often quoted as an authority in Gallop's wholly imaginary projection of the history of feminism from a university chair (mis)readings of random and peculiar texts, without noticing that Robinson's exclusion and demonization utterly undoes her argument. Gallop's fantasy of a feminist history she missed in prime-time reality tries to prove that the collective anthologies of essays, which are a trademark of the movement and were adopted by other groups of intellectuals as well, were as individualistic as the work of one critic working alone for narcissistic acclaim rather than political education. For those who came to feminism after establishing themselves through psychoanalysis or other highly rewarded mainstream theories, it may have seemed that feminism had more power than it did. But the collective work was not and

is not a myth, and Gallop's willful and unfounded assertion that our collective work was a fiction has already caused untold damage to the possibility of a creating a usable history.

22. "Arnold's Ethnographic Politics" presented paper by Robert Young, Oxford University, at the 1994 Warwick Conference in honor of Edward Said. Young points out that Arnold always uses the word "pregnant" when discussing race. He argues that the fear of hybridity, of interracial sex, was at the heart of nineteenth-century European racial science discourses. Seeing 1848 as "the year of the war of the races," he claims that questions of racial knowledge were behind the setting up of academic disciplines and discourses. As such, race is an academic invention, as is racism, and the organizing principle behind all culture.

23. See Aphra Behn, *Oroonoko and Other Writings,* edited with an introduction by Paul Salzman (Oxford World's Classic, 1994). This is the edition used throughout this paper. Many of Salzman's points are made by Vita Sackville-West in *Aphra Behn, The Incomparable Astrea* (London: Gerald Howe Ltd., 1927), though she is not listed in his bibliography. The passage Virginia Woolf lifts for *A Room of One's Own* is from p. 12, as Angela Ingram has reminded me: "The fact that she wrote is much more important than the quality of what she wrote. The importance of Aphra Behn is that she was the first woman in England to earn her living by her pen." And Woolf's character sketch benefits as well from Sackville-West's adoring heroine-worship: "Gay, tragic, generous, smutty, rich of nature and big of heart, propping her elbows on the tavern table, cracking her jokes, penning those midnight letters to her sad lover by the light of a tallow dip—this is the Aphra of whom one cannot take leave without respect" (p. 85).

24. *The Diary of the Lady Anne Clifford,* with an introduction and note by Vita Sackville-West (London: Heinemann, 1923). Vita Sackville-West deeply admired the stubborn, tough administrative qualities of Lady Anne, who liked a legal fight and always won, unlike Vita herself, consolidating her lands and properties all over the country and refusing to sign them over to her husbands, despite tremendous pressure. "Certainly she went through life permanently embattled, whether her quarrel lay with her husbands—for she had two and fought with both of them—with her servants, her tradesmen, or her tenants, to all of whom she spoke her mind on some occasion or other, or with Cromwell, whom she defied, or with Charles II, of whom she disapproved, or with a mere canvasser for parliamentary election, to whom she wrote, "I have been bullied by a usurper, I have been neglected by a court, but I will not be dictated to by a subject" (xxxvi—xxxvii). She spent a fortune suing a tenant whose rent traditionally included a hen, and enjoyed serving him the hen in a victory dinner. Lady Anne was a major counterexample to Woolf's portrait of the Englishwoman as a slave.

25. Lucie Duff-Gordon, *Letters from Egypt* (1865; reprint, London: Virago, 1983), pp. 39–40.

26. See my *Virginia Woolf and the Languages of Patriarchy* for a discussion of Woolf's colonial heritage. Also "Britannia Rules *The Waves,*" in this volume.

27. *International Herald Tribune*, Saturday–Sunday, September 18–19, 1993, p. 1. See Freyer, *Staying Power*, and Paul B. Rich, *Race and Empire in British Politics* (Cambridge, England: Cambridge University Press, 1986, 1990), and Beverlie Bryan et al., *The Heart of the Race: Black Women's Lives in Britain* 2nd ed. (London: Virago, 1989).

28. See *Nancy Cunard: Brave Poet, Indomitable Rebel 1896–1965,* edited by Hugh Ford (Philadelphia: Chilton Book Company, 1968), and Anne Chisholm, *Nancy Cunard* (New York: Knopf, 1979).

29. Leonard Woolf, *Empire and Commerce in Africa.* Wayne Chapman's paper at the 1992 Virginia Woolf Conference in New Haven indicated that Virignia Woolf's participation in the research and writing of this book was extensive.

30. J. H. Willis, Jr., *Leonard and Virginia Woolf as Publishers: The Hogarth Press 1917–1941* (Charlottesville: University Press of Virginia, 1992).

31. See Bonding and Bondage: Nancy Cunard and the Making of the Negro Anthology, in this volume.

32. George Macaulay Trevelyan, (London: Longmans Green, 1926), pp. 260–261. Trevelyan writes that wife-beating was "a recognized right of man," and he cites a popular manual for the treatment of a scolding wife: "He smote her with his fist down to the earth. And then with his foot he struck her in the visage and brake her nose, and all her life after she had her nose crooked that she might not for shame show her visage it was so foul blemished. . . . Therefore the wife ought to let the husband have the word, and to be master."

33. This phrase and the argument it makes derive from Lisa Marcus, "A White Woman is Being Beaten: The Rac(e) ing of Whiteness in Pauline Hopkins's *Contending Forces,*" paper presented at the American Literature Association Symposium on Women Writers, October 3, 1993, San Antonio.

34. For a brilliant analysis of racism see David Theo Goldberg, *Racist Culture: Philosophy and the Politics of Meaning* (Oxford, England: Blackwell, 1993).

35. Virginia Woolf, *Letters,* edited by Nigel Nicolson and Joanne Trautmann (London: Hogarth Press, New York: Harcourt Brace Jovanovich, 1977).

36. Roger Fry, *Vision and Design,* (1920; reprint, Oxford, England: Oxford University Press, 1981).

37. Marianna Torgovnik, *Gone Primitive* (Chicago: University of Chicago Press, 1990), pp. 14–15.

38. Helen Calloway, "Purity and Exotica in Legitimating the Empire: Cultural Constructions of Gender, Sexuality and Race," in *The Colonial State and the Pursuit of Legitimacy: Essays in Honor of A.H.M. Kirk-Greene,* edited by Terence Ranger and Olufemi Vaugh (Oxford, England: Oxford University Press, forthcoming).

39. Claude McKay to C. K. Ogden, May 18, 1920, Ogden Papers, McMaster University, quoted in Josh Gosciak's dissertation, CUNY, 2002.

40. For a discussion of Woolf's interrogation of the idea of whiteness and her representation of the workings of imperialism on a home culture, see Britannia Rules *The Waves*.

41. John MacKenzie, *Propaganda and Empire: The Manipulation of British Public Opinion 1880–1960* (Manchester, England: Manchester University Press, 1984). See also *Anthropology and Photography, 1860–1920* (New Haven, Conn.: Yale University Press, 1993).

42. Ian Jeffrey, *Photography: A Concise History* (London, 1981), pp. 63–64.

43. See *The Diary of Virginia Woolf, vol. 2, 1920–1924.* Edited by Anne Oliver Bell. (New York: Harcourt Brace & Co., 1980). Entry for 3 July 1924, note 2, which says that the Woolfs went to the Empire Exhibition on May 29.

3. BRITANNIA RULES *THE WAVES*

My thanks to Louise Yelin, Patricia Laurence, Mary Ann Caws, James Haule, Regina Barreca's seminar at the University of Connecticut, and Ruth Perry. Thanks also to audiences at Harvard, CUNY Graduate Center; SUNY, Purchase; the University of Hawaii; and Texas A & M, Mary Mathis, and students in my seminar at City College in fall 1987, where this reading of *The Waves* was first worked out.

1. Virginia Woolf, *The Waves* (New York: Harcourt Brace Jovanovich, 1931). It is ironic that a novel that critiques the canon-making process should appear among the first classics in Cambridge Univeristy Press's 1986 World Literature series.

2. See the appendix to Raymond Williams, *The Politics of Modernism,* for the responses of Said and Williams to the question of gender. His well-known attacks on Bloomsbury reveal a need to maintain a muscular macho modernism of the working class. As late as 1965 Leonard Woolf answered Queenie Leavis's claim that Virginia Woolf's novels were not popular with sales figures to show that they were (*Times Literary Supplement* (London), March 2–8, 1990, p. 211).

3. The classic essay on romanticism and *The Waves* is Frank McConnell's "Death Among the Apple Trees," *Bucknell Review* 16, (1968). Also relevant is J. H. McGavran, "Alone Seeking the Visible World," *Modern Language Quarterly* 42 (1981), pp. 265–291, and J. W. Graham, "Mss. Revision and the Heroic Theme of *The Waves,*" *Twentieth-Century Literature* 29 (1983) pp. 312–332. See John Moses' 1988 dissertation, Miami University (Ohio), for further documentation of the passages from romantic poetry incorporated in *The Waves.* When Lytton Strachey read *Jacob's Room* in 1922 he told Woolf she was "very romantic." She replied, "Of course you put your infallible finger on the spot—romanticism. How do I catch it? . . . some of it, I think, comes from the effort of complete representation. One flies into the air." *Virginia Woolf and Lytton Strachey: Letters,* edited by Leonard Woolf and James Strachey (New York: Harcourt, 1956).

4. James M. Haule and Philip H. Smith, Jr., in *A Concordance to The Novels of Virginia Woolf.* (New York: Garland, 1991), cite eleven instances of "O," twelve of "Behold," and five of "alas."

5. Mikhail Bakhtin, *The Dialogic Imagination* (Austin: University of Texas Press, 1981), p. 238. In the monological discourse of *The Waves,* the dialogic operates as Bernard's intertextuality with the "great books" of English culture. Like his hero, Percival, he regards words as quarry that he hunts: "How tired I am of sto-

ries, how tired I am of phrases that come down beautifully with *all their feet on the ground"* (emphasis added).

6. Michel Foucault, *The History of Sexuality, vol. 1, An Introduction,* translated by Robert Hurley (New York: Pantheon, 1978), pp. 103–105. Foucault does not include a category for Louis, the colonial figure, and his exotic sexuality, but this is an appropriate addition.

7. For other popularizations of the new scientific theories Woolf may have read, see Arthur S. Eddington *Space, Time and Gravitation: An Outline of General Relativity Theory* (Cambridge, England: Cambridge University Press, 1921), James Jeans's *Eos, or The Wider Aspects of Cosmogony* (New York: E.P. Dutton, 1929), and his *The Universe Around Us* (Cambridge, England: Cambridge University Press, 1929). The connection between *The Waves,* relativity, and wave mechanics was first suggested to me by Carol Donley.

4. LAUGHING AT LEVITICUS: *NIGHTWOOD* AS WOMAN'S CIRCUS EPIC

This essay was written in 1983–1984 for *Silence and Power: Djuna Barnes, A Revaluation* (Carbondale, IL.: Southern Illinois University Press, 1991), edited by Mary Lynn Broe, but given as a talk and widely cited from manuscript, beginning with Shari Benstock's *Women of the Left Bank,* in dialogue with others working on Bakhtin's idea of carnival, the revision of modernism, Kristeva's concept of abjection, and Freud on the uncanny— and it bears the marks of that historical moment. Versions were read at the 1984 Modern Language Association, American Literature Division; for Shari and Bernard Benstock and their students at Tulsa, Oklahoma; and audiences at the University of Wisconsin, CUNY Graduate Center, New York; Northwestern University, University of Utah, Grinnell College, the University of Houston, the University of Arizona as well as for Susan Lanser and the Georgetown Critical Theory Conference in 1987.

My thanks for the University of Texas (Austin) research grant that allowed me to work at the Barnes collection, McKeldin Library, University of Maryland; Donald Farren and his helpful staff for making the materials needed for this study available to me, and for permission to reproduce materials in the collection, as well as to the Author's League Fund, Herbert Mitgang, holder of the Djuna Barnes copyright. I am indebted to Beverly Stoeltje for introducing me to Bakhtin's work and the circus, and to the students in my Feminist Theory Seminar at the University of Texas (Austin), especially Lee Mellick, Patricia Rezabek, and Ingeborg O'Sickey.

1. Julia Kristeva, *Powers of Horror: An Essay on Abjection* (New York: Columbia University Press, 1982), p. 100.

2. See Mikhail Bakhtin, *Rabelais and his World,* translated Hélène Iswolsky (Bloomington: Indiana University Press, 1984).

3. Mary Douglas, *Purity and Danger* (London: Routledge & Kegan Paul, 1966).

4. The quotations are from Djuna Barnes, *Nightwood,* introduction by T. S. Eliot, who edited the first London, Faber, edition (1936; reprint, New York: New Directions, 1977).

5. See Victor Brombert, *Victor Hugo and the Visionary Novel* (Cambridge, Mass.: Harvard University Press, 1984).

6. Aphra Behn is one of Barnes's few precursors whose work survives. Most women's bawdy humor available to us is oral, as in Bessie Smith and black women's music, but see *Last Laughs: Perspectives on Women and Humor,* edited by Regina Barreca (London and New York: Gordon and Breach, 1988).

7. Emily Coleman's essay, with Djuna Barnes's comments and objections, is in the McKeldin Library, University of Maryland. The Emily Coleman papers are at the University of Delaware.

8. Brombert, *Victor Hugo and the Visionary Novel,* p. 109.

9. For another analysis of Barnes's excremental imagination, see Louise De Salvo's essay on *The Antiphon* also written for *Silence and Power.*

10. Brombert, *Victor Hugo and the Visionary Novel,* p. 116.

11. Michel Thevoz, *The Painted Body* (New York: Rizzoli, 1984).

12. Kenneth Burke, *Language as Symbolic Action* (Berkeley: University of California Press, 1968). Burke notes the God/dog reversal in the last scene of *Nightwood.*

13. Eugène Sue, *The Wandering Jew* (New York: Random House, 1940). A full study of the influence of Eugène Sue on Djuna Barnes remains to be done. It is clear that Sue's career as doctor/sailor/writer is a major source for the character of Matthew O'Connor. The description of Morok, the lion tamer, with his beasts, Judas, Cain, and Death, in chapter 1 of *The Wandering Jew,* begins with a three-sided chapbook illustration of his conversion from beast to human, a savage fleeing from wild animals, transformed to their tamer in the last picture. It is not difficult to imagine the young Djuna Barnes's identification with outsiders deriving from the novel after which she was named. Her early journalism produced memorable portraits of misfits and outsiders and the chapbook or broadsheet is an important motif in her writing and drawing.

14. See Frederic Jameson, *The Political Unconscious* (Ithaca, N.Y.: Cornell University Press, 1981). While I find Jameson's categories valuable for this analysis, one must point out that he does not count feminism as part of the political nor does gender appear in his system. For a good discussion of these issues, see Judith Gardiner's review in *In These Times,* October 28, 1981.

15. Hans Mayer, *Outsiders: A Study in Life and Letters* (Cambridge, Mass.: MIT Press, 1984). Naomi Schor's essay is in *The Female Body in Western Culture,* edited by Susan Suleiman (Cambridge, Mass.: Harvard University Press, 1986).

16. See "Berlin in Person," *Times Literary Supplement* (London), 28 December, 1984, p. 1507. Heinrich Mann, from whose novel of *The Blue Angel* script was taken, was surely an influence on Barnes in *Unrath* and *Der Untertak.*

17. For feminist discussions of the importance of transvestism to women artists, see Susan Gubar, "Blessings in Disguise: Cross-Dressing as Re-Dressing for Female Modernists," *Massachussetts Review* 22.3, Autumn 1981 pp. 477–508; Sandra Gilbert's "Costumes of the Mind," *Critical Inquiry* vol. 7(2), (winter 1980), and Shari Benstock's response to and revision of their arguments in *Women of the Left*

Bank. To this debate among feminist critics on the function of transvestism in women's culture, I would add that Barnes's presentation of a male transvestite as hero is a very clever way of privileging the female. Radclyffe Hall's *The Well of Loneliness* (New York: Covici and Friede, 1928) was clearly an influence on *Nightwood,* and I maintain that the structure of *Nightwood* is based on cabaret "acts." *The Well of Loneliness* also gives a guided tour of gay bars in Paris in the twenties. I believe that the novel's title is a play on the name of a well-known homosexual and lesbian club in London in the twenties, called the Cave of Harmony after the club in Thackeray's *The Newcomes,* famous for impersonations, improvisations, and dirty songs. Radclyffe Hall's tour includes Monsieur Pujol of the Ideal, who "collected inverts," and entertained his straight clients with photographs of his gay customers in a sinister locked leather notebook in which he cataloged his "collection" (Hall, pp. 441–442). Like Dr. O'Connor he tells stories, but their object is not the same. At Le Narcisse, the Patron is a transvestite who sings both sentimental and lewd songs. At Alec's, the whole "miserable army" of inverts is gathered. He sells cocaine to his "*filles,*" and Stephen is called "*Ma Soeur*" by a dying young addict, of whom she thinks, "It's looking for the God who made it" (Hall, p. 449). The contrast between Hall's tragic, despairing vision and Barnes's comic approach is instructive. Barnes never reifies her outcast figure into an "it." Yet Angela Ingram points out that Hall's line repeats the earlier scene, in which the fox is hounded to death as "scapegoat" and she is referring to all outcasts as hounded beasts, a view she and Barnes might have shared.

18. The figure of the lesbian lover as a fair-tale prince or page is a common one in women's writing. In Antonia White's *Frost in May* (1933; reprint, New York: Dial, 1982), the heroine's adored friend in a Catholic girls' school in England, Léonie, is seen as "a young prince, pale and weary from a day's ride, with his lovelocks carelessly tied in a frayed ribbon. . . . Her feeling for Léonie was one of pure admiration, the feeling of page for prince, too cold and absolute to be called love" (White, pp. 79, 80). Antonia White was part of the Peggy Guggenheim circle at Hayford Hall, where Djuna Barnes wrote part of *Nightwood.*

19. Sigmund Freud, "The Uncanny" (1919), in *On Creativity and the Unconscious* (New York: Harper & Row, 1958), pp. 122–61, 123.

20. See Nancy Harrison's 1983 University of Texas thesis on Jean Rhys.

21. For "The Sandman," see the *Selected Writings of E.T.A. Hoffmann,* edited and translated by Leonard J. Kent and Elizabeth C. Knight, 2 vols. (Chicago: University of Chicago Press, 1969). The tales are in vol. 1.

22. See review of Freud-Fliess letters in the *New York Times Magazine,* March 17, 1985. As Freud repressed physical evidence of father-daughter incest to write his seduction theory, so Marx rejected earlier nonrational socialisms to create Marxism as a science. Consequently, in each ordering and theorizing of self and history, an important component is left out and made other. After Freud, the real incest victims are neglected until quite recently. "Other" socialisms were denied by Marxists. See Barbara Taylor's *Eve and the New Jerusalem: Socialism and Feminism*

in the Nineteenth Century (Cambridge: M.A.: Harvard University Press, 1993), for feminist socialisms in Pre-Marx English history.

23. I am indebted here to a paper read by Gareth Stedman Jones at Texas in March 1985 on the nonrational origins of socialism in French thought. In a type-script of *Nightwood* in the McKeldin Library, after Robin is called "the infected carrier of the past," the phrase "the *magnetized* beastly" is crossed out; it is clearly a reference to the magnetic theory of somnambulism of Anton Mesmer. Bernard Benstock points out that Marx discusses these thinkers in *Capital*. See "Making Capital Out of Vampires," *Times Higher Education Supplement* (London), June 15, 1984.

24. I suspect that both her father, Wald Barnes, and her grandmother, Zadel Barnes, were deeply interested in Fourier, Mesmer, Hugo, and Sue, and that the family experiments in living on their farm owed much to the influence of Fourier's ideas.

25. This information was supplied by Nancy Levine; Wald Barnes's novels and musical compositions are in the possession of Kerron Barnes and Duane Barnes.

26. Freud says that the mother of a girl he had cured regarded psychoanalysis itself as "uncanny." Helplessness causes one to feel "uncanny," he argues, and tells the story of being lost in the streets of a town in Italy on a hot afternoon. Three times, while trying to get out, he returns to the same place, a street where "nothing but painted women were to be seen at the windows" (*The Uncanny*, 143). This hardly needs a feminist analysis. Though Freud says he has "drifted into this field of research half involuntarily" (*The Uncanny*, 160), I suggest he was writing the male fear of being castrated by the father as a cover for his own guilt at having mishandled his women patients. For a brilliant analysis of the power of the mesmerized woman and of Freud's relation to hysterical women patients, see Nina Auerbach's *Woman and the Demon: The Life of a Victorian Myth* (Cambridge, Mass.: Harvard University Press, 1982).

27. Jean Rhys and Diana Atill, *Smile Please: An Unfinished Autobiography.* (New York: Penguin, 1995), pp. 20–21.

28. The typescripts *Bow Down* and *Nightwood* are in the McKeldin Library, University of Maryland. When it is possible to quote from T. S. Eliot's letters, a full study of his cuts and corrections to *Nightwood* should be made, with the aim of restoring and publishing the text as Barnes wanted it. While Eliot did have to think of the censor, many passages could be restored. He corrected her French and German, marked out many passages on Jews, on King Ludwig, and a scene with the doctor in jail, as well as passages that might be considered obscene. He crossed out on page 202, "You can lay a hundred bricks and not be called a bricklayer, but lay one boy and you are a bugger." He told her to think over whether she wanted to say of Jenny, "when she fell in love it was with a perfect fury of accumulated dishonesty," and told her to take out Matthew calling himself a faggot, a fairy, and a queen in the scene in the carriage. He crossed out "and the finger of our own right hand placed where it best pleases" and the McClusky passages

on a girlish boy in the war. In the description of the "Tuppenny Upright" he crossed out "letting you do it," but she restored it in 1949. He wanted to change "obscene" to "unclean" on the last page, and said he couldn't understand why Robin had candles in the chapel at night. Barnes's penciled note says "Sample of T. S. E.'s 'lack of imagination' (as he said)." Also cut is a homosexual courtroom joke in which the judge asks, "What do I give a man of this sort?" And the clerk replies, "A dollar, a dollar and a half, two dollars." The whole of Matthew's circumcising the regiment scene is cut. The collection also includes Barnes's library. Inside her copy of Eliot's *Collected Poems* she wrote "He said 'Someday they will say I copied you,'" and in his *On Poetry and Poets* she wrote in 1981, "Mr. E. said of the last act of *The Antiphon* that it was one of the greatest last acts he had ever read. But he did not so write of it."

29. I have discussed this aspect of *Nightwood* in a review of Andrew Field's *Djuna* in *Women's Review of Books* 1, no. 8 (May 1984). See also Paul Bouissac's *Circus and Culture: A Semiotic Approach* (Bloomington: Indiana University Press, 1976).

30. Note the resemblance of Robin as a beast to the description of Charlotte Brontë's Bertha in chapter 26 of *Jane Eyre:* "What it was, whether beast or human being, one could not, at first sight, tell; it grovelled, seemingly, on all fours; it snatched and growled like some wild animal."

31. For discussions of carnival, see *The Reversible World: Symbolic Inversion in Art and Society,* edited by Barbara A. Babcock (Ithaca, N.Y.: Cornell University Press, 1978), in particular David Kunzles's "World Upside Down: The Iconography of a European Broadsheet Type" and Natalie Zemon Davis's "Women on Top: Symbolic Sexual Inversion and Political Disorder in Early Modern Europe."

32. Marguerite Yourcenar, *Fires* (reprint, New York: Farrar, Strauss and Giroux, 1981); Susan Gubar, "Sapphistries," *Signs* 10, no. 1 (1984). See also Colette's *The Pure and the Impure* (New York: New York Review of Books, 2000), for further connections between woman, circus, cabaret, and lesbianism.

33. For a contemporary version of Barbette's story see Albert Goldbarth's prose poem, *Different Fleshes* (Geneva, N.Y.: Hobart and William Smith Colleges Press, 1979). Writing of the painter Chaim Soutine, Goldbarth says, "No one had ever prayed before in Meat Cathedral," which also recalls Barnes's Rabelasian use of the butcher motif.

34. Bouissac, *Circus and Culture,* p. 8.

35. Brombert, *Victor Hugo and the Visionary Novel,* p. 202.

36. Yvonne Mitchell, *Colette: A Taste for Life* (New York: Harcourt, 1975), p. 177.

37. See Robert H. Abzug, *Inside the Vicious Heart: Americans and the Liberation of Nazi Concentration Camps* (New York: Oxford University Press, 1985), pp. 56, 128–129, 132.

5. Bonding and Bondage

1. Moira Ferguson, *Subject to Others: British Women Writers and Colonial Slavery, 1670–1834* (New York: Routledge, 1992).

2. Nancy Cunard, *Negro* (London: Wishart, 1934). Hugh Ford's abridged version (New York: Ungar, 1970), was reissued by Continuum. This edition lacks more than one third of the original and is problematically presented with photographs of Cunard, against her decision specifiing that *only* photographs of blacks were to appear. See also Ford's *Nancy Cunard: Brave Poet, Indomitable Rebel, 1896–1965* (Philadelphia: Chilton, 1968). Cunard was coeditor with Edith Sitwell of an annual anthology of poetry called *Wheels,* 1916–1921. Cunard's published work includes *Outlaws* (London: Elkin Matthews, 1921); *Sublunary* (London: Hodder and Stoughton, 1923); *Parallax* (London: Hogarth, 1925); *Black Man and White Ladyship: An Anniversary* (London: Utopia, 1931); editor, *Authors Take Sides on the Spanish Civil War* (London: *Left Review,* 1937); with George Padmore, *The White Man's Duty* (London: W.H. Allen, 1943); *Men-Ship-Tank-Plane* (London: New Books, 1944); editor, *Poems for France* (Paris: La France Libre, 1944); *Grand Man: Memories of Norman Douglas* (London: Secker and Warburg, 1954); *G. M.: Memories of George Moore* (London: Rupert Hart-Davies, 1956); *These Were the Hours* (Carbondale: Southern Illinois University Press, 1966). Her late poems, numerous essays, and an immense amount of journalism have not been collected. The biography is by Anne Chisholm. *Nancy Cunard* (New York: Knopf, 1979); she is discussed in Shari Benstock, *Women of the Left Bank: Paris 1900–1940* (Austin: University of Texas Press, 1986), and by Susan Friedman in Bonnie Kime Scott, ed., *The Gender of Modernism* (Bloomington: Indiana University Press, 1990), pp. 63–68, and Sabine Broeck, "Do White Ladies Get the Blues?" in *IEAS Women's Studies Newsletter* 2, (Frankfurt, 1992).

3. See James Clifford, *The Predicament of Culture: Twentieth Century Ethnography, Literature, and Art* (Cambridge, Mass.: Harvard University Press, 1988), and *Writing Culture: The Poetics and Politics of Ethnography,* edited by James Clifford and George E. Marcus (Berkeley: University of California Press, 1986), Michel Leiris, *Manhood: A Journey from Childhood to the Fierce Order of Virility,* translated by Richard Howard, foreward by Susan Sontag (Chicago: University of Chicago Press, 1984), Michel Leiris, *Journal 1922–1989,* edited by Jean Jamin (Paris: Gallimard, 1993).

4. See Henry Crowder, *As Wonderful as All That? Henry Crowder's Memoir of His Affair with Nancy Cunard 1928–1935,* with the assistance of Hugo Speck, introduction and epilogue by Robert L. Allen (Navarro, Calif.: Wild Trees Press, 1987). The typescript of this peculiar volume is now (1992) in the Humanities Research Center at the University of Texas. Ernest B. Speck, Emeritus Professor of English in Alpine, Texas gave the unpublished manuscript to Allen after the death of his brother, a white journalist based in Paris in the thirties for Universal News Service and Paris correspondent for *Variety.* They speculate that the book was not published for fear of a libel suit from Lady Cunard. My own hunch is that Speck took the disillusioned Crowder under his wing and produced the "as-told-to" "autobiography" as part of an effort to discredit Nancy's Left politics. The book is badly written but not consistently badly written; that is, it may have been pro-

duced by more than one author. Her FBI file shows that she was watched closely by British and American intelligence. The production of the *Negro* anthology was clearly viewed as subversive and its progress was reported. Without claiming that there was a conspiracy at work here, one may speculate on the extent of the perceived threat involved in the circulation of Negro poetry and history by a leftist. Letters in Texas from Claude McKay in North Africa about his contribution to the volume include descriptions of being watched and his house being destroyed by intelligence agents. These enthusiastic letters introducing her to his friends and family in the West Indies are hard to square with the portrait he paints later in his memoirs of a grasping white woman who refused to pay him for his contributions to the volume (when he knew that nobody was paid.) I believe that Henry Crowder had a story to tell and that Speck helped him to tell it. What we don't know is who may have encouraged Speck to produce this slander on the reputation of Nancy Cunard. Harassment by intelligence agents and the collection of information on the sex lives of radicals was routine practice. The extent to which it may have been used against black poets like Langston Hughes remains to be seen. Henry Crowder's language justifying his attack on his ex-lover is odd. He says he "owes it to (his) race" to "disclose all of the sordid details" because of "the dangerous and sometimes harmful nature of her activities." Right. Dangerous activities. He hopes the story may be "of some value to colored men who become enamored with white women."

5. Val Williams, *The Other Observers: Women Photographers in Britain 1900 to the Present* (London: Virago, 1991). Barbara Ker-Symer's photographs reproduced here are from the Photography Collection at the Humanities Research Center at the University of Texas.

6. See the catalog *Alone in a Crowd: Prints of the 1930s–40s by African-American Artists,* from the Collection of Reba and Dave Williams (American Federation of Arts, 1993). The lynching theme is represented very powerfully as a hanging tree with a waiting noose in the background of Charles White's *Hope for the Future,* a 1947 portrait of a black madonna and child (p. 24), and in Elizabeth Catlett's *Mother and Child,* 1946 (p. 25).

7. See the introduction to my *Suffrage and the Pankhursts* (London: Routledge, 1987) and "Laughing at Leviticus: *Nightwood* as Woman's Circus Epic," in *Silence and Power: Djuna Barnes, a Revaluation,* edited by Mary Lynn Broe (Carbondale: University of Southern Illinois Press, 1991), pp. 221–251, and "The Asylums of Antaeus; Women, War and Madness: Is There a Feminist Fetishism?" in *Feminism and Critical Theory: The Difference Within,* edited by Elizabeth Meese and Alice Parker (Amsterdam and Philadelphia: John Benjamins, 1988), pp. 49–81.

8. Further materials, typescripts of some articles, and the like, for *Negro* are in the archives of the Atlanta University Center Robert W. Woodruff Library. My thanks to Minnie H. Clayton for her help in locating them.

9. Nancy Cunard's correspondence with Arthur A. Schomburg is in the Archives of the Schomburg Center (Microfilm R2798, reels 2, 6, and 10); thanks to Betty

Odulashian for help in finding materials. Their copy of *Negro* also contains a printed insert on Jesse Owens at the Olympics. Thanks to Lois Overbeck, associate editor of the Beckett letters, who also noticed that the essay on the "Negress in the Brothel" by Rene Crevel was not listed in the contents of *Negro* but had been separately printed and bound into the text without pagination.

10. One of the curators at the Humanities Research Center told my class that the hate mail had included envelopes full of lead printers' slugs with no stamps on them. The receiver was supposed to pay for the postage.

11. See Scott Braverman, "Isaac Julien's *Looking For Langston:* Hughes, Biography and Queer(ed) History," *Cultural Studies* 7, no. 2 (May 1993), pp. 311–323. Also, for a counter to Rampersad's biography of Hughes's playing down of the importance of Nancy Cunard and radical politics in his life, especially his struggles against fascism in Spain, see Cunard's *Three Negro Poets, Left Review* 3, no. 9 (1937), pp. 529–536, which includes the text of Hughes's speech before the Second International Writers' Congress in Paris. A student gave me a description from a bookseller's catalog of a presentation copy of *Fine Clothes to the Jew,* inscribed "For Havelock Ellis, with deep admiration, these songs and poems of a simple people. Sincerely Langston Hughes, Lincoln University, March 10, 1927." Included in the volume, which is offered at fifteen hundred dollars, is a letter to the sexologist, dated April 14, 1927, thanking him for his comments and for his own work: "Your books (the ones I've been able to get and read) have meant much to me. I feel that they have helped me better see and understand life."

6. LAYING DOWN THE WHITE WOMAN'S BURDEN

This chapter was written in Calcutta in January, 1997 at the Indian Statistical Institute, where my husband was Visiting Researcher in Mathematics. I am grateful for their hospitality. A version was read at the Rockefeller Institute's Bellagio Study and Conference Center at the Villa Serbelloni in March, and I am grateful to the fellows for their responses, especially Ayappa Panniker, Anna Deveare Smith, Regina Schwartz, and Barbara Sicherman. Thanks also to Gay Wachman and Claire Tylee for subsequent readings.

1. Angela Ingram, "Un/Reproductions: Estates of Banishment in English Fiction After the Great War," in *Women's Writing in Exile,* edited by Mary Lynn Broe and Angela Ingram (Chapel Hill: University of North Carolina Press, 1989), pp. 325–348.

2. For a discussion of the mother-country metaphor in colonial discourse see "Liberty, Sorority, Misogyny" in my *Virginia Woolf and the Languages of Patriarchy.*

3. The European painters' representation of the white woman's breast is discussed in my *Black Books, White Looks: Nancy Cunard and Modernist Primitivism* (New Brunswick, N.J.: Rutgers University Press, forthcoming).

4. See "A Very Fine Negress" in this volume. A version of part of the argument appears in "Registering Objections: Grounding Feminist Alibis," in *Reconfigured Spheres: Feminist Explorations of Literary Space,* edited by Margaret Higonnet and

Joan Templeton (Amherst: University of Massachusetts Press, 1994), pp. 33–63.

5. Virginia Woolf's research notes in purple ink from the British Museum, for Leonard Woolf's *Empire and Commerce in Africa* (1920) are in the Leonard Woolf Papers at the University of Sussex.

6. For instance, she did not see herself as a feminist; on the other hand, she did not make common cause with feminists. So the histories of the relations between black men and white feminists are not fully appropriate as examples of Cunard's politics.

7. Term used by Anthony Appiah *In My Father's House: Africa and the Philosophy of Culture* (New York: Oxford University Press), 1992.

8. See also Doris Lessing's *The Grass is Singing* (American first edition, New York: Thomas Y. Crowell Company, 1950).

9. Sybille Bedford *Aldous Huxley: A Biography,* vol 1, p. 213 (Chicago: Ivan R. Dee, Inc., 2002).

10. This and the following quotations are from Bedford's *Aldous Huxley: A Biography,* vol. 1, pp. 132–133.

11. For suicide and other social problems in England after the war, see the sequels to Helen Zenna Smith's *Not So Quiet . . . Stepdaughters of War* (New York: The Feminist Press, 1989), and Angela Ingram.

12. Nancy Cunard, *Grand Man: Memories of Norman Douglas* (London: Secker and Warburg, 1954), pp. 70–71.

13. The Eurasian misfit is a staple figure in both Anglo-Indian and Indo-Anglian fiction. See Kipling's *Plain Tales from the Hills* (1890), Orwell's *Burmese Days,* or the Ranee of Sarawak's *Lost Property,* 1930).

14. Wyndham Lewis, *The Roaring Queen* (New York: Liveright, 1973); introduction by Walter Allen. Scheduled to be published by Jonathan Cape in 1936, the book was withdrawn in proof for fear of libel suits. Arnold Bennett, the writer and reviewer satirized as Shodbutt, had been dead for five years, but Rhoda Hyman (Virginia Woolf) was alive and still smarting from Lewis's charge in *Men Without Art* that *Mrs. Dalloway* was a "pathetic crib" of *Ulysses,* a "sort of undergraduate imitation" of Joyce's masterpiece. Mrs. Lewis told the editor that Baby Bucktrout was based on Lewis's friend, Nancy Cunard, who had wanted to publish *The Roaring Queen* at the Hours Press when it was censored, despite the satire on herself, her friend Brian Howard, the "Roaring Queen" himself, and her friend and publisher of her poems, Virginia Woolf—but he needed an advance she couldn't supply.

15. A term I use in "Britannia Rules *The Waves.*"

Index

Crevel, Rene: "Negress in the Brothel"
in *Negro* anthology, 139
Critical Guide to Virginia Woolf (Jane
Goldman), 18, 183n12
Crowder, Henry, 126, 136 passim;
Henry-Music, 136, 143, 153
Culture and Anarchy (Matthew Arnold),
31
Cunard, Lady (Maud) Emerald, 123,
148, 159
Cunard Line, 141
Cunard, Nancy, 1, 3, 8, 17, 19, 45, 46,
119–149, 150–178; activist, 7; and
African diaspora; British identity, 7;
descriptions of, 161, 162, 166;
"Equatorial Way," 137; images of,
163; influenced by black poets, 137;
left-wing champion of rights of
blacks, 7, 123–149; Pan-Africanism,
31, as a poet, 148; *Outlaw,* 148;
scapegoat for white rape of Africa,
125. *See also* Africa; diaspora; *Black
Man and White Ladyship; Negro* anthology; George Padmore
Cunningham, Michael, 11. See also
The Hours
Cunningham, Valentine: excludes
Cunard from history of 1930s, 126
curse: on the clitoris in *Nightwood,* 105
cutting and writing, 34

Daily Herald, 2
daughters: white, 49
Darwinian: battle at Kew, 10; social-
Darwinian plot
death: death of the author, 66, 79; as
liberator of oppressed women, 30. *See
also* Toni Morrison
decline of the West, 81
*Decolonizing Tradition: New Views of
20ᵗʰ Century British Canons,* 17,
183n11

desire, 4, 5, 113, 161; acting out of, 22;
lesbian, 13; unacted racial, sexual, po-
litical, 14, 17; white women, 13;
women writers and, 102; of young
Clarissa, 10. *See also* race; fantasy
De Salvo, Louise, 82
Devi, Mahasweta, 6, 8
deviance, 99
Diana of Ephesus, 109, 116
Diaspora: African, 1
Dickens, Charles, 29. *See also* Governor
Eyre
Dictionary of National Biography, 7, 183n4
Die Fledermaus, 89
Dietrich, Marlene, 103; and Robin
Vote, 104; voice, 104
difference: class gap, 2; homosexual, 16;
racial, 20, 31, 97
documentary, 1; ethnographic and an-
thropological, 7
doll figure: in *Nightwood,* 106–117,
Olympia, 107; prince/princess, 106;
smashing of in women's writing, 110
"domestic obscene," 130
dompteur, 114
Dora (Freud's case), 99
Dostoevsky, Fyodor, 9
Douglas, Norman, 127
Dreadnought Hoax, 45, 64
dreckology, 117
Duff-Gordon, Lucie: Nubian girls, 39
Dubois, W.E.B., 121, 129
Duval, Jeanne, 24

economics, 2, 4
eco-terrorism, 9
elegy, 64, 80; editorial cuts in *Night-
wood,* 95. See also *The Waste Land*
Eliot, George, 110
Eliot, T. S., 20, 181
Ellis, Havelock, 96
Elvedon Hall, ix, 61, 78

About the Author

Jane Marcus is the author of *Virginia Woolf and the Languages of Patriarchy,* and *Art and Anger: Reading Like a Woman the Young Rebecca West* and the editor of several books of essays about women writers. Distinguished Professor of English at the City University of New York and the City College of New York, she is working on a book for Rutgers on Nancy Cunard called *White Looks, Black Books.*